All in a Day's W

Danny Danziger's intervie
appeared in all of the majo
and he now writes for the S
He is also the author of *Th*
Book, and is currently writi
called *Eton Days*, which is a series of interviews with people who went to Eton, and a book about the medical profession.

Danny Danziger

All in a Day's Work

Fontana/Collins

First published in 1987 by Fontana Paperbacks,
8 Grafton Street, London W1X 3LA

Set in Plantin

Made and printed in Great Britain by
William Collins Sons & Co. Ltd, Glasgow

This book is dedicated to:

My mother and father,
my favourite brother, Jimmy,
and Clare

They know why …

Contents

Acknowledgements

My special appreciation for all their hours of hard work, and without whose commitment I might never have dared embark on this book: Emma Sainty and Sally van Hasbroeck.

Thank you to: Lord Forte, Adrian Pennink, Susan Raven, Dr Christopher Tyerman.

My thanks also to: Janet Ashton; Nic Barlow; Ann Barr; Victoria Battersby; Iona Cairns; Julian Calder; Lucinda Chambers; Barnaby Conrad; Helen Cormack; Harry Lee Danziger; Josh Dixey; Toby Eady; Rina Girardi; David Godwin; Ron Hall; John Hopkins; Charlotte Hutley; Michele Jaffe; Rob Jenkins; Len Joseph; Penny Junor; Celia Kilner; Rupert de Klee; Jane Krivine; Katie Law; Paul Manduca; Mollie Martin; Martin Miles; Beatrix Miller; Dominic Milroy; David Moorhouse; Sarah Motion; Celestria Noel; Anne Norman-Butler; Robert Orr-Ewing; Amanda Ramsbottom; Gay Rendell; David Roodyn; Rachel Semlyen; Jerome Stonborough; Johnny Stonborough; Linda Sullivan; Sue Taylor; Studs Terkel; Tessa Traegar; Nina Train; Susie Ward Thomas; Ann Weltmer; Carly Whalley; Anthony Wilmot-Smith; Richard Wintour; Peter York.

My deepest appreciation to everyone I have interviewed, all of whom appear under their real names.

Introduction

Last year, for a series in a Sunday newspaper, I would do a different person's job and write about my experiences. One week I was a waiter in a London restaurant, another week I was teaching seven-year-olds in Salisbury; one time I was on a factory line making Yorkie bars! I tried my hand as a radio disc jockey in Nottingham, donned top hat and tails as a doorman at a smart London hotel, I became a travel rep in Corfu, looked after the rhinos at Whipsnade Zoo, and patrolled the clock gallery as a museum warder in the Science Museum.

I was paid to write about how I felt doing their jobs, but I felt frustrated. The real story, I realized, was how *they* felt doing the job, what they felt about their work and how that work affected their lives. I was only an itinerant actor: after I took off my uniform, my top hat, Wellington boots or whatever, my role was over, yet obviously the story didn't end there. More than anything, I wanted to talk to people about *their* jobs – hence this book.

The motives for working are as infinite as the variety of jobs, or occupations, or careers, crafts, or callings that exist. What I hope these interviews reveal are the dreams and the hopes, the victories, the worries and the fears of a working group of people, the strong and the frail, the optimistic and the defeated.

I have tried to pinpoint how work affects fifty individuals through the one activity that physically if not mentally shapes our existence on this planet. Whether we relish it or evade it, work is one of life's main preoccupations.

What is work? And *why* work? The writer Ian McEwan asks, 'Is writing really work? It certainly makes you hungry, it makes you tired and you know when you've had enough …' And the advertising director: 'Grown men flogging Angel Delight, you know it belittles you. You think, "How can an intelligent person turn out this garbage to people?"'

Father Paul mentions the penitential aspect of work, pointing out that in Genesis, work is a part of man's penance for his rebellion against God: 'Thy should earn thy bread by the sweat of thy brow.' 'Nobody says you've got to go to work every day, five days a week, and bring home so much money to pay the bills,' says the restaurateur. 'We just accept it. That is the norm ... I'm living my life the way I choose to live it.'

What surprised me was how few people were motivated by making money for money's sake. Certainly they recognize that remuneration is essential for their existence, but they regretted the mercenary obligations which compel people to work. Andrew Seaman the gamekeeper: 'Really and honestly, I often look at my job, and I get more out of the three thousand acres that I look after for my guv'nor than he does himself ... Sometimes I consider it work, but truthfully, if I had a nine-to-five job, I'd have to have a piece of part-time keepering to do, and I'm really being paid for what I'd be doing as a hobby.' The tour guide would be a very unhappy man if he couldn't show people around his precious Hampton Court. The patients of the dentist have become as dear to him as his own family.

Of course there are exceptions. The prostitute, Sonya: 'When I was nursing, the money was atrocious. I must have been mad to do it. I mean it was about £25 for a forty-hour week, and it was working really hard as well. There's nothing wrong with wanting nice jewellery, nice clothes, nice wages, and when I moved down to London it hit me how much money there was, and I thought, "I'll have some of that – why not?"'

Sometimes I spoke with people who had never reflected on what they were doing, or why they were doing it, and I know that causing them to think, to explain, to account for their existence – which is after all what people are doing in a book which discusses work – made them unsettled and depressed. 'I get very frustrated and wonder what the hell I'm doing, sitting on that seat doing the job,' says the taxi driver. 'I feel I could handle something a lot better than driving ... in circles from Knightsbridge to wherever. You don't need much of a brain for that ... I hate the job, every minute of the day.'

The television producer hopes that by deliberately immersing himself in work he can escape from the problems of life. 'I think it's part of not exactly knowing now what your function is outside of work ... I know what I'm supposed to be doing when I'm at work, I seem to know less and less what I'm supposed to be doing outside of work. I seem to become less and less capable of being a friend or a father or a husband or a whatever, and so I get more and more scared of trying, I just go back to the office where I know what I'm supposed to do ... at least I know what I'm bloody supposed to do there, and I can more or less do it ...'

But for those who love work, retirement is very difficult to come to terms with. Peter Carey, the dentist: 'By now I don't have any patients that I don't like so it's all fun, and that's why I don't want to stop doing it; I'd miss them all terribly, I mean, what would I do? Sometimes during the weekend one does feel one's age ...' The criminal: 'I'd still be involved in the crimes for the crimes' sake because it gives me a fucking boost, keeps me going, keeps me alive, keeps my mind young, keeps me thinking. Why should a man retire when he's sixty-five?' The lexicographer, having completed a thirty-year task updating the *Oxford English Dictionary*, is preparing a new project: '... In a quite hard-headed way, when you are sixty-two, you have reasonable expectation of eighteen years' day-to-day activity. In my case I will concentrate on grammar. I don't play cards, I don't propose to learn how to play chess, I propose to go on with work.'

It can sometimes be the job itself which reminds you that time is passing. The tour guide: 'When I sit on the coach, especially after leaving Hampton Court, and we go back to London, sometimes I think to myself, "I've done this job so many years now" ... and I remember the days when we used to be on forty-nine-seat coaches, perhaps even smaller ... I can't remember any driver who started with me, and I think to myself, "All the years I've done this, am I mad?"'

The people in my book have come by their work in many different ways. Some by design: the television producer again, 'I decided I wanted to be in this business by the time I was eight. I imagined that much more than I imagined being married or having children or living in a house. I never saw myself in any other context.' Others landed their jobs by chance. The taxidermist: 'When I was a child I used to do quite a lot of birdwatching on the Broads here, and as you go about you tend to pick up dead birds and that sort of thing. In a lot of cases they were quite pretty and it seemed such a shame to throw them away, and it was quite coincidental really that I happened to find some books in the attic with instructions on taxidermy.' The golfer: 'You read about people who say when they were twelve years old they decided they were going to be something or other. I always sort of thought I'd like to be a professional golfer, but it was more a question of I couldn't really think of much else to do, to be honest.' The doctor: 'I had a choice between music or medicine and I'd have preferred to do music in some ways because it's aesthetically more pleasing, but it wasn't secure enough, especially in Coventry where I'm from. I just wanted to do something where I went to work every day, and I happened to be good at the sciences ... I'm not like some people for whom medicine is all-consuming, you know, it's just a job really.' And Dave the diver: 'I originally started out wanting to be a mechanic but girls didn't like the filth under my finger nails and diving seemed the second best job ...'.

For some people, the decision is made for them, like Lord Brocket. 'I inherited the title age fifteen from my grandfather. I didn't understand what it meant, I'd only met my grandfather twice in my entire life.' And Nigel Harvey the game dealer: 'I didn't really have too much choice about going into the business ... by the age of fifteen my father was very ill. He had Parkinson's Disease and it was becoming more and more difficult for him to carry on with the day-to-day running of the shop. After having two brain operations, he had problems with his voice, but I could understand him, so I would be standing next to him acting as an interpreter.'

Work is the medium through which society judges an individual's worth. You are born into a particular geographic and socioeconomic group, and you have certain expectations. Now those expectations can remain the same, they can get greater, or they can diminish. Fifty years ago your domestic environment and your job would very closely mesh, like in mining villages, or domestic service, and there was little mobility in the social or financial hierarchy. Nowadays it is work – the job or profession itself – which influences or determines the rise, flow or ebb of these expectations. There is, thus, nothing which so completely defines a person as what they do, although, it must be said, class preconditioning often dictates the socioeconomic level of a profession or job.

But the spirit with which work is undertaken transcends that prejudice. Character triumphs. The dustman enjoys telling people what he does. 'A lot of people have said, "You don't look like a dustman," so I usually say, "What does a dustman look like?" ... I'm proud to be a dustman. I wouldn't like to say, "I'm Philip Ridgen the great dustman." I try and be a good dustman. I sweep roads to earn a living to make some money so I can pay my bills, full stop.' The plumber is well aware of his traditional standing in society: 'It's a funny relationship. The people look down on you, and yet they don't take any notice of the trouble that is in the drains is actually of their doing, and they try and put on this superior act: you know, "Well, you're only here to clean the drains," and I'm looking at them thinking, "But it's you that caused it ...".'

The 1980s is a timely moment to consider man's relationship to work. It is not merely unemployment which is the great issue of the rest of the century, but the entire activity of work. The great fear for the future is the decreasing amount of work. We can restructure the economy, but can we restructure the human psyche?

And as new technology develops, and the working week is shortened and the number of unemployed increase all over the world, the very word 'work' has taken on a new meaning. There is an attendant connotation that aggrandizes the word, it has become associated with a new nobility: work now means 'hope', 'freedom', 'liberty'. Perhaps this is a return to the Victorian age and values, the strict work ethic and devotion to duty. Or perhaps it reflects man's reliance on working, or doing, to impose some sense of order on a life which might seem empty and meaningless without it.

Advertising Director
Malcolm Gaskin

I hate work, I'd much rather not work, but unfortunately life has ordained that I've got to work, and I might as well work at something I quite like doing and where I'm allowed to do what I'm allowed to do and get paid for it. Man wasn't brought up to work, he's been brought up to run around the fields with the beasts of nature. Animals weren't meant to work either.

I was brought up in a town where not working wasn't a slur on your character because it was an unemployment blackspot. When I was fifteen I had to choose whether to stay on at school or get a job at the pit or something. The town was only about forty thousand people and the week when I had to decide whether to leave or not, seven thousand people got fired at the shipyard and two thousand blokes got paid off at the coalmine. All my family were alternately out of work, their fathers were in and out of work, their mothers were in and out of work. Work for the working class is not a thing to be enjoyed, whereas, say you're the son of a doctor, work might seem like it's a good thing, it's rewarding.

I left school. Most people I knew worked hard. My dad worked abroad and my mother supported the family and she had to work hard, and I got a job in a brickworks which was like Belsen but very hot. Maybe you were getting paid good money compared to the regular blokes there because you weren't paying tax and that, but it was hell. I also used to work for joiners and brickies and that was hard – it's cold and wet and dangerous. Who needs that for the rest of their lives? You could see all the people you knew, and your family, dying of work. Life's not killing them, it was work that was killing them, and you thought, 'There must be a better way.'

But when I was a kid, about twelve, I had decided I wanted to be an ad man. In this drab, horrible town I lived in, at the bottom of our street of terraced houses, just between us and the shipyard, were some hoardings – you know, billboards – and we used to play on the back of those, and it was like an adventure playground.

I used to climb up the back, but I'd look at the front of them and see these ads for Persil and VAT 69 and I used to like that because that was the only contact with the outside world, the only bit of glamour in the whole town was what was on those billboards. So I knew quite early on that was the kind of job I'd have to do because I'd got this impression it took in weirdos and paid them a lot of money.

A creative person in advertising is usually a nonconformist; can be any shape or form, any colour, any kind of weird person, anything's accepted, and if you look normal you're usually a nonconformist by looking normal. And they let you get on with it.

Of course advertising is soft. A lot of people in advertising sit around and moan about what a terrible day they've had. Now there's not many jobs where you can walk about with funny haircuts, and a lot of people walk about drunk and go on holidays and spend a lot of money and have quite a lot of direct power over a lot of money. Not many people have got that, it's a unique business.

I first started working in a really terrible agency, an American-based agency, and it was a nightmare, just as hard work as the brickworks, except you had beautiful surroundings and lots of free booze and perks and stuff like that. But psychologically it was hard because of the futility of the work. I was building slummy adverts.

For example, with bricks, you can build a fine Georgian building or you can build a slum. With the same amount of bricks and the same amount of windows, you can either build something nice or something nasty. I couldn't understand why you had the bricks, the actual products and the amount of money you needed, and you were forced into building something that was totally ugly or misguided, when you knew too well that the advertising you were doing was going to be wrong and was going to insult people and wasn't going to work.

I worked on a well known brand of toothpaste once. Most toothpaste advertising is pretty dreadful and I could never understand why, because everyone brushes their teeth, nobody's got any objection to brushing their teeth, and nobody's got any objection to toothpaste. So why is the advertising terrible? Anyway, we were set to work on all this terrible stuff and it was all very formulated American stuff. We spent years doing this, 'Well, that one doesn't have enough smiling people in it, it needs a mother and a father.' You know, it's complete claptrap. So eventually, after bashing your way through this, you get the opportunity to produce some of your own ideas. So we did some ads which were quite funny, animated teeth. There's one where it's a young tooth talking to an old tooth, and it was in a Western setting like cartoons, and the young tooth was talking to the old cowboy tooth (all full of lead, i.e. fillings, because he hadn't been using his toothpaste), and it was all very good copy – 'When a tooth's got to go, a tooth's got to go' – and that worked really well. They put it in a test region and overwhelmingly people loved it, 20 per cent of that would sell 20 per cent more toothpaste, just like that. So, I was really pleased with myself; after all these years, we'd done commercials that really worked and were proud of and actually sold more toothpaste. And they cancelled them, stopped the advertising. The advertisers told us, 'We don't want to sell 20 per cent more, we only want to sell 2 per cent more. Because if we sell 20 per cent more we'll have to build another factory, we'll have to employ another thousand people, we'll have to buy twenty more lorries and that'll take five years to do.' So basically, you've been spending all this time trying to sell and then you find out that they're not really interested in selling – and that's sort of warped.

There's no enjoyment in advertising because it's a war, it's total war. Every day it's a struggle. When you think of the ad, it's all pure, and then you've got to get it physically made, you've got to deal with photographers, typesetters, printers, stylists, prop-makers, block-makers, the whole caboodle, and every one of them can screw your work up, your perfect image. If you're an artist you paint a painting and that's it and nobody can do anything with it. On an advert there's a lot of people who work with you, and every one of them can screw up what you've done, and usually it'll happen.

I usually believe in a product. I may not believe in the people who are selling it but I usually believe in the product. We don't work on products that we don't want to work on. I never do work on cigarette advertising or anything like that. I wouldn't work on British Nuclear Fuels who would have been paying a lot of money. But most products are pretty inoffensive because the people in Britain aren't starving and it's neither here nor there if they have fizzy water that's orange or fizzy water that's lemon. Either way we've got a choice, we're quite a sophisticated society and we just eat or drink this stuff, or not, and it's no big deal.

Charles Revlon said that in the factory we're making the product and in the stores we're selling dreams. It's a hard world for most people and they don't want reality. I mean, why do people watch 'Dynasty' when they could be watching people starving in Ethiopia? It's human nature, people are optimists. People want to believe that life can be a bit better. Unless we wove an artificial web of non-reality we couldn't exist.

We worked for CV Ltd who make cookers, and they always used to be in terrible trouble. We had to do a commercial for them to revive them or else they would get sunk. We went to this factory, and it was a terrible place, really Dickensian. We wrote this humorous commercial, went up to the factory and presented it to the Managing Director and he said, yes, fun treatment of his cookers, and he took us round this awful factory, thousands of people toiling away in all this grime, and he'd say, 'This is Fred Whatnot and he's been here fifty years and he's got three kids and one's got an iron lung, and this is Young Whatnot, he's got two kids, his wife's expecting and he's got a big mortgage.' He took us around the factory and we met all these people working there and he said, 'If this doesn't work, all these lot are going to be out of work, right?' Really serious. If this commercial doesn't work the whole factory shuts down and all these people are out of work and there's no chance for them because it's a terrible place. You know, it's no big deal for anybody else, it's life or death for them. It's very easy to be frightened, there's so much depending on your ad succeeding.

Say if I was a dentist. When you put down your tools at the end of the day you've stopped work, right? But if you're an ad man, everything that you see, everything you experience, is part of what you're going to use when you're advertising. You've just got to keep your eyes and ears open and train yourself into doing things. I'll go to an opera even though I can't stand opera, I'll go to anything just for the experience, just because I know it will benefit in the long run by knowing about these things. I'm a zealot, right? I'm mad keen, I want to do it, and I'm totally committed to the job.

All most ad people want to talk about is advertising, so you stay away from them. It's too much pressure to talk about your work all the time. Most people do it because they're sycophantic or they think they're better than everybody else. It's pure 'Emperor's New Clothes', because once you tell each other that you're so good, eventually people will believe it. Everybody outside your field probably thinks people in advertising are a bunch of wankers. They're right actually. People in advertising – 90 per cent of the people – turn out crap; you know, adults, grown men, writing Angel Delight commercials which a moron would be ashamed to write, and being paid a lot of money for it.

I'm going to be out of work when I'm forty, right? There's no such thing as a future in advertising, generally, because no matter what targets you set, things happen, things come along that make it not work. You either get burnt out or pushed out. Grown men flogging Angel Delight, you know it belittles you. You think, 'How can an intelligent person turn out this garbage to people?' After a while it must get to you.

I went to a funeral at home once, and I was talking to one of my aunts and I hadn't seen her for a while and she said, 'I hear you're down in London and you're doing all right.' I'd been at it for about four years, and she said, 'Well, what do you do?' So I explained what I did and how I went about it and all this, and she seemed quite interested. And she says at the end, she says, 'In advertising, are you?' And I said, 'Yes,' and she said, 'I always knew you'd turn out rotten.'

I feel as angry now as when I started, which is one of the motivations of work. I'm angry that people make us work like this and people stop me from working the way I want to do, and I'm angry because I have to work.

Air Stewardess
Camilla Clarke

Well, I needed a break because I had been nursing for ten years. I thought, 'Nothing ventured, nothing gained.' I'd travel a bit.

I hadn't travelled before. On my nurse's salary I'd never been able to get round the world, like I already have done in six months. I've been down to Australia, just come back from San Francisco, I go to South Africa next week, Singapore after that, so I've really travelled a long way. And they pay me very well.

It's not all glamour or fun, there are some very hard moments as well, mainly the hours. Jetlag I don't find too much of a problem because I can sleep day or night, no problem, because I'm used to shift work. There is a lot of night flying. Nearly all our flights back into London are flying through the night and there are the massive time changes. For example, you can be plus ten hours on GMT one week, and the next week you'll be minus ten, or you can jump the date line if you go to Japan and over via Alaska, which means you lose a day, and that really messes you up. But on the whole I love it.

A lot of people are bored with it after a few years, and I'm glad I've done a job beforehand. If I had started at twenty I think I would have got into a way of life that I couldn't have broken out of. I would have been paid a lot of money, I'd have been spoilt, and I wouldn't have had any qualifications to fall back on should anything change in my life and I wanted to be back home.

It does disrupt your life, and you have to forfeit weddings and parties because you only know about a month ahead what your schedules are. People have stopped ringing me because they know I probably won't be here, so I think much of the effort has to be by me. I'm glad I'm doing it now, because my friends are friends that I've had for a long time and they won't abandon me, but if you were younger, it's possible that you would lose a lot of friends. I know a lot of relationships break up because of the job. People can't take the other person being away. We do anything from a one-night stop to twenty-one or more days away, and about three or four long trips a year.

It's what you make of the job. I think you could get away with doing just the minimum, but you can also put yourself out. For example, you can make yourself freely available and not sit all night in the galley with the curtains drawn across, which I must admit some people do, and when a film is on, OK you don't want to be parading up and down every two minutes, but at least be around, be available, be approachable.

Sometimes I feel really tired. The cabin is pressurized at six thousand feet so you tire more easily than if you were on the ground. The cabin pressure makes you feel a bit odd sometimes, and if you go very high you find you can get headaches and a bit short of breath, and if you run around it makes you feel pretty bad.

I think a lot of people when they get on an aeroplane tend to become totally helpless. They let you take over, a bit like the schoolmistress role, and they ask you silly things. Maybe it's because it's a new experience and quite a lot of people are scared of flying, but they do take on this helpless attitude - you know, crying out for water when it's readily accessible.

Stewardesses talk about the 'punters' coming on. I'm afraid that nickname is used all the time. And the punters vary according to what part of the world you're in. You go to New York, for example, you have a lot of businessmen, and they just want a good efficient service while they are getting on with their work. And when you go down to Australia, you've got an average age of about seventy. The grannies are going down to see their children, and they love to chat about their families and show you photographs. They know they may never see them again. Then you get the holiday-makers. St Lucia, it was all honeymooners, so that was a completely different lot of people. Every race is different. The Indians and Pakistanis you bring back from Delhi and Karachi, they're completely different, there is a language problem, communication is somewhat difficult. The Arabs, of course, treat women as very servile, and they are very demanding and it's 'Give me', 'Take this', 'Do that', they treat you like a slave, and that is difficult; you do have to adapt to each sort of person, each passenger that you are dealing with. I think patience is a good virtue.

If you are nice to people, some of them take it that you fancy them or something. And there are a few people who ask, 'Where do you stay?'

and 'Would you like a drink this evening?' And those that drink too much, which is quite common because it is all free booze now, they tend to keep calling your name out and asking you out and giving you their cards, but I haven't had major problems.

A lot of people do get quite ill on the long flights. Because of the pressure problems, the altitude, they need oxygen, or they get anxiety attacks – quite a lot of people faint. Then there is air sickness, and I had one woman who went into premature labour. You always hear about babies being born on aircraft, it's because of the pressurization. Nose bleeds, asthma attacks, I had one lady who had a blood vessel burst in her eye. But I can easily cope with all that. The senior crew members like to have a nurse around; with over ten hours flying time to the West Coast, or whatever, it is jolly reassuring to have an SRN on board.

There are similarities between nursing and this job. The hours, obviously, shift work and long hours, long hours of being on your feet, eating on the run – if you get a chance to eat. Things that are dissimilar are a lack of continuity. For example, on a ward you have people coming and going, but it wouldn't always be a complete change of people, like every trip. Often here, you are too busy to sit and chat to people, and I think the atmosphere is quite claustrophobic. If you don't get on with someone or they are rude to you, you can't just walk away and get out. You're stuck with them for the next ten hours or whatever. You have got to be polite and courteous, and they are always right. After all, they are paying your wages.

Sometimes it's difficult to be smiling and nice and polite. I think there are some people who are so demanding and so trying, and it's 'Give me, give me' all the time, that you just feel like telling them where to go, but you can't because it would come back on you.

When people are coming in, getting on board, I look around, take note of what passengers I've got, children or people who are on their own. Some people tell you they are scared stiff of flying, and it may even be on the printout, 'claustrophobic', 'doesn't like flying', or whatever.

We are taught that if there is an emergency, and you have to make an emergency landing, you need to rely on someone in your section, because when the chute goes out the first two people down are supposed to wait at the bottom and help people off the plane. We are actually taught to look at the passengers in our area and, in case of an emergency, pick out those that you could rely on if you needed to. But the thing is, a nice friendly person who seems to be responsible and reliable might then turn out to drink more than anyone else and be totally incapable if something did go wrong.

It's nice if you've got nice people. But more often than not you'll say, 'Oh, I've got an awful demanding lot.' Before they have even sat down, they want drinks, they want something to eat, they want to know when the film will be shown, why there is a delay. Because of all the problems that they have had in getting to the airport, the checking in, you know how stressful it is, well they take it out on us. Maybe they have been given a non-smoking seat when they want to smoke or vice versa. Or if they are next to children they complain, but if you have thirty children on board, what can you do?

I think the single thing that annoys me the most is the sheep factor. You can be going down the aisle and one person asks you for a cup of tea, and you've just done the meal, just given tea and coffee to two hundred people, and they have all had two cups. One person will ask, and the next person will think, aaah, that's a good idea, 'Did I see you making a cup of tea? Do you think I could have one?' And then the next person and the next, and everyone just follows on and they all start asking for drinks. It takes just one person to do it. I wouldn't mind if two dozen are going to ask you for tea because then you might as well make a pot, but they wait until you come back and then the next row will ask you.

Of course I will go and make them a cup of tea, that's what I'm there for. That's the difference between how much you put into it and how much you don't. I'll willingly make tea, but I think it's pretty annoying.

I don't like telling people I'm a stewardess. I always say, 'I work for British Airways.' I suppose it is because I'm so used to saying I'm a nurse. I get mixed reactions from people. Some like to tell me what a crummy job it is and how awful to be a flying waitress, and I often think they are slightly jealous because they know I'm one week in the Caribbean, the next week in Africa. They think you're name-dropping when they ask where you've been recently in your job, or where you got your suntan from, and they don't like it when you explain that you have a permanent suntan. A lot of my friends think it's wonderful, though.

I think I'm getting well rewarded for the hard work, not just in terms of money, because I've always survived on my nurse's salary, but with the travel. After a year I will be able to go anywhere in the world for 90 per cent discount. That to me is fantastic. I just want to do it for a couple of years to see the world and travel to the Far East and Australia and places I would never ever go in my life.

I do miss being a nurse. I miss the satisfaction of doing everything for somebody who's not well. I think that is it, really. For example, I'm quite pleased to help someone when they are ill on the aircraft. I don't wish them ill, but you do get satisfaction from helping people. Mind you, I like people to be properly ill. You get a lot of neurotic types, hysterics, although I suppose they are ill in their own way.

It's terribly different for me because I was in charge of a ward for four years, and now I'm just one of fourteen crew. I'm nobody really, and I'm not my own boss any more. I have lost responsibility although I haven't minded that too much. I quite enjoy getting off that plane and thinking, lovely, that's behind me, it was a good trip, a bad trip or whatever, I've got something different the next day. Whereas nursing, well certainly on a ward, you go back home and worry about that patient, you know, are they going to be there the next morning or are they going to be dead. It was never close one door, open another one, which it is in this job.

I've met so many people who have said they were only going to do it for two years – but they're still doing it ten years later, because it is a way of life that they have got into and it's very hard to leave. I think I will review the situation when I have done it for two years. I shall carry on doing it for as long as I'm happy doing it, and I'm not starting to say, 'Oh no, not Bermuda again.' Then I'll know it's time to stop. Or if my circumstances change and I get married and want to have children, then obviously I would leave.

I recently had four days in St Lucia and three in Barbados and it was lovely. You're in a holiday resort with beaches, everything paid for, you're given local currency when you get there for all your meals, so there are not really any bills to pay. So you find yourself in the most beautiful surroundings, but you're not with anybody you want to be with, and you wish you could share it with someone from home, some friends – or someone special. It can be a very lonely job.

I might think I'd had enough just at the end of a long flight or at the end of a difficult flight, difficult passengers and nothing seems to go right. Sometimes then you are so tired, and you have some angry person going on at you for no particular reason, they are just taking out their annoyance at something on you, and I'll think, 'That's the last straw, I can't take it, I'm fed up with it.'

Money isn't that important to me. I have always survived on my salary. I live within my means and I don't owe anybody any money. But it is lovely to have a car, have a bit more freedom, so my poor old bike is redundant. It hasn't changed me. I don't go to any more expensive shops, but it just means I don't have to worry. The money's there if I do want something. I think the biggest difference is having a car, and being able to think in terms of getting an answer phone or a video or owning a telly.

I did think it was unjust that I was being paid what an eighteen-year-old secretary would get in her first job for all the responsibility and hard work that I put in as a sister. Ridiculous, but I had to live on it. I'm earning almost double what I was getting as a ward sister, for a lot less responsibility – and better perks.

I quite often think I'm shallow to do this job. That's why I'm glad I have qualifications, and I had a good job before, because I don't see this job as a career. Maybe I feel slightly ashamed of saying what I do, and because I'm just doing it to see the world. Of course that was the last reason I gave British Airways for wanting the job. I never mentioned travel, and of course it was the main objective.

The hardest part of leaving my nursing job was plucking up the courage to say what I was going to do. I suppose I felt slightly ashamed that I was going to be a stewardess and having to tell my consultant not only was I leaving, but I was going to work for British Airways. He immediately thought it would be in the medical department and he said that would be good for my career, but when I told him what I was going to do he was horrified. 'What a waste.' Although the director of nursing services was very nice, and said she could appreciate why I wanted to do it, she advised if I wanted to go back into nursing not to leave it more than two years and I would be able to step in fairly easily.

I think I'll give it two years and then I'll have to see. I probably wouldn't go back to nursing, money wise. It's a shame, isn't it. I mean if they could increase the nurses' salary by double it would be justified, it would be about right compared to what I'm getting now. It seems unjust that nurses have to suffer.

Bank Manager
Brian Lightowler

I was at grammar school in the old traditional grammar school sense, left at sixteen, and I had a burning ambition to work in a bank for some obscure reason. The only thing I can put it down to is that I was a keen stamp collector as a child, and an adult stamp collector befriended me, we did swaps, and he was a bank manager. I don't know. I could be wrong there. It could've just been that I much preferred maths to English at school – maybe it was as simple as that.

I started at the very bottom. I cleaned drains, I made the tea, I cleaned the mess in the banking hall when anybody was sick, or a dog was... you know. It was the lowest of the low in those days. I stoked the boiler. Very accomplished boiler-stoker and tea-maker.

I dreamed about being a manager. What a smashing life. He seemed to have time to think, he seemed to lead a very pleasant life, he seemed to have knowledge about such a wide variety of things, and he appeared to have power, sorry, responsibility is a nicer word for describing it.

I was a very poor performer at the start. I was very slow. I learned afterwards that there was a distinct possibility that I would not continue after my probation. I don't know what saved me. I think the manager was too weak to chop anybody out.

I worked at a three-hander for the first two years and then I did national service, and then came back to another smallish branch, a nine-hander. I was now getting on towards twenty-one and I hadn't been allowed on to the counter to service the public. Nowadays we put people on the counter within six months of coming to the bank.

I just wasn't progressing. I found I was still the junior, still doing the same things. Stoking the boiler, perhaps with a bit more finesse, and sharing the tea-making duties, but there was a lot of frustration, and after a year, I said, 'Can't I do something more responsible in the Midland Bank, please?' With which I was despatched on what then was an enormous journey from Bradford to Rotherham and I had to move house – I'd just got married – and move to Rotherham where my career, in any sense of the word, began.

It was a larger office, and there was the flexibility to move people around and give them other things to do. At Rotherham, which was a forty-hander, I was allowed to look after customers' statements and go on the counter, and in a very short period I went on to what was regarded as very senior duties, looking after people's valuable safe-custody items, dealing with the security that's taken by the bank for lending, and looking at how the bank lends money. So I literally saw a lot of other aspects of the bank. It was an excellent way to start. Very mundane chores, but they stood you in good stead later on when you became the administrator of an office, because you knew what the shop floor was doing because you'd done it. I mean, today's entrants from university who come in as management trainees don't have the benefit of having done that.

The manager at Rotherham at that time was a very senior man. He'd been through the bank properly, through head offices and things like that; he was a real banker. And he recognized that he had three of us on the staff – there were two other lads of my own age – who were very keen. He would take us back to his house after work for a cup of tea and teach us how to look at balance sheets and things like that. He was very good to us, he encouraged us. In those days we opened the bank up on a Saturday morning, half-staffed, and we were given a chance to run the office on Saturday mornings, things like that. We were given a real sniff of responsibility, and we all three responded. Mr Renshaw – Mr Bert Renshaw was his name – he was a quality banker, his own reputation within the senior banking people was well respected. And so if he recommended you, it carried some weight. Two of the three of us were put forward for special training; and I was given an appointment, and to get an appointment meant something; you were on the first rung of the ladder. And so I went from Rotherham to Brighton, with no car and two babies.

Nowadays, that is not an untypical posting. In those days, it was very unusual to move outside your own patch and I had expected to remain within West Yorkshire all my life. It's a bit like the army, although there's one big difference, you can say no. But if you say no, you could be turning down promotion. And you're not sure if or when the next opportunity will be given. So, if you're ambitious, as I was, then you don't turn it down.

One saw little, if anything, of friends, particularly when we moved to the south coast. I began to think of them less and less. It became a Christmas card situation, nothing more. I'm sure my parents were extremely disappointed when we moved from Yorkshire to the south coast with their first two grandchildren. But they were never anything other than encouraging. They had a great deal of pride in the fact, if you like, their son had progressed.

I don't really know what made me ambitious. I only had a limited ambition in the sense that I don't think I ever wanted to be the boss of the bank. But I'm sure this applies to organizations other than the banks, if you get into the promotion stream, you can be carried along. It reaches the stage where you are perhaps offered more senior jobs than you necessarily want, because the organization feels it has trained you for those things and has the impression you can do them. If you're honest with yourself, you know it's going to be a struggle.

For over twenty years work has been the most important part of my life. In fact it overwhelms other things. I found quite early on in my career that I was spending evenings and weekends doing banking work, on the lounge carpet, at the desk at home. Since then, it has gradually become almost a twenty-four-hours-a-day job. I'm very interested in it and I get tremendous satisfaction from working in the bank. Sometimes perhaps one would like to get off the treadmill. There are many times, when life gets difficult, that you wish you could step off, and you contemplate all the things that other people do. Wouldn't it be nice to have a country pub or a village post office, where the reponsibilities were a lot less; or even, why didn't I finish up with a job in the bank that wasn't so taxing?

There are times when the wife wishes I would devote a little less time to it. She obviously thinks that it is not good for one's health to be as involved as I am.

I think one has a level of competence which enables you to do certain jobs. The problems are very complex, they stretch you mentally, and the challenge of selling a multiplicity of services I find difficult. I have a narrowish mind in the sense that I'm not a good delegator. This is why the bank takes up an ever-increasing part of my time, because I am not a good delegator. I like to know everything which is going on within my own particular domain, and so unless the day was lengthened to forty-eight hours, I couldn't take on a larger function – unless I changed my character and personality radically, which I think is no longer possible.

Although I'm ambitious for this area, I feel I've reached the height; my abilities are not such that they would lend themselves for me to go any further in the bank. I think it's a sensible person who recognizes their own limitations. I have moved around the country. I've come back home now. The truth is that I have no burning desire to go and do anything else. I feel that there is enough here to challenge me for the remainder of my stay in the bank.

My strengths have taken me to where I am. My weaknesses are keeping me there. I accept it. To progress in the bank is likely to mean returning to London, and I have never enjoyed the anonymity of big-city life. I've always enjoyed being part of the community, and being accepted through my position into the community.

I'd say I've achieved my ambitions – in fact I've surpassed them. I'd seen myself, with luck, becoming the manager of, say, a twenty-hander, with a reasonable spread of business, instead of becoming, if you like, senior manager of a very large business where I'm in charge of seven banks in the West Yorkshire area.

I've certainly felt guilt that in order to achieve my ambition of getting to a responsible position in the bank, I've had to put my family through the traumas of moving all over the country. We've lived in Birmingham, Reading, Maidenhead, Brighton, everywhere, and the stability that I enjoyed as a child, growing up in a small district in Bradford from four to eighteen, my children never got that stability, and I often worried that it would affect their ability to be happy in life. But it doesn't seem to have done so, and they're both married and they found their partners through having lived in the different places we've lived in. So at the moment my guilt is assuaged.

People are very disappointed if you won't go along with their ideas sometimes – and that is the hardest part of being a bank manager, saying no to people. It's very, very hard because all human beings want to be liked. But it is what I call the 'element of steel' in them which differentiates the good bank manager from the not so good. I feel a little stretched emotionally sometimes, a little upset, particularly if the man won't accept your decision, or you know that it has angered or hurt him.

Some customers are aware you have feelings, and play on it. They will occasionally blackmail you by suggesting that they would take their business elsewhere, and that's again where you need strength of character to say, 'Well, that is your decision.'

I suppose the worst part of the job is dealing with terminal situations, the financial demise of a business or a person. You can be making decisions that might cost five thousand redundancies, and I have found that a source of heartache. But it has to be done because it is the correct thing in stewarding resources.

In the old days, going back thirty years, the Inland Revenue was regarded as 'fair game', if you like, and people were generally honest with every other organization that they came into contact with. But I find that is not the case now. People will try to take advantage of many other organizations, and banks in particular. Sometimes I do take it personally, yes. Where you've dealt with somebody and you've been conned because events showed later that he clearly was misleading you. I sometimes feel quite bitter.

I think man is becoming increasingly dishonest. Perhaps it's because banks are now faceless institutions. In order to offer a cheaper product, we have become very much more anonymous and less approachable. When I began in the bank, nearly everything was done across the counter. Banking now is done by post or telephone, machines in the wall. It has had to be done like that because if we had continued to provide a full personal service, the cost of wage rates would have meant that bank charges would have been prohibitive.

If the customers don't regard the banker as having, if you like, the wisdom of Solomon, then they aren't going to respect his decisions. We are not only protecting our money, but the vast majority of our decisions are made with the customer's best interests at heart. We can perceive, as an outside observer, what he is doing wrong with his business, or what he is planning to do wrong, or what may go wrong. A lot of customers will come and talk over things which don't necessarily call for the bank to be an integral part but simply because they respect the views of a banker. Yes, that's important to me. That is one of the facets of the job which makes it so satisfying, I think that's the pride angle coming out, isn't it? One wants, if you like, to be respected for one's judgements.

I think that one of the things which the population still looks to in a bank manager is confidentiality, in the same way that they go and tell their doctor a lot of intimate problems in the knowledge that he won't go and tell everybody else, people will tell their bank manager the majority of their situation, because they recognize that you won't go and spill the beans.

Occasionally I wistfully wish that I had been the manager of the branch in the days when I began. It was a wonderful life he seemed to have, all the time in the world, and no pressures. It was traditional for the manager in those days to have a half day off in the middle of the week, he didn't appear on a Saturday morning, so effectively he worked a 4½-day week on a 9.15 to 5 o'clock basis, whereas the majority of bankers now work very long hours. Life wasn't as complex, business wasn't as buoyant, competition between the banks was a fraction of the present time, there was no competition from any financial institutions such as there is now, life was very cosy in my view. Perhaps it was because I was looking at it from the other side of the office, it may not have been, but it appeared so.

Bookseller
Christopher Stephenson

It's fulfilling an ambition. I was always a book buyer, always frequenting bookshops, and when Enid and I married we both had the feeling that we would like to do this at some future date. We were both working at the *Observer*, but our life circumstances changed when I contracted an illness. I went to teacher training college for a few months, but I just realized it wasn't me. So when I pulled out from that, then we said, 'All right, now we'll do what we always said we were going to do.' Enid had a number of publisher friends and they looked out for places where they thought a new bookshop was needed. We like East Anglia, but because we are both city people it had to be in a town, not in the countryside, and in fact, living up here in Norwich, I've become more urbanized than I realized; I'm lost without petrol fumes up my nostrils.

We had an idea of what sort of bookshop we wanted to run, which was a general bookshop with a large children's section. We originally looked for the typical bookshop premises, one floor above another – very impractical, lots of thievery goes on, and you can't really feel that you've got control over the place. Then this suddenly came up, the premises here. We were a bit worried about the number of people passing, and I spent days standing outside loitering with intent, watching how many people came in, but yes, everything's working fine.

I couldn't sell anything else, it must be books. It's one of the few things I really care about, selling books to people, and sometimes I feel I could give them away, quite honestly, because I think books are so important. So this has certainly fulfilled by expectations, and it's also given me a wonderful chance to read all those books I've always wanted to read. I'm always reading a book, I walk along the street reading a book. I think I can only see the world through a book sometimes.

Before you come into a business like this, you think that working in a bookshop is just selling books over the counter to people, but of course it isn't. It's getting the books into the shop and seeing the reps and listening to their patter, and doing the windows, sweeping the floor, all these things have to be done. It's damn hard work if you do it properly, but I think we're halfway there. It is rewarding, but like all jobs it has its dull moments, it has its routine. The main thing for me is customer orders. A customer comes in and orders a book which we haven't got, and we can get up to fifty requests a day, and they all have to be written up and sent off to the publisher. Publishers are not as efficient as they should be in getting their books out: a fortnight is the usual sort of time between an order going from here and the book arriving, and it's absolute nonsense, there is no need for that. All the publishers' excuses for not sending the books have to be relayed to the customer – and even sometimes the books – so it is mundane things like that, and just finding the time to do it. Sometimes I have to do it at home because there is no other way if we are very busy in the shop.

Then there are the reps. It can be a damn nuisance when you're getting into some nice work and suddenly you're interrupted by a rep who hasn't made an appointment. But most of them do, and it's a very important part of the day, because although some will only bring a book jacket, they are usually able to fill you in on the background and show a few pages from the book. We try only to order books that we like. And the gratifying thing is that a lot of the books we like might be slightly odd and out of the normal run, but they are usually picked up by our customers and they're the ones that go.

I suppose there are about ten very good publishers, there may be more but I can only think of ten, and usually the best publishers have the best reps, and the best reps know what it's all about. You see somebody like the rep from Faber and Faber who comes with an immense amount of books all of pretty high quality, lots of poetry, lots of theatre and new novels, and he can tell you when the play's going to be in production, or when he met the poet last. Some reps just come in with their little, they call them 'blads' – I don't know why, those little plastic notebooks – and they stand and read it out to me... well, thank you very much, *I* can do that. I do sometimes wonder whether reps are necessary. The best reps are a joy to see because they don't come in talking about percentages and sales, they're interested in the books, or they give the impression of being interested in the books.

Money is necessary to live on but it isn't very important to us. You never make a fortune bookselling, and for a medium-sized independent bookseller like us, there is no thought of making any money out of it. We pay ourselves a very minimum wage each week. Money doesn't worry me, I'm middle class so I suppose I can afford not to worry about money – not that I've got any. I'm so bad with money. For example, people ask me how the book token system works. I sell them, I accept book tokens, but if you ask how it works, I've no idea.

It's lovely when somebody comes and buys fifty pounds' worth of books, but that's luck, it doesn't really matter; they could buy a £1.95 book and I still get a kick. It's being with books. One of the greatest joys is a new box of books coming in, that wonderful moment when you open it and there they are! But my greatest pleasure is when a box of new Penguins come in, and immediately of course I find ten I want to read.

There is always a basic stock of books that you try to keep on the shelves, I don't just mean the *Wuthering Heights*, but things like the Booker Prize books of the past years, that sort of thing. One of our main interests is new fiction, and I don't know how true it is, but the rep from Jonathan Cape actually told us that outside Cambridge we stock more new fiction than any other shop in East Anglia. I don't know if he was buttering us up, but we certainly do stock more than we've been told is good for us, because when we first started, one of the things that we were warned about was to stay off hardback fiction.

There is a number of authors you know you can rely on, but it is still wholly a gamble. You're not given a book and told to take a pile away and read them and the ones you like you order. You have to order them sight unseen. I'm not bad at that, though. Getting better, more canny as we go along. When we first opened, we knew all the books we liked and ordered them. We also listened to the reps praise some books: 'Oh, yes, this is definitely an important book,' they say. We've now begun to step between their terminology, 'important book'... absolute nonsense. I remember one rep came round with a book saying, 'Now *this* is an important book,' and immediately the hackles rose and I thought, 'What's he going to show us?' And he said, 'It's a book about the Redgraves,' and I was thinking, 'Maybe it's a book about Michael Redgrave and I would be interested in that,' and it turned out to be by Deirdre Redgrave who was Corin's wife, I think. And I mean it's our money we're spending. And he said, 'You'll be asked for it... ' And of course I never read a review of it, nobody ever asks us for the book, and we were quite happy without it.

I sometimes try and guess what people are going to buy. I can do that much better with the people we know, of course, and you can also guess that some people are not going to buy anything. It's the way they look round the shop. I mean if somebody is interested in the books they actually look at a book on the shelf, they take it down, and look at it on the table. Some people come into the shop, and I don't know why they do it, will walk around it without seeing anything. You can see there is not a thought of buying a book or indeed looking at a book. People who come in and say, 'I could spend a thousand pounds in here,' you know they are not going to spend a penny, it's a very strange thing.

There is a man, I've never actually found out what he does, I think he might be in the film world, he lives in America but comes over about every three months, and I know precisely what sort of book he's going to buy. So when I see this man come through the door, and he always has a long cigar and says, 'Hello,' I know he's not interested in looking at the shelves, he is only interested in the books on the tables, which are usually the larger books. There was a beautiful book Thames and Hudson did called *Leaves*, photographs of leaves, and I thought, that's the book for this man – now how am I going to put it in front of him without actually saying, 'Here's the book for you'? So I took one book off the table and put *Leaves* there instead, and I watched him come along, and pick it up, and he said, 'Would you gift-wrap this for me?'

There are a whole group of customers who are friends now, purely through the shop. They don't come just to buy a book, but to chat, sometimes about the books, or things that are happening in Norwich, sometimes about Mrs Thatcher, although they usually pick up a book or two.

I'm a fan of P.G. Wodehouse, there's no one greater, I think. Well, we try to keep P.G., usually in Penguin, on the shelf, and if somebody arrives at the cash desk with a Wodehouse, I feel, here is a friend, here is a man worth bothering about. Quite a few young people, I'm pleased to say, buy Wodehouse, and I usually have a bit of a chat and see how much he's going to quote of Wodehouse to me before I quote it back. They usually can, and there is a warm feeling, definitely. I'm very fond of a novelist called Brian Moore, he's an Irish Canadian, a very fine novelist. I read his new book a couple of months ago called *The Black Cloak*, and a few weeks later a chap who I know vaguely came in and bought it – and immediately the day opened up for me – because you get hobby horses about certain things, and Brian Moore, he's a very, very good author, but he's little known, and it's a wonderful moment when somebody agrees with you.

The bad moments come, as they do in life generally, from rudeness. It happens very rarely, but it sticks out because I get hurt. I can think of one man particularly. I cannot stand the man, I find him a bully, and a bore, and he's rude, and I'm uneasy the whole time he's in the shop. We have little postcards of authors on the wall from the National Portrait Gallery, and my greatest joy came to me when he was showing off in front of his two sons, and as he walked out of the shop he said, 'Look, George Orwell,' pointing to a portrait of T.E. Lawrence, and somehow I thought, 'All right, good, that's the measure of you, sir.'

If I've made a mistake, of course I get worried about that. We get quite a lot of school orders, you know, sixty-five copies of *Practical Technology,* Book 2, Teacher's Notes only sort of thing, and occasionally it happens that I order the wrong book. But this is all very mundane stuff, on the whole it is pleasant, people are pleasant, people are interesting, they like chatting, I like chatting to them, I just get annoyed with the rude ones.

I get very het up at busy times, the lead-up to Christmas, for example, which is very busy indeed. At Christmas you get a queue of people who come round, and it's book-grabbing time, desperation sets in and there is something almost animal-like about that, and I feel we are not functioning properly then, because our job, as I see it, is to talk about books as well as just sell them.

Well, I was thinking as I was walking in this morning, 'I wonder what he is going to ask me... is work important?' I could in truth give it up tomorrow quite happily because I'd still carry on reading, I'd still be in touch with books. But I suppose, if the truth be known, I'd have liked to have been a writer, but I tell myself, and it's true, if I really had been a writer I would have done that rather than sell books. I can't think of anything else I would prefer to do – I'm not saying I wouldn't have preferred to have *been* something else – but I can't think of anything else I would prefer to do.

Car Salesman
Rob Shellard

Originally I worked for my father who sold the family business, foundry engineering, and made me redundant so he could get the capital and retire. I'd worked for him for nine years and I considered it my birthright to take over the business. Anyway, that wasn't to be.

After that I just needed a job and I went to Volvo's in St John's Wood who had advertised in the evening paper for a service receptionist – the people who you go and see when you take your car in for a service. So that's how I got involved with Volvo, I just needed a job. I didn't last very long there, about eighteen months, I couldn't stand the aggravation. Then I went off and did other things, played tennis and what have you, came back five years later and needed a job again, so I went back to the original place in St John's Wood just so I could start earning some money. A position came open selling, so I came along for an interview, they were very short of staff, and although I had no selling experience, they took me on.

I started about six years ago when business was very buoyant. In my first week I sold ten cars, there were more customers for Volvos than there were cars. It was a question of if you had the cars you could do the deal. So I stormed away, no problems at all, and from earning a very meagre salary as a service receptionist I was earning very good money indeed. I'd only actually planned to stay a short time because I was thinking of going to Canada, but with the sort of money I was earning I decided to keep going. And now, although the market has changed and it's far more competitive to sell cars, I'm still earning very good money, and while I'm earning good money I'll stay. How long that will be I don't know.

I think I'm suited to selling something a bit more up-market than, say, Fords. I think Volvo is a very good product and I'm happy selling it. I don't think I'd be happy selling something like Renault or Citroën because I don't actually believe they're a very good car.

My accent goes down very well, but I think you've got to be able to deal with anybody. I mean, we get people in here from Rastafarians to Royals, so you have to be able to adapt to whoever. Most of the time you try and be as up-market as you can, but there are times when you have to change the accent and come right down to dealing with market traders or whatever. Any good car salesman has to be an actor because you've got to get on with the person you're dealing with. I quite enjoy dealing with Joe Blow from down the road, but I probably find it easier to deal with the up-market people.

All the salesmen that have been successful here seem to fit into a certain image. You've got Mark out there who's a university graduate in economics, and we've got two other ex-university guys. They're all mid-twenties to mid-thirties – I'm probably getting a bit too old now, I'm forty. All very smartly dressed, all really the same sort of characters, prepared to work hard, but also to play hard as well. I mean we do have a laugh selling cars. For example, with the different people we deal with, you can set them into categories, and that's funny. You know, you've got your Mr Patels and the Wally Brigade and the Hooray Henries we deal with. There's probably a dozen different categories if you actually worked it out.

There are basically two techniques in selling cars. There's the soft sell, which is to get to know the chap you're dealing with and try and be as he wants you to be – friendly, helpful, and on a par with him. That works a lot of the time, but then you have to go to the other end of the scale when somebody is actually wasting your time or haggling over twenty-five pounds.

You have to get very tough, you have to become a hard salesman and close the deal. You give them an ultimatum and actually force them into signing a deal because otherwise with certain people you can go on too long playing the nice guy.

It's difficult to tell who's a time-waster, because you get a lot of people just wandering around the West End and they see a Volvo showroom and think, 'We'll wander in here and have a look.' But I would say that anybody you actually start talking prices to, they're 75 per cent of the way there. The next 25 per cent is getting them to like you, because if they like you they'll buy the car – and not necessarily at the cheapest price.

All I've ever read about car salesmen is that they're a fairly shabby crew, and I think it's a pleasant surprise for anybody who comes in here to meet somebody who is responsible and who they can trust. It's not so bad for me working up here in the West End because it is the most up-market you can get in the car-selling game, but yes, you're still a car salesman. It doesn't really worry me, because the money's there at the end of the day. Looking back on it I wish that I'd gone into something else, but at the time I needed a job and needed the money. Sometimes I wish I could go back into engineering and pursue that, but having been out of it for fifteen years I'm probably terribly out of date anyway.

Being married with two children and running a very high mortgage, I'm certainly under pressure. Providing business is good, and providing you're performing and acting well, then you can earn the money and pay the bills. But if I slip, or the product slips, or there could be a strike in Sweden or a strike at the docks this end, any number of things could cause your money to be cut by half or more in one month, so there's a lot of pressure on actually keeping up with your commitments. But we're not a sour-faced serious lot.

Basically there are three levels of commission and they vary according to what level you are on. I'm on the top level which means I get paid a higher basic rate of commission on the profit of the car. If you keep performing at your targets, which for me is about 245 cars a year, then you're OK. It's done on a quarterly basis throughout the year. If you don't make a quarter's target then you receive a warning from the sales manager, and if you fail to make your target the next quarter, you're then down-graded. Then if you fail to make the next target you're down-graded again, so you're down on the bottom rung of the ladder. If you then fail to make that, you're out. Anybody coming in and starting has got three months to make their mark; if not, out. So because of my commitments I have to perform well over my target a lot of the time, and it's a lot of pressure to keep performing regularly and continually at those numbers.

You've got to keep an air of confidence and that it doesn't really matter, you're not going to suffer if you don't do the deal. I think grovelling is the worst way of selling. You've got to exude the fact that you are successful, and that in the customer's eyes will make you look good, and he must have confidence in you. But if you're down on your bended knees he's not going to have a lot of confidence.

You've got to be good at gauging people. That's the secret of success.

I think I'm good. I don't know whether it's luck or not, but I can usually tell as somebody's coming through the showroom door whether they're a time-waster or not. They may ask for one particular model of car, and then perhaps they might drift on after a minute to another car, or 'What is that car over there?' If they're being very non-specific then it's time to try and ease them out the door or say, 'Right, that's that one, and that's this one, that's so much – do you want to buy it?' You get tough then. But if you have someone who is after one particular model then you know you are on the right track.

Also, you can tell just by the various types that come in. If they come in loaded with brochures under their arms it means that they are actually shopping around all the different dealers. All you can do with them is to be polite, give them the brochures to add to their collection and send them on their way. Time is quite an important thing. Lunchtime is not a good time, you get a lot of time-wasters. If you were to have somebody come in about now, 11 o'clockish in the morning, smartly dressed in a suit, then he's obviously come out of his office specially. So it's a number of things.

Then there's the chap who buys a car once every seven or eight years and, no matter how good you are, he will not trust you – you're still 'the car salesman'. And he would be a civil servant, or something along those lines, and when he comes into the showroom, he's got everything organized, a list of questions he's going to ask you two pages long. They're hard work to deal with.

I tend to enjoy the country crowd with the Volvo Estates and the nice houses, and you make an excuse for going down there to hand it over, because they are always very appreciative, and they are just generally very nice to deal with. Like the Chelsea set who have a house in Chelsea during the week and use the car for the country estate at the weekend. And City people are normally nice to deal with: they're too busy to haggle over the last few pounds. If you give them a good deal you can do the deal very quickly.

As a franchise we get 17½ discount. We can give up to 15–16 per cent which leaves you 1½–2½ per cent profit in the car, of which you get 10 per cent. So basically you're on 10 per cent of fuck all. But with accessories, we get 10 per cent of the invoice price. So if you came to me and we agreed a deal of 15 per cent on an estate car that would leave about £250 profit for the company, of which I would get 10 per cent, which is £25. You may then say to me, 'Well, I want a sunroof, I want a stereo, a tow-bar and I want a dog guard, spotlights.' I might invoice you for accessories for up to £1300 or £1400, so at the end of the day you end up making a total of about £150 on the car for your commission. Because of the commission structure we work under, we're not really interested in what money we make on the car, it's more whether we can make it on the accessories or on finance – if you're buying a car on HP, we have finance commission where you can earn again £100, £200 a car.

Most members of the public go about buying a car all wrong. You should get the price of the car from a book, and you work out roughly 12½ or 15 per cent off that price and keep that figure in your head. You do all your research first so you know exactly what you want. You might want to test drive two or three cars. Now a lot of people will come in and be afraid to ask for a discount and they will duck and dive and phone three or four dealers and get comparative prices, but it's all a waste of time, because if you're totally straight with the salesman and say, 'I will buy that car if you give me 15 per cent discount,' the salesman will sell it to you for that money, because that's the market we're in today.

There's an overproduction of cars in Europe and they've got to be moved. There's only a couple of franchises of the mass-produced cars you can't do that with, people like BMW and Mercedes. But any other car, virtually, providing you're not being silly and asking 17½ per cent – the salesman would throw you out then – but at 15 per cent, yes, the salesman will do a deal.

In twenty years' time I'll be coming up to retirement age. I would hope by then that I would have some sort of small business of my own. This present house-move I'm going through hopefully will be the last one, and then gradually with time I shall have some capital over, but I would like to get into some aspect of the car business on my own somehow, probably buying and selling.

Chimney Sweep
Edward Bull

It's my name that's on the vans. Although I'm Edward Bull, I trade as Yorkshire Chimney Specialists, but that name is still my trading name and I don't want people going out and saying, 'They're a useless firm.' I get a great deal of satisfaction when a total stranger rings me up: 'Will you come and clean my chimney? Mrs So and So has recommended you and she said you've always done a very good job.' That's very very satisfying because I always say that word of mouth is the best advertising – and cheapest.

To a certain extent it is a dying craft. When my father was doing the job, going back twenty-five years, every house had one or two coal fires, there was a chimney sweep almost on every street corner. Nowadays there are three or possibly four full-time chimney sweeps covering Huddersfield and the whole surrounding areas, covering probably a ten-mile radius. So a spin-off of that is my work tends to be more spread out so I'm having to travel about a lot more.

We cover a wide area, last week I went to Keighley which is about thirty miles away. It takes an hour to get there, an hour to do the job and an hour to come back, and the reason why we go that far away is because I've got the brains – I don't mind saying that – and the equipment and I know the chimney; all the local chimney sweeps have looked at it and couldn't clear the chimney, so we go along four times a year and do it. I take pride in being able to do it, I always go along and make a good job.

I'm not greedy, I'm getting a comfortable living out of it, I'll not grumble at all. Obviously money's important because it's survival, isn't it? Without money you can't live nowadays. I did a job this week and I made a great deal of money on it and that was satisfying. I think to a certain extent money is a yardstick of the success of your business. But money isn't everything. I've got a lot of commitments just at the moment. I've started with this new house, new mortgage, both children are fairly small – I've two daughters, the youngest's three the oldest one's six – so I'm at a time in my life when I've got to be working as hard now, I would imagine, as at any time in my life. And once or twice it's come to my mind that I'm working incredibly hard, long hours purely to pay for all this, and I've said jokingly to my wife, 'I could pack it in, sign on the dole and go walking every day.' But I don't mind working hard because it's my business and I'm getting the rewards for it.

I've got a conscience and if I was not working, and I could see everyone else working, I wouldn't be happy at all. I like paying my way. I mean, bringing it down to basics, going into the pub, I want to pay my round. I don't want to be relying on someone else, I don't want to be beholden to anybody.

When I'm chimney sweeping I never take a flask with me because it's a very unusual day when I don't get offered a cup of coffee. Some days I can be drinking a dozen cups of tea or coffee. I never say no, I'm a talker a little bit, so when dear old Mrs Jones puts the kettle on, if I can afford five minutes I'll sit down and have a cup of tea and a chat with her, and I enjoy it, I enjoy being with pleasant people. I've had my dinner made for me, sat down to a Sunday dinner on jobs more than once, although I don't often work on a Sunday if I can help it.

I always feel conscious of being dirty, I'll never sit down even if they ask me to; we're not terribly dirty but I feel conscious of it, I wouldn't sit down in my own house, so I don't want to do it in theirs. But with farmers, it's 'Never mind, it'll not harm, sit down lad, get your feet under the table,' it's lovely, I like working for people like that, very, very pleasant. A lot of people say farmers are difficult to get money out of, but you work hard for them and do them a good job and you'll find it very rewarding, that's my opinion. The farmers that I've worked for have paid me no problem whatsoever, full amount.

I'm a Yorkshire man born and bred and I'm proud of it. I find the further south the less friendliness there is about. Yorkshire people are friendly. I go down to London occasionally to do with work. I'll just mention it in passing, I'm one of the founder members, founder executive member in fact, for the Yorkshire Area National Association of Chimney Sweeps, and we go down about half a dozen times a year to London to meetings. I always drive down, and I feel myself changing as I'm driving down the M1, like Jekyll and Hyde. I drive totally differently as well. Hyde Park Corner – I'm aggressive, driving just like a taxi driver, I get taxi drivers moving out of the way for me. I get more and more tense as I'm walking through London, everything's a rush to get there, nobody's talking, everybody's hustle and bustle... and then coming back home I feel myself relaxing slowly as I'm coming up the M1.

It's beautiful country up here. When I'm very very busy I never even see the sides of the road going from one job to another, I'm just thinking about the next job or thinking about the last job. Whatever is round me I'm oblivious to it, and I'm just wanting to get on with my work. But if I can relax in the slightest, I'll drive around looking at the moors, and I love it.

The other side of Holmfirth, which is very very well known nationwide for 'Last of the Summer Wine', once you start getting over the moors there, that's fabulous. I could grow old sat up there quite happily. I've stopped many a time beside the road at lunchtime, get my sandwiches out, and I just sit back for half an hour, and then I find it very very difficult to get back working again, I've relaxed, I've settled down and I'm enjoying it. I like the rough moorland round here very much. A lot of people find it a bit too rugged, but I get my Wellingtons on and I'm up through the marsh bogs, yes, fabulous.

Traditionally chimney sweeps are lucky, touch a chimney sweep and you get good luck – that's one of the traditions. Probably the best known of all is a chimney sweep at a wedding is supposed to be good luck; if a chimney sweep kisses the bride it's good luck, although the only time I tried, everything went wrong. I was best man for one of my friends. I didn't go in my working gear which is probably the mistake I made, you're supposed to go in with brushes and covered in soot, and we had all sorts, taxis breaking down, telegrams left in the church, this, that and the other, and it was all a bit of an upset.

I don't know about luck. I think you have to go out and get it. I'm not terribly much into these traditions, I don't fill in the pools, this sort of thing. I think the only way I'm going to make money is to go out and make money myself.

If the business is not handed down in the family, it's going to be a nice little nest egg to sell the business and retire on, so whichever way, it wouldn't upset me too much. Okay, we're living on dreams here – but you've got to have something to work for, haven't you? I would like to see the business handed on but I wouldn't wish my daughters to go out doing the jobs I'm doing. I don't know, I'm not really sexist, but to me it's not the sort of job that you'd expect a girl to be doing. If they want to do it, all well and good, but it's not particularly feminine.

One thing I get pride in away from chimney sweeping is chimney building, chimney repairing. There's a great lack of knowledge about chimneys nowadays. They'll build a house and put in a fireplace and a chimney which are totally unsuitable for one another. One of my boasts is that I can cure anything with a chimney and I've gone along to cases in question where no one, not even the Coal Board, can cure it, and I'll look at it and I'll say, 'If I can't cure it you won't owe me anything,' and never yet failed. So I get a great deal of pride from that, a great deal of pride, and satisfaction, and pleasure. Mind you, I'm a chimney sweep at heart, that's the first love.

I used to do the job part-time with my father on school holidays and weekends. The first job I did when it was my business, my name, was an old woman. My father had been looking to retire for a long time, so his prices had gotten a little bit out of touch, and the first thing I had to do was revise all the prices – not a terrific amount – probably twenty per cent, twenty-five per cent, something along those lines. And the very first job I did, the woman went, 'Oh, you've put your prices up so much.' I mean, obviously you get people grumbling about the price, but on the very first job I did, it was a poor start. I thought, 'If this is what working for myself is going to be, I'll finish now.' I made excuses why the price had had to go up, this, that and the other, but I wasn't used to dealing with people then at all. My father was with me, so he was a great help of course. But it was a little bit off-putting.

Father died about three years ago. I don't like to have regrets in life, but the only thing I do regret is that he can't see me now. My father always did the job in a small way. In a way I admire him for it; he was happy to just go along, and do enough work to make the minimum amount of money that he needed. He wasn't greedy, he always wanted to be fair with people, which I still like to be, but I'm trying to get that little bit further in front, and I'm probably turning over now about twenty times what my father was turning over when he retired. I'd like my father to see what was happening now with the business, which he can't do, obviously... well, I don't know, can he?

Some of the things I do, he'd look at me and say, 'Son, you're barmy.' But I mean, to make money, you've got to spend money, you've got to speculate to make it, haven't you? My bills have soared. I mean petrol this week alone, and we haven't done a great deal of running around this week, I must have spent nearly one hundred pounds on petrol alone this week. My father put five pounds in on the weekend and if he had to put some more in before the weekend, he'd had a bad week.

I'd like to think he would be proud of me. I think he would, yes, I feel sure that he would.

Criminal
Jack Maxwell

It's just a job. It's what I was brought up for. I was brought up as a criminal. I don't like harping on about people being hungry and all that carry-on, but my first conviction was when I was arrested at nine years of age at 5 o'clock in the morning, stealing bread out of the baker's. I was stealing the bread because I was hungry, and we used to eat the bread, no butter or nothing, just lumps of bread. That was fifty years ago – I'm celebrating my anniversary, fifty years a criminal.

My father wasn't a criminal but all my family bar my father were engaged in criminal activities. Back where I came from it was just a natural way of life, it was a way of stopping being hungry, a way of being the best-dressed guy in the district or something like that. None of my acquaintances that I know ever thought of taking a straight job, because straight jobs, what do they pay today? Say a miner, people just can't live on these things. My expenses before I can have a cup of tea or a packet of cigarettes is £500 a week at the least, because if a person has got any principle, any character at all, he looks after his family, which is my job, being that I'm considered the best money earner, and it's a large family, and somebody's got to feed them, and if I went out and took a job at £200 a week, there's no fucking way in the world I could feed crippled brothers, cancer-ridden mother. I'm the one considered responsible ...

All through my fifty years as a criminal I've enjoyed it. I've spent a lot of time in prison, I've looked at it as part of the game, no complaints, get your bird over and get back out, get on the phone and get a bit of action going. After an eight-year sentence which I finished five years ago, I just walked out the prison gate to the nearest telephone and I was criminally active within three minutes, at the most, of coming out of prison.

I'm not clever or anything like that, I've got no O-levels or A-levels or any of that rubbish, but I am ambitious, I would like to line everyone in my family up and give them a lump of money for their start in life, because if you don't have any money, you don't have any start in life.

The street knowledge that I have gained through being fifty years a criminal, it even leaves the fucking police surprised. I'm proud of that, of course I'm proud of it, it's my job.

There's crime being committed in this country which is bringing too much heat on the likes of us as quiet people, we like our crimes to be committed and no trace of them left behind, non-violent crimes. We used to charge into a bank and people were nearly fucking dying of fright and all that carry-on, then the big sentences came and supergrasses and all that, and most people have moved out of violent crime. Most of them doing violence now is kids; we've all moved into a nice little business where there's no crime being committed unless you're actually caught doing it, and we're getting a pound out of it. We're getting a living and not causing any harm that we can see, and we intend keeping it going.

My type of criminal, I leave here at the same time every afternoon. Just like an office worker, people know not to phone me at certain times because I won't be in the house, I'll be engaged in my work. I'm abroad a lot now, I'm just back, had a nice little trip to Germany, got myself a pound note there. I was over on a little bit of criminal business; it was the best crime, it left no trace, the thing was done, I came back here with my share of the money and nobody was hurt, somebody was short of a few pounds, that's all.

I can't afford to have a conscience. Well, take for instance shoplifting, which I've done, and I'll give you an instance. I had an order for a couple of suede coats. I went in and I took twelve suede coats, it was at a C&A which was just opening up; the place is jam-packed with people, and I went and wiped out one rail. Unfortunately the girl in charge of the rail, she got the sack, but the girl, she was unknown to me, how could I have a conscience about her getting the sack? I mean the likes of that wouldn't keep me awake for one second and it wouldn't stop me going into another shop and stealing again and for someone else to get the sack. I mean, if you have a conscience like that you're just not a criminal, you don't do these things if you have a conscience about it.

I would say that my hunger comes before anybody else's hunger. If I was robbing a till I wouldn't fucking leave anything in it, I would want the lot; if I was going to steal anything I wouldn't steal one article, I'd try and steal ten or maybe twenty. I'm greedy that way, but I'm not greedy for myself, because what do I need? I don't drink, I don't go out of the house, except on criminal activities. I don't spend anything.

Prison is part of the job. You don't go out committing a crime with the full expectation of getting completely away with it. Everybody would be committing crime then, there would be too many fucking people in the game then, we don't want that, in fact the less people in the game the more we like it. We'd rather the whole police concentration was on us, providing the game was left to us, because we know how to handle police. You don't go out fucking shooting policemen and all that, you pat a policeman on the back – that is a saying for you don't fight with policemen.

Being a professional criminal, when you are planning a crime you're also weighing up your sentence for each crime. Just yesterday I was offered a part in a nice little caper and I would have got a few thousand pound out of it, but I didn't think the risk justified the chance that I would have to take on it, so I didn't get involved. When I was going over the pros and cons of the caper with the little firm, I asked, 'What if this or that happens, is the security man going to get it?' Well, if he gets it we're going for a ten- or twelve-year sentence for a couple of grand, it's not worth it. You can get a couple of grand out of any shop if you want to go shoplifting and get three months for it, why go after ten or twelve, there's just no sense in it.

I wouldn't say I was a hard man, I've got a bit of a reputation, I mean nobody will fuck with me, especially as I've got the family. I've got fourteen children, thirteen boys, I've been married three times, I've got a daughter of forty.

I don't mind my sons being involved in criminal activity if they listen to me and they don't go out with guns and all that fucking rubbish. I don't mind because being a criminal, it's not a bad life.

I think a non-criminal who is hungry and wouldn't resort to crime to fill their belly has got to be a fucking imbecile as far as I'm concerned.

If my sons are going to be criminals, there's clean criminals and dirty criminals, same as there are clean businessmen and dirty businessmen. I've always drummed it into their heads, violence is never a part of your crime, violence should never be part of any crime.

You read about the bullion robbery, 25 million pounds' worth of gold. Now to be prepared to set people alight, even for 25 million fucking pounds, it just wouldn't be in my book. If it were 100 million pounds I could never do it. Maybe I could set fire to an enemy, somebody who had done real damage to me, maybe I could do that, but to go and do violence for money, I just don't see any fucking sense in it because I can get people's money without committing any violence.

But if anybody insulted me or any of my family, or if somebody spoke bad of my friends, then I'm a different person altogether, I revert back to animal stages where I was brought up and what you've got to do with cunts like that. It's only temporary, I revert back and go fucking mad. Six weeks ago I made a meet at the pub, two friends had flown over from Spain to see me and I ordered a bottle of champagne and everybody started laughing. And I said, 'What's the matter?' They said, 'Champagne in here . . . ,' and they were all laughing, and I didn't like one of the guys that laughed and I just went over and said, 'You, you cunt, I'll cut your tongue out if I fucking hear you laugh again,' and he shut up immediately. I would have done, too, soon as look at him.

I was violent at one time, but if I hadn't been violent, then I couldn't have survived. It's as simple as that. People talk about the Gorbals in Glasgow, I used to go to the Gorbals on holiday. I'm telling you, I used to go to a nan of mine for a week's holidays every year. The Gorbals at its worst was Anderston as its best, for violence, hard drinking, cheap women and all that stuff, my district had to be the number one in the whole world. You just didn't exist in the district if you weren't violent, you'd be jumped upon. You had to be an animal. It was only when I moved to England that I realized that other people didn't fucking want to cut me up or stab me in the back, whereas in my home town, twenty-four hours a day you had to be alert. If you were a Protestant the Catholics were out to get you; a Celtic supporter, you had to watch for Rangers supporters . . .

I work a lot harder than nine-to-five workers. These people have got easy fucking jobs, that's why they don't get any money for it. I want to get more money than them because I work a lot harder than them; if my job requires me to spend eighteen hours a day on it and just six hours sleeping, then I will do my job. I went three days once without food, staked out on a caper, no sleep, no fuck all; you know, you're getting into a heavy one, and your bottle's going and you want to go to the toilet and you're nearly pissing yourself, and you can't move, now that's what you call work.

When I was in the army all I was was a thief in uniform. I just wanted to rob dead bodies and go into jewellers' shops with guns. I had a licence to do what I wanted in Germany. That was the kind of action I liked, where you could commit a crime, commit whatever crime you wanted, you had a licence for it because you were working for the government. I could go and shoot fucking people and rob them, I could do what I wanted. I shot one guy in the back. I don't know if I killed him, well, he shouldn't have died, he was hit high in the shoulder. It's funny. It comes back in my mind. You ask if I have a conscience, it's come back into my mind for forty years, I keep bringing it back into my mind. I shot a guy, and the only reason I fucking shot him was because he was running – if he wouldn't have been running I wouldn't have been interested, but I saw him running, and he was prey to me, I was the hunter, he was prey. It was instinct made me shoot him, out came the gun and bang. I wasn't a great shot or any fucking thing like that, but the guy went down and I ran up, and when I'm spinning him, going through his gear and that, and took his ring and his watch, I take his wallet out and it fucking hit me, his little kids, two little kids, beautiful blonde wife, and I fucking went and shot him. What for? For nothing, just instinct made me do it and that has come back. More than anything in my whole life was that regret. There's no way in the world I could bring the guy back to life and fucking say that was a stupid thing I done and I shouldn't have done it.

That is the only crime that ever comes back. Crimes where I've robbed people and fucking stripped people of all their wealth, burgled people's houses and got in among people's private possessions and all that carry-on, I didn't have no conscience about anything like that, but a needless crime, there was absolutely no need.

I don't give one monkey's fuck about the people's feelings. But I wouldn't go out in the street and take money off old women or anything like that. That's not crime, that's fucking vandalism on a person. Sex offenders, we don't think of them as criminals, they're all fucking head cases, something's wrong with their minds.

I am getting the urge, now I'm nearly sixty, I want to make sure a bit of money is left here when I die. No tax or anything gets paid, I don't believe in any fucking tax. Tax! How can you possibly go out and work for a hundred pounds a week and have some invisible cunt take thirty or forty pounds out of the hundred you've knocked your brains out getting. They'd have to take a gun to me before they get my money.

I'll be a criminal right to the day I die. I like it, I enjoy my life. I go into prison now and again – what is prison? I enjoy my own company, so a prison cell holds no fears for me.

I've been around the world about ten times, and that's another thing, if you're a criminal you can go anywhere. You're not restricted. I can and I have gone to Heathrow Airport, and just looked up at the board to find out where I was going shoplifting. I love nothing better than going to an airport and getting on a plane to another country.

What is a successful criminal? Is Biggsie a successful criminal? He's on the run, can't come back to his homeland – I'd be heartbroken. He's a successful fucking prison escaper, yes, but no way in the world can he be classed as a successful criminal. Am I a successful criminal? I'm not rich so I can't be very successful. I've got a pound note, I've got enough to get by on and I'm still working. I've got potential, my potential is better than anyone I know, including big businessmen. My potential at sixty years of age is better than my sons', even at their young age.

I've got to work till I die, haven't I? The dream, what is a dream? The dream was always money in my life, always after money, but that seems to have faded now. I'd still be involved in the crimes for the crime's sake because it gives me a fucking boost, keeps me going, keeps me alive, keeps my mind young, keeps me thinking. I want a bit of the action. There's no fucking action going into your Ford's down the road and putting nuts and bolts on cars and all that carry-on.

There's no danger I won't make the money, for a very simple reason that I've got credit in Morocco for two hundred kilos of dope. Two hundred kilos of dope over here, you're talking about a million and a half street price, how can I lose? At least I know I've got that coming, my final act, take the money, and that's it, and be satisfied with the little bit that I've got. I don't want to retire, but forces of circumstances may be getting me in a corner, I may have to retire, this may be a fucking compulsory retirement I'll have if they get hold of me.

How can I retire? A human body is just not fucking built for retirement. If you're ill and you've got to retire, that's a different matter altogether. But why should a man retire when he's sixty-five? People just don't want to retire because what can you do? You can go to Spain or Italy for six months of the year, but you get bored to fucking death. In my opinion people should be left with a bit of the action when it comes to retirement age, they should be shoved into something constructive where their minds can still work. Their minds still do work, you know.

Once you start getting up into the big five-figure bracket, money loses all its value, so what do you call the big one? The big one wouldn't stop me, I'd carry on. If I get busted, when I come out I'll carry on. Until I die I'll keep going, I'll keep going for the rainbow, for the pot of gold, it's my job. You're trying to write a good book, I'm trying to commit a good crime, that's all.

Dentist
Peter Carey

My father was a doctor, a general practitioner, and so all my life it was automatic that I was going to be a doctor. We went along, my father and I, to see the dean of the medical school and he said to my father, 'I presume that your son can matriculate,' and that was all the formalities required then to get into medical school.

And then after about a year, my hearing began to deteriorate, and it was thought that I might not be able to hear through a stethoscope, and the suggestion was that I should change to dentistry. My father said, 'There is money in it, and you won't have to get up at night,' and so that's how I became a dentist, and one might think that I could have regretted that but in fact I haven't. I've thoroughly enjoyed being a dentist for forty-five years now.

The training hasn't changed a lot in this country since I trained, I'm afraid, because I think the training of dentists in this country is appalling. It's a little better now than it was, but all dentistry I know now I've learned since I left dental school.

I'm very disappointed when I see new patients and I tell them what they ought to know about care of their mouths, expectations for their mouths, and it's all news to them. They say to me, 'Not bad at my age' – say a man of forty-five with rather a broken-down ruin – and in fact everybody should have all their teeth all their life, ninety per cent anyway could have. The public have too low an expectation. It comes as a surprise to people to learn they can keep their teeth all their lives.

It is something I've always dreaded at parties when they ask what I do because it's rather a conversation-stopper being a dentist, and you get very facile replies. 'Oh, my God, I don't want to talk to you,' or 'Whenever I go to the dentist it hurts.' Somebody asked, 'Where do you practise?' and I said, 'In Sloane Street.' 'Oh,' he said, 'my dentist is in Harley Street,' and walked off, so I didn't have a chance to say that I thought Sloane Street was just as good an address. A lot of people think to practise in Harley Street you have to have special qualifications, that the address in some way endows you with knowledge or expertise.

But in America, where I worked for a few years, it's quite different. To be a dentist in America is to be quite a social lion, and to be a dentist with an English accent, you were very much sought-after – 'Come and sit next to me and tell me all about yourself,' sort of thing. I think it was the regard Americans hold for their dentists, dentists seemed to enjoy a higher status even than doctors, and certainly lawyers. It's difficult to know which comes first, the standard of dentistry offered, or the esteem with which the public holds their dentist. They seem to go to their dentist for dental care rather than with toothache, because they are so good at preventative dentistry.

It's more than just a job, it's very much a social service. I think I'm an educator, a guide, philosopher and friend. A lot of people talk to me of things other than their teeth after a period. I don't make friends of my patients outside the surgery, but within the surgery they are my friends. I don't have many friends, and my wife offered an explanation, she said, 'You do all the work of making friends at the practice and you're tired of socializing by the end of the day, and you don't really need friends,' and I think maybe she has a point. She doesn't mind I don't have friends, I mean *we* have friends, but I only really have a couple of chaps that I would go out for a beer with. I have a friend who was a student with me, he lives in South Wales, practised all his life down there, he's now retired, and I do his teeth, and when he comes up to London to have them cleaned, we have a day together.

When I am here I put everything I've got into it, but I don't work the way some dentists do. My friend in South Wales worked in a mining area, he worked a twelve-hour day, and when he first started his practice in the Health Service he might see sixty patients in a day. He has never seen a private patient in his life, and I have never seen a Health Service patient in my life. My friend has earned much more money than I have, but he's worked a great deal harder and he's hated every minute of it. It's been an absolute treadmill for him, because the kind of work you have to do on the Health Service, you don't have time to get to know anything about your patient.

When I asked him whether he's enjoyed being a dentist, he said, 'No,' but he is proud of the service he has provided over the years to his community, I mean he sees a very big difference in the health of the miners and their children from when he started.

I see much greater expectation of life in teeth than he does, because he doesn't have my facilities. He can't deploy the skills I deploy, not because he hasn't got them, but that the state won't pay. It's not his fault, it's the fault of the Health Service that they won't pay for preventative service. In the Health Service you get paid for a filling or an extraction or some false teeth, piece work, but you don't get paid for advice. Now if a child comes to me they book an appointment for half an hour and I may not do any work on that child's teeth because I'd be talking to it, reasoning with it, chatting it up, making it amenable to dentistry. The parents will get a bill for half an hour's treatment although they won't have had any actual physical treatment. Now in the Health Service you'd get nothing for that and of course you should get something.

When I came here as an assistant, the chap who employed me was the smartest, most fashionable dentist in London, he was the Duke of Windsor's dentist. I still have a patient who was sent to the practice by Wallis Simpson – she's getting on a bit now. My patients are mostly educated, and they have to be willing to spend some money on their teeth. But I fondly believe that being my patient is no more expensive than being a Health Service patient in the very long run, because I think my patients have less wrong with them so they have to pay less. It's very expensive for them to have their teeth cleaned by me, but on the other hand if they only have to come once a year that's not very expensive.

I talk about the people the way one would about one's friends. If you're a general practitioner for the length of time that I've been, you come across the most dreadful tragic stories, and it makes you feel very lucky that you've got through life with so little trauma. I look frequently at that photograph over there which is of a girl who has been a patient since she was four years old; we took nine years to straighten her teeth, and then she had a dreadful road accident when she was thirty in which her husband was killed, and she was paralysed from the waist down. And she's so brave and marvellous, which is why I have her photograph there. So if anybody starts moaning about their lot, I point over to that desk and say, 'How about this ...'

It impresses me how well my children patients do, I can't think of any who have gone on the drug scene and taken to drink and made a bloody nuisance of themselves, and they all seem to have done well at university and their careers after that. I can't explain that.

I should think I've been generously rewarded for the work I've done, although I haven't charged enough. All my life I've charged much less than I could have done and I don't feel deprived by that, I've always had enough and I've not got expensive tastes. I've never done what a lot of posh dentists do, they fall into the trap of trying to emulate their patients, living like they do, and if you do that then you're in trouble, because you don't earn the kind of money that they earn, you don't have the kind of money to spend that they have, or I don't have at any rate. But I've been amply rewarded really, I quite often think that I ought to pay my patients I so much enjoy seeing them.

I have one family that has forty-five members and I know more about that family than any one of them does, and they will ask me about someone who they may have not seen since the last family wedding. They have referred each other to me; they all have the same dentist, but that's all they do have in common.

If I meet one of my patients in Sloane Street, I might not remember their names because I'm not very good at remembering names, but I'll still know what their teeth look like. Because they are dear to me, I worry about them a bit more than I should, I think, because doctors and nurses are not supposed to get personally involved with people and I do, I mind very much when they've got a pain and I mind very much when I hurt them.

It's a bit like being on stage, because my patients have a lot of time to look at me and one is very aware that one is on view, and you can't be cross or careless. I think I am more equable now, but I think it's been very trying for the girls who work for me, because 'There's Mr Carey all charm and grinning and cheerful as the day is long, and he comes back here in the office and all he can do is bawl us out.' I see their point, and I'm not so irascible now. I put on a performance for the patients *and* the girls now, where I used not to bother to perform for the girls.

I may have a pain or rheumatism or stomach ache or headache, or there might be a frightful noise going on outside the window, but once the patients come in, I'm completely oblivious to the noise outside. There was a chap working the other side of the wall with a hammer drill, the noise was absolutely deafening, I didn't think I would be able to work, but when I started work I didn't even hear the noise, one is so concentrating. I think that makes it a bit tiring, you really do have to pay attention to what you're doing.

Modern equipment has been a tremendous boon. I mean, I wouldn't be practising now if I was doing it standing up, I'm sure of that. I keep reasonably fit in that I ride a bicycle in the summer and I ski. Last bus strike I cycled all the way from Kew and I wondered why I don't do it more often. But I get a free ticket now, and so the railways cost me nothing.

I think the dentistry I most enjoy doing is scales and cleans, funnily enough, which bores most dentists to distraction. But I enjoy doing it because I think it does more good than anything else I do. I like doing extensive restoration work, bridges and crowns, because that is a kind of test of skill and patients are usually pleased with the results, and I'm pleased with the result in that I feel I have saved them having to wear false teeth. I don't much enjoy taking teeth out, in fact that is the least enjoyable part, it's sort of like going to a funeral.

By now, I don't have any patients that I don't like, so it's all fun, and that's why I don't want to stop doing it; I'd miss them all terribly, I mean, what could I do? I could find something to do because I always do find something to do. There are so many things I have never had time for. I've never been to an auction sale and I would like to go, but I'd much rather come here than go to an auction sale, because I feel so well when I'm here. I'm doing four days a week; I'm not planning to do any less than I'm doing now, although I might have to go down to three. I don't want to have to give it up altogether but there are some nasty tricks up the sleeve of Providence, you know, like Parkinson's and multiple sclerosis. One never knows, you could have a stroke.

Sometimes during the weekend one does feel one's age, but I don't feel my age here because everyone says I don't, which is a great boost. 'You haven't changed a bit since I've been coming here,' they say, and I say, 'Well, I hope to God I didn't look like this forty years ago!'

Diver
Dave Moore

I originally started out wanting to be a mechanic, but girls didn't like the filth under my fingernails, and diving seemed the second best job. But as soon as I got into diving, there was no other job for me. I started diving commercially for the excitement, for the travel; I mean, I've done three years in Angola, I've worked in Nigeria, I've been all over the world, Japan, China, Russia, all through diving. I've been doing it now fifteen years. Every dive's exciting, it's as simple as that, it's an exciting job.

Money has never been important to me, it isn't important to my generation of divers. When I first started going offshore it was £13 a day, stay on for as long as you could, dodge the taxman. But the money is quite good now.

Every single body of water is different. We did two years on the Thames barrier, and there you were working in absolute zero visibility, and everything was done by touch. It was so dark, you could be burning under water with a massive arc welder, six inches in front of your face, and you couldn't tell whether it was on or off, it was that black.

Every single dive is different. No matter if you are doing the same job every day, there's always something different down in the sea, the currents are different, you've got tide, temperature, you've got visibility, you've got whatever's in the water, fish, wave action, all these things are different every single day, you never get two days the same.

Your mind does do very strange things; if you have got a vivid imagination a bit like myself, you can imagine if you're diving in an area with no visibility that everything you touch has got something on it that could hurt you, and so it's a question of going in the water and controlling the fear, and getting the job done.

Of course, it's dangerous because you are working in an alien environment, but I should think it's safer down there, in that you have more safety checks and you are more aware of danger, than you are in an ordinary job where it's repetitive and nothing happens until there's an accident.

I started my own company three years ago; this is my fourth year now. Started off with a very small trailer and we've built up to quite a large trailer. We're a marine maintenance company, we do underwater cutting, inspections and surveys. The unfortunate thing about it is you don't get the chance to travel in the job. Brighton is as far as I go nowadays, company headquarters.

But I don't want to go abroad too much now simply because I've got a girl aged four, another aged one. I suppose I didn't want to be away as they were growing up and saying, 'Who's that strange man?' when you come home. I even tried a couple of other jobs to get out of diving completely, but that didn't work out. I sold insurance policies for a while and then – a great one for a diver – I sold fire extinguishers. Then I started in kitchen fitting. I did that for three or four months and I couldn't stand it, it was too boring, so I just went back diving again.

I suppose I'm very selfish in that I do what I want to do workwise, but I'm very lucky that I have the perfect wife, because she never moans, never grumbles, she accepts it. I was diving when I met her and I'm still diving now. She has never said stop, so really, I'm luckier than most, because divers have probably got the highest divorce rate there is going.

I have to work. If I don't go to work I get ratty. If I haven't got anything to do then I get bored, and once I get bored I get in a bad mood. I wasn't doing anything today, so I worked on the car all morning just to give me something to do.

I've been brought up to accept the fact that you go to work to earn your money, it's the way you live. When we leave here to go to Brighton to work, there'd be myself and one or two of the other divers who help. We get to Brighton. If the weather is bad and we're weathered off, we get half a day's pay and we come home. We don't work. So you end up down the pub. But it's not a very nice pint, it's just a pint of beer. Now if you've gone down there and done a real day's collar, a real day's work, then you think to yourself, 'Well, I deserve a pint now,' and you go in the pub and have the same pint – and it's a good pint, you know, because you've earned your money for the day, and deserve a pint, sort of thing.

Everyone knows me as Dave the Diver, that's it, I mean I'm not Dave Moore, I'm Dave the Diver, and I accept it because I've only ever really had any great success at one job, and that's diving.

Diving gives you a bit of pride in yourself, doesn't it? I mean you're good at what you do, you're a specialist, also there's not a lot of divers about, so it's a bit of an individualist's sort of thing. People ask, 'What do you do?' and when you say you're a diver, they think that sounds interesting, so then you have to go through the whole performance of telling them everything about your job, because it's interesting for people to talk to you. It's a bit of an ego trip, I suppose.

There's always the same two questions. 'How long can you stay down with those oxygen tanks?' which is stupid, really, because you don't breathe oxygen, and, 'Have you ever seen a shark?' It's the same two questions, I don't know why.

As it happens, sharks are absolutely superb. There's nothing to worry about with sharks. Jellyfish are the worst. In the Gulf, there's a jellyfish called a sea wasp that will kill you, it's very small and if it catches you on your throat or your mouth, you convulse in about fifty seconds and you're dead.

I'm an old sweat, as they call you, I really am an old diver: thirty-nine. The only thing that defines whether you can carry on diving is a medical, and you have one medical a year. There are only six registered doctors in the country that can do it; if they pass you fit you can dive for another year, if they pass you unfit, that's you finished. So your medical is the most important thing that you could possibly do once a year.

They started collating these medicals eighteen years ago with every commercial diver in the country, so they're now getting a picture of what this is doing to divers *en masse*.

There are some real problems emerging. For instance, because they decompress you with oxygen on the surface, it tends to cause a problem with your memory. It's very bad in a lot of older divers which they're only now starting to discover. I've got short-term memory loss; if you told me a telephone number, I'd forget it immediately. You've told me your name twice now, but I had to ask Jenny my wife to remind me again before you walked in; it's not being disrespectful to you, I just can't remember it. Funny thing is, I can remember every dive I've made.

I always look at the sea life, never take my eyes off it. It's fascinating. I mean, at Brighton at the moment we've got lobsters and crabs, as per normal, spider crab, shrimps, prawns, all floating around the water, we've got conger eels, lots of bass. And the thing about sea life is it's not frightened of you. You get near a bird, it will fly away, but put out a bit of bread in your hand and a fish will come and eat out of it because it's not frightened. And they just come straight up to you, and when you're trying to work there will be loads of them swimming in front of you all the time. It's fascinating.

I saw my first Angler fish about three months ago and it frightened the living daylights out of me. It was a monstrous, horrible-looking thing. I went up to tell the other diver, and he came and had a look at it and poked it and the thing went for me, and didn't go for him. There's a thing I'll never forget in the Gulf that I saw, used to see a lot of them. Small hole in the sea bed and in that hole lives a little tiny fish at the back of the hole, and at the front of the hole lives a little lobster, can't remember the name of it, but they are two individual creatures living together as one. The fish catches the food and shares it with the lobster, and the lobster keeps the hole clear, and when there is any danger the fish goes in and the lobster sits outside and protects the fish.

One of the nicest places you can be is down there because it's quiet and there's nobody to bother you and you are your own boss. When you come out, it's just back to ordinary. I mean, you even get colours under water you don't get on the surface. It's so much more exciting down there than it is up here. Most of the colours are fluorescent, so you get unbelievable fluorescent mauves and oranges and yellows that you wouldn't even dream of on the surface. The only colour that comes near to the yellow that you see under the water is the yellow rape that you get in big fields that almost hurts your eyes when you look at it, that's the yellow you get under water.

Divorce Lawyer
Charles Doughty

I'm a grandfather, and fifty this year. I got married when I was twenty-two and I'm still married to the same wife.

I specialize in matrimonial law which is divorce, and divorce has now been made so easy that one is basically talking money: what the husband should pay the wife or what the wife should pay the husband, and a few cases about children, which are always the unhappiest.

Some young or middle-aged women arc very miserable when they thought they had a happy marriage and the husband has suddenly said, 'I want out,' for good reason or bad, and they are left absolutely without any roots at all. You may talk about the equality of the sexes, but for those people it's amazing how little they know of what makes the world tick. They've just presumed their husband will pay the bills and have no idea of the struggle he's had to get where he is, and they've criticized like hell, some of them. They've complained they had to go out to do business entertaining, that they were forced to go abroad on business promotions, but equally they get upset when it suddenly stops.

I do get a little cynical when they start blubbing. I make the fairly standard remark, 'If you want to cry I'll give you a cup of tea – and I will charge you double for the time you are crying.' It's amazing how they stop. If you let some people become very emotional about their own problems they can't help themselves.

If you're talking to a woman who's been married for many years, she has had, her judgements formed, developed, twisted by her husband: 'Whatever my husband says,' 'My husband wants me to do this,' 'My husband wants me to do that.' And then one says: 'Well, stop, just a minute; at the moment you and he are not on the same side, you are trying to organize your own futures apart. Now I've got one hour or a very short time to superimpose the views that I think you should hold over the years your husband has had, and if one lets emotions get involved then you've got a great deal of uncertainty, uncertainty leads to bad temper, bad temper leads to trouble and trouble leads to expense and litigation.'

The husbands, for their part, look pretty blank when you show them the wife's calculations of what she thinks it's going to cost to maintain herself and a couple of children. There's a great big gulf and one never knows quite who is the least inaccurate in their recollections.

If you have an exciting or difficult or bad-tempered case, the adrenalin does flow a bit, but if you're not dispassionate and sit back and say what is correct, what is the law, you don't give sensible advice.

I think I most enjoy the initial interview with a new client, about whom you probably know little more than his or her name and telephone number and perhaps who recommended them, and seeing just how that person lives and what the problem is.

A lot of people come along and say, 'This may end in divorce, what would happen if I separated from my wife?' You give them general advice and answer any specific questions they may ask. You see some of them again when they come back and say, 'Now I've made up my mind and I want to go ahead.' Some you never see again, because they've decided they didn't want a divorce or decided they didn't like you and go somewhere else when they've actually decided to do something.

There are three common reasons for divorce: alcohol, boredom and secretaries. Which order they come in I don't know. Boredom I think comes fairly high and therefore one flits from flower to flower until somebody gets cross. Alcohol – married to an alcoholic, it just wears one down, according to clients who've had that misfortune, and everything goes, money, self-respect, appearance.

What makes a successful matrimonial lawyer? Good clients. I say disparagingly about matrimonial lawyers that they are fairly near the bottom of the tree in that the law involved is not enormous. One has to have a certain amount of common sense for the obvious pitfalls of conveyancing and Capital Transfer Tax, and that's why it helps to be in a big office because you've got other specialized partners who can avoid you falling into all the pitfalls. But the old adage about if you are dealing with the problems of the rich there is no problem, if you're dealing with the problems of the poor there is no solution, rings very true.

I'm sure I could find better ways of spending my time than working, well, dammit, wouldn't you? Would you work if you were in a position of being no burden or expense or trouble to anybody else?

I maintain glibly that 20 per cent of my work I would pay to do, 20 per cent I would pay not to do and 60 per cent is where the bread comes from. Now whether that percentage is a bit wrong one way or the other as a principle depends on what sort of day I've had.

One feels terribly sorry for some of the clients. Women because they've been bereft of any roots. Men sometimes, because one feels that if they pay what they're required to pay, they're left with a very bleak future. It is very seldom that one can do anything which in Wilson's phrase, 'at a stroke', would make all the difference.

The most painful situations arise from those who have married too young and it's a disaster; they've mucked up everything, they end up with two small children and no money, and you can virtually predict that they cannot have a happy life now, separate or together.

I hope I don't become cynical, I don't want to become cynical. But certainly one sees people who have remarried, and the old cliché about remarrying somebody very much like the first spouse is only too true, and one sometimes wonders why they bother. It's simply an additional expense.

I've spent my entire working life doing matrimonial work. When people come here and seek advice, the vast majority of them have already decided that they want a divorce and they are asking you to arrange it in the best possible way, whatever the best possible way may be to that person. The number of times that *you* say, like a surgeon, 'You must have it out, get rid of him,' against that person's wishes is very seldom.

The burden comes when one sees the end result, where people are separated from their children, or they're living in very much less comfortable surroundings, or they have a financial burden which they find difficulty in meeting. Then one asks, 'Could I have organized that differently? Have I got a result that is sensible under all the circumstances and in accordance with the law?' And you remember that business you learnt at law school, the moment you become a solicitor, and they tell you to take a decent holiday, because you'll never actually sleep 100 per cent through the worries that you have for the customer.

Doctor
Richard Warner

You've come at a bad time. Well, you see we admitted somebody yesterday, somebody who was poorly, and we didn't know what was wrong so we left her on the ward to see if things got better; but it became obvious she'd got an appendicitis which had perforated, so the bowel contents were leaking into the belly. Once we decided what to do, we went straight ahead and booked the theatre, booked the anaesthetist, and at half past two I rang the ward to see whether the patient had been seen by the anaesthetist, and she hadn't, so I had to find out why. And we've had a huge bunch of people in Casualty, two of whom had stopped breathing. One was a road accident. I went down there to try and find my anaesthetist and it was like bedlam, people throwing things through the doors and running around the department, just awful, so I decided eventually that the best thing to do was to bleep the second on-call anaesthetist. He was delivering a baby, and, can you believe it, the third on-call anaesthetist was also delivering another baby, so we were stuck, we didn't have an anaesthetist. So I had to sort one out, and eventually I met my registrar in the corridor – he's like the guy next up from me – and we went down to Casualty and we actually went into the scrum and winkled out the first anaesthetist and said, 'Come on, you must operate on our girl because she's going off quickly,' and he said, 'Yeah, sure,' and as we were going out we rang the theatre who told us they had put another case where we were supposed to be because it was busy! It's just like juggling, and it basically means you spend ages on the phone, and because they have always got so much going on in Casualty and bleeping so many doctors, we call them with a special code on the phone, but every time I used the code it was engaged, so I was literally taking about ten minutes to make a call.

And even then there were things going on in the ward, because I cover the wards during the day, and at the moment I happen to have got about three or four ill people and have to do everyday things for them like blood tests and forms and things like this. It just means you get bombarded from all directions, and you've only got one brain and one pair of hands, and when everyone throws things on you in a big heap, you just have to try and put things in order of priority, and when the thing you are trying to put first in order of priority is impossible to organize, like getting the girl to theatre, it's a nightmare.

She's on the wards now. I mean she's quite well, she's got everything she needs at the moment, she's got pain relief and fluids going into her veins and she's got somebody looking closely at her in case she becomes iller, but what we really need to do is stop the bowel contents leaking into the peritoneum – which you can only do by sewing up the hole. She's only going to get worse, she won't get better if she's got a hole in her bowel.

I don't think she will pop off, I mean it would take her a couple of days to go, but the point is it's the weekend coming up and over the weekend there's just on-call people; there's two house surgeons and a registrar and a few medics as well, but that's it. I mean, the whole of the hospital winds down over the weekend and if anything bad happens your facilities and your ability to cope is considerably reduced, so you want to get things sorted out before the weekend, and that's why today there's such a rush on. I was going to go out this evening but it doesn't look like I'm going to now ...

I get hassled, everyone gets hassled occasionally, but all it is really is the limit at which you can pretend you're not hassled, if you see what I mean. You see I'm not hassled at the moment even though there is quite a lot going on, but if you put a little bit more on to me, heap me with a little more work, I would be hassled, yes. But everybody's got their own limit and some people's are quite low and some people's are very very high. I'm about in the middle.

I've been in the job three months. As it turns out, all I do is very minimal sort of easy things which isn't how the general public think of a doctor. Really all I do is clerk people when they come in, do routine tests, and occasionally do very simple techniques to help people, nothing which you would consider to be particularly glorious or clever, nothing sort of prestigious, but I enjoy it anyway because they're just little things that make people more comfortable.

I'm a houseman. It's a beginning, I'm twenty-three and it's the first step on the ladder. In the medical field you can either just drift and try and end up in something good, or you can go hell for leather for a certain career. Some people have just got it in their heads right from the beginning they are going to be brain surgeons and they attack that idea, you know, very aggressive about it: they have to get the right job for the next stage in their career ladder. I'm going to be one of the people that just drifts and I might even end outside medicine, I'm not really sure yet. I'd quite like to be a physician, but at the moment my heart's not really in it.

I love doing the job, but my heart's not in the sacrifices you have to make in order to go for the one particular career. For instance, having to do one and twos in hospitals for the rest of your life. One and twos is when every other night you're on call and they are supposed to be made illegal but people still have to do them if they want to get on.

It's a very self-destructive process. People who are quite senior surgeons and physicians have said, 'For goodness sake don't do it, you know my kids are strangers to me, I don't enjoy my job because I'm still not doing what I want to do, I'm still scraping and bowing to senior people at the age of forty-four.'

I had a choice between music or medicine and I'd have preferred to do music in some ways because it's aesthetically more pleasing, but it wasn't secure enough, especially in Coventry where I'm from. I just wanted to do something where I went to work every day, and I happened to be good at the sciences, and also I quite like the glamorous idea of being a doctor. I'm not like some people for whom medicine is all-consuming, you know, it's just a job really. I felt I had a choice, and because I actually enjoy doing it, it means that it was the right thing to do, but if at some point I decide I'm not enjoying it, I'll go off and do something else. And if I don't become a consultant, it's not going to be the end of the world.

I really don't believe that I'm a doctor, it's all come as a big surprise. I was a student and now suddenly I'm a doctor. It takes a lot out of you, you give too much and you end up being drained emotionally and physically. Giving all the time can destroy you and people become embittered by the fact that they always have to be reasonable and rational when things happen which aren't reasonable and rational.

Things like, somebody who has a small little lump in their bowel, and you say, 'Oh, well, we should be able to cure you,' and then the house report is something horrendous... a horrendonoma! You can't really say, 'That's tough, I'm sorry,' you have to talk to them and be nice to them. It's the same situation as if you have just finished with your girlfriend and she wants to keep seeing you and you have to keep going along and saying hello and being nice, but really it's just making you feel sick inside 'cause you've really been nasty to that person. You feel, 'If I hadn't given you that horrible disease... if I hadn't discovered it for you...' It would have been discovered anyway, but in some way you feel you're to blame. And also the fact that every time you don't actually cure someone, no matter how you deal with it, you always think, 'Well, maybe if I had done so and so... '

Well, I still feel totally young and stupid, I don't feel the least bit grown-up yet, because every single time somebody talks to you, either a nurse or a physio or a pharmacist or a senior member of the medical staff, every single comment is tailored to someone who is still a schoolboy. I really do feel like a new boy at school. An experienced nurse, for instance, knows a lot more than a newly qualified doctor does on a ward. The best people to work with are the people who are able to tell you what you are doing wrong without destroying your confidence.

I feel terribly embarrassed all the time saying, 'Look, I really haven't a clue what's wrong with you, I'm sorry.' A look of bewilderment comes over their faces and they think, 'Surely, haven't you got any idea at all? My wife thinks it might be so and so...'

I personally don't worry about things nearly as much as I used to because this job alters your perspective on what's serious and what isn't, and I think that in terms of personal trials and tribulations it certainly gives you good experience in actually coping with life.

Sometimes you just feel so sick about the whole thing you just sit there and have a quiet think about things, or you go and talk to somebody. I mean there is a tremendous spirit amongst the junior staff, you know, everybody supports each other, every time anything bad happens everyone knows about it, and things can be done within the sort of infrastructure of the hospital. But it still doesn't alter the fact that some things that happen are just appalling.

Youngsters come in, kiddies, and die in Casualty, you know, and I haven't actually had to do it yet, but I can't imagine going out there and saying, 'Listen, sorry, but your five-year-old is dead...' What then? You really haven't got anything to offer, all you can say is, 'We did our best.' The way I could cope with it is to actually say to myself, 'Well, there wasn't anything I could do, I didn't do anything wrong, so it's just tough.'

I always used to think you have to come up with something brilliant to put everyone at their ease, and I now know all you have to do is sit there and not get too embarrassed when people are telling you things which are upsetting them, or when people are going to die and you've got all the sort of high-tension emotional scenarios. They are actually not as critical as I thought they were. I've always thought maybe I couldn't produce the goods but really I don't have to produce any goods, I just have to sit there and I don't say anything concrete, I just have to be there and as long as they feel that somebody has actually bothered and is doing something about it, it's enough.

I like Casualty, Casualty is fun because you don't know what's coming in, it's a challenge. You often don't know what's wrong with the person, so it's up to you to find out. What I don't like is covering other people's patients in the middle of the night. We do two sorts of on-call work: we do the Casualty call work, and then we do the second on-call work, as it's called, where you cover the patients whose doctors have gone home. So you get called in the middle of the night to someone you don't know from Adam who is 'going off' (these are the phrases the nurses use: 'I don't like the look of Mrs So and So, she looks a bit peaky'), and you go down there and her blood pressure is in the boots and it's just a nightmare then because you don't know the background to the patient and you've got to go to notes which sometimes haven't been filled in for a few days, and then you are faced with a difficult problem which you've got no idea about, and I don't like that, it's a bit unfair really. You haven't got the benefit of people to look over your shoulder to see you're doing everything right, and although the X-ray machines and the ECG machines work at night, you've got to wake up people to get them working, and although they are on emergency call, that takes time, and you have to transfer the patient across to the main X-ray block, so the time involved in getting things done at night is just a bit too long and it's frightening from that aspect.

Drunks are the bane of my life because they very rarely have anything wrong when they come in, but you have got to keep an eye on them for a certain length of time to make sure they don't bleed inside their brains, and the police are always around because they've perhaps got into a brawl or something, and they're abusive and smelly and you've got to put them into bed and look after them, and in the middle of the night, it's the last thing you want if you've had a busy day.

Well, I like to think I work very hard. Sometimes I'm sitting having a coffee about half past three in the afternoon and there's absolutely nothing going on. The job comes in fits and starts. Some weeks you can be really quiet and you've got a bit of time to sit and think and have a lunch hour, and some weeks you can be up with the lark and go to bed half past one, two in the morning, be up two or three times in the night, and start work again at seven. That can go on for a good week's stretch, and it's after that that you really need your time off.

I make valiant efforts to meet people outside medicine because you do find you become totally blinkered and introverted. I can only go out every other weekend and every two nights in three during the week, so of course it cuts into my social life. But the thing is, I have a philosophy of making the nights off harder work than the nights on because otherwise if you let it stop you doing things, like having a beer in the evenings, if it stopped you doing that then it's interfering too much. So some people go home and at nine o'clock they're in bed because they are tired. But even if I'm tired I get on the tube and go into London and come back even more tired, but at least I've done something, I've gone out, I haven't sat in the hospital, because that can be a really negative, destructive process.

I have got nurse girlfriends, but it's because they are forced on you, because they are the people who are around. I'd like to marry an opera singer or something, that would be fun, it would be an escape when you got home from the hospital.

There are some things I would rather didn't happen to me until I'm experienced enough to cope with it. I really hated it when one of the guys on the wards had this big belly wound that went from the umbilicus to the super pubis region and had a great hole there with what looked like just a little bit of infection, and the registrar stuck his probe up and into it, and it went into a big cavity at the top and a big cavity at the bottom, and he took a knife then and there in the ward, because there are no nerve endings in a scar, and he opened up the scar with his knife and it fell apart and all this stuff came out, green muck, pus, and pieces of nylon which is the stuff they use to sew it with. I'd had too much to drink the night before and I just sort of had to go out of the curtain and have a breath of fresh air, because of the smell basically, but I mean even the sister who had been there for twenty-five years found it a bit much.

I'm less upset about death now. Some people should die, I mean I'm not going to make them die, but they are sitting there, they're blind, diabetic, demented, they've got pneumonia, they have a colostomy bag, they've got nothing going for them, they don't understand what's happening to them, they just plead all night and all day to die, and they get a chest infection and you give them a course of antibiotics; and in some ways you feel you're being immoral doing that, but it's not really for you to judge, it's just for you to help. And when they die I'm positively glad sometimes and it's only humane to feel that really.

I've only had to tell one person so far that they were going to go, it's Good Night Vienna, it upset me a lot. Well, I just felt really unhappy, a bit depressed for a few hours, I mean I didn't cry my eyes out, but I really thought it was a bit off.

My personal beliefs are unchanged, I believe there is a God, but I haven't experienced anything tangible. It's quite nice in some ways for patients to think, 'Oh, it's the will of God.' It takes the responsibility off me.

It's made me more appreciative of health and happiness, you know, seeing so much going on around you really makes you enjoy being happy and well, and it's also given me a strong feeling of fate, you know, sometimes Somebody has got it in for a certain patient and no matter how good you are, no matter what you do, things keep going wrong, and you just get this feeling that it's a bit beyond your control really.

I feel like I've aged about ten years in the past three months. I feel like I've got grey hair, lines. I feel like all the sort of carefree student existence has just evaporated. One minute you don't have to get up in the morning and you don't have to take your work too seriously, you can enjoy yourself if and when you want; next minute you're being screamed out of theatre for doing something. The whole world changes as soon as you qualify and they expect you to just cope.

I was not prepared for the onslaught. I had my expectations of what the job was when I was a clinical student, I thought I knew what was going to happen, but I didn't quite realize the ferocity of such responsibility. I mean everything really comes on to your shoulders in a big way, like making decisions instead of in a theoretical context in front of the consultant, 'Well, we could make a laparotomy... '

Suddenly it's you that's doing it, and it makes things totally different, it sharpens up your wits and your instincts no end. Immediately you become a lot more astute, not because you become cleverer, but because you have to put what few bits of knowledge you've got into some sort of semblance of a rational decision. I hated it at first because it was so foreign to me, but now I quite enjoy it, especially when you get it right, it gives you a nice feeling afterwards.

Driving Instructor
Ray Johnson

I was doing music before. I wanted to buy a house, but I couldn't get a mortgage, being a musician. So I needed to get a job where I could have a trade and be qualified fairly quickly, and driving instructor seemed to be the best idea, so I went into it. All you need is to have a current driving licence which has been clean for four years, then you've got to take some exams. Six months after qualifying, I got my mortgage.

Sometimes I'll start at eight in the morning and I'll finish at eight in the evening. You've got to be on the ball because it doesn't matter how many pupils you had or how long you've been working that day, they'll expect you to be like they are the first pupil of the day. Mentally it is very tiring because you have got to be alert all the time, you can't afford not to be, because it's a life-and-death situation really.

Because it is so demanding you'll find that most driving instructors' marriages don't last, because of the hours they do, and the problems it can cause. We are working Saturday and Sunday sometimes as well. So the social life is not very good. It can cause a lot of problems. It really best suits the person who is single and hasn't got any other commitments. I've seen people working seventy hours a week and from the strain I know it puts on me doing fifty-odd hours a week, it's just not worth the exhaustion. You may not actually feel wound up while you are doing it, it's when you stop and you get home and you try to unwind and get rid of all the tension which builds up, because not everybody gives you a beautiful, perfect drive.

I put my home life first and if it's affecting that, I will cut down the hours I do at work, but it's easy to neglect the home life. My wife works, so she's not too bothered, but I've just got to make sure that I take notice of her and not take her for granted when I am around.

I've got a house I'm working on now, so if I have the time I shoot home and try and do some work there, otherwise I'll just clean the car or sit around the office and look at how many pupils I've got, moan about the situation. The office is supposed to book pupils in for you as well as you getting them yourself, because it's difficult a lot of the time to make any headway in getting pupils if you are out on the road all the time. So you need the office to give you the bulk of your work.

I've only got something like three lessons today, one that starts at eight-thirty in the morning, one at lunchtime and one in the afternoon and really it's just the same as working the whole day through. It actually feels worse sometimes just sitting around, I mean you get more tired.

You definitely cannot judge people from what you see, without a doubt. The thing about the job, you get to be a sort of social worker cum psychologist, because a lot of pupils will tell you things that they won't tell their husbands or wives – I don't know why. Some people have driving lessons just to get out and talk to somebody, particularly older people. Maybe it helps them, and when they tell you personal things, it's best you just listen and don't actually make any comments.

I remember a young lady telling me that she was leaving her husband. I mean *he* didn't know, but I knew, which I thought was totally wrong, and I just felt sorry for the guy. But it wasn't my business to say anything. I suppose my reaction inside was, what are you telling me for?

It is quite an intimate relationship. I mean they're trusting you with their lives, for a start. The majority of people taking lessons haven't driven before, so they are leaving it totally up to you.

Women are easier to teach because they are much more concerned with safety, which is one of the main things you've got to get across to any learner. Blokes tend, once they can move the car and change up and down the gears – right that's it, they can drive – and it takes a lot to make them concentrate on the actual rules they need to pass the test.

You've got to feel that you are in control. I have a set of dual controls which consist of a brake and a clutch pedal, and the only thing we can't control is if a pupil stops suddenly. In general you are going to grab the steering wheel or hit the brakes or use the clutch a few times a day. People tend to think the better the driver is, the less the instructor has to worry. That's not true. Usually, the better they are, the more you tend to relax, but there's always the chance of something happening, because after all, they're still learning, and they can do something totally out of the blue. Also, you mustn't hit the brake or grab the steering wheel until the last moment, because you've got to give the pupil the chance to do it. No pupil likes an instructor taking the controls. But it does make it difficult for the instructor, because he's got to wait until the last possible moment before he can do anything. I had a lady hit me because I stopped her from going into a car. She said she was just about to stop, but I actually made her get out of the car and have a look at how close she was to the vehicle. There was no way she could have done it in the time, because I'd only just done it in time. But she still told me not to do it again. You've got to keep your sense of humour.

It does count whether you like your pupils or not. For example, you can have a pupil that smells. Now they're paying their money and they expect you to give 100 per cent, but if you don't like the way they smell, or if you don't like them, you don't want to have them in your car. You're better off telling them to go to someone else rather than trying to give the lesson because you won't teach them properly.

There might be personality clashes, race might be an issue. I've only ever had one pupil who didn't want me because I'm black, and she was an Indian lady. In actual fact, age is more of a concern than colour, because a lot of people prefer an older instructor, at least older than themselves, to take instructions from.

Many times I've told a pupil, I will just make a tape and play it because you are not listening to what I'm telling you. It can get on your nerves if you are repeating the same thing for the whole lesson and they are still not taking any notice.

The only thing you can do is know if your pupil is ready to take the test or not, that's as far as you can go. You cannot predict how a pupil will do. I mean you can have a diabolical pupil and think that there is no way they will pass, they might as well cancel it, and they'll go up there the next day and pass it.

I suppose the main thing that the pupil will fail his test on is driving too slow, because most people try to be too careful, and that's the one thing that the examiners really hate, because it is very difficult to judge somebody's driving ability if they are only pootling along at 15 mph, waiting too long to turn and being overcautious.

We don't feel as if we are regarded as a qualified profession should be regarded for what we have to do, and the amount of strain the job puts on you mentally and socially. I mean it's a qualified profession, we've got to take exams and go through all the rigmarole you need to get qualified, we are putting our lives on the line every day of the week, and I think we should be held in higher regard than we actually are. In

European countries like Germany and places, a driving instructor has the same social standing as maybe a doctor or lawyer, and they do nine-to-five kind of hours. You'll do your job much better if you feel more appreciated.

I'd like to see a different situation completely for driving instructors and for pupils. I think it would be much better if it were government-controlled and there was a set fee across the board for driving lessons, and it was a nine-to-five situation.

There are good times. I know I've said quite a lot that doesn't make it sound good, but you have nice times as well. I mean when the pupils say things like, 'It's all because of you,' and that sort of thing, it's ego, I suppose, but it's also self-satisfaction, and that is the biggest bonus the job has got.

Because I've got a wife and mortgage to think about, I cannot afford to do the music and not have money coming in on a regular basis, so I'm biding my time sort of thing. In actual fact I'm doing a record at the moment, and once it's finished I'll try and sell the song. If I can get a deal off that, then I'll quit, but I need to have something concrete, in writing, for me to stop driving-instruction.

It's definitely something I won't be doing for the rest of my life, because first and foremost I'm into music. I know music is unpredictable, but the thing is, I can always do the driving as well, just to tide me over sort of thing. I could do a couple of lessons here and there if I had my own car. You remain qualified as long as you renew your papers every four years, so I've got that trade to fall back on.

I'm not the type of person to be sitting around and working all the hours God sends and just having a terraced house at the end of it and a gold watch. I'm not into that. I think there is a lot more I can do with my life.

Dustman
Philip Rigden

I enjoy it, but like any other job it gets a bit of a routine after a bit, you know. But I get up in the morning and pull myself up and say, 'OK, you know it's a good job this really.' I mean it's handy for me, it's only five minutes down the road, and I get up on the hills and it's gorgeous, especially in the summer.

The area around here is lovely. It's turning into a town now, but it used to be a tiny village, the sort of place you stopped on your way to somewhere else, a journey's resting place. It's just a nice little town with a few of the old Yorkshire cotton mills.

A lot of people have said, 'You don't look like a dustman,' so I usually say, 'What does a dustman look like?' When I go out I dress in right with-it stuff, I suppose that's it, I've always been very smart in my appearance. I get a perverted sort of pleasure out of saying I'm a dustman. I'm proud to be a dustman, any road.

I don't put a lot of mental activity into it. I work hard physically, but I wouldn't like to say, 'I'm Philip Rigden the great dustman.' I try and be a good dustman, I'm conscientious, but it doesn't take a lot up here to be a good dustman. It's not the most important thing to me. A job is a job. I need to pay the mortgage and pay my other bills. I wouldn't say I sweep roads therefore I must be this sort of person, I'd say I sweep roads to earn a living to make some money so I can pay bills, full stop.

It's all go, from as soon as you get there. You get the wagon ready, go pick the lads up, and you're out, and there's not a minute to spare. Sometimes to keep up to your bonus, you're running, there just isn't enough time. You've got to empty so many bins in your allotted time for the week, you get so many hours for each round and you're timed for one minute, forty-five seconds for each bin, and you have to keep up to that all the time. Management says if you get your full bonus, you should be absolutely shattered at the end of the week. To achieve top bonus regular is very hard work. The average dustman walks twenty-two miles a day. I'm not kidding. The time-and-motion man came round with our gang a couple of weeks back and he clocked twenty-two miles on his chart, and that's as well as humping bins.

Because you're walking so much and carrying so much, your legs and your hips feel the strain. A few weeks back I hadn't done any dustbins, I'd just been driving for about a month, and when they put me on bins again, I had to go and sit in the cab after about an hour, I felt dizzy and I was out of breath. They took me home, actually, I was that bad.

A lot of people who I talk to, they say, 'Well, dustbin men never speak to you nowadays, they're right surly, they just come and empty your bin and they're off,' but it's because we're so busy.

I'm on the perimeter round at the moment, and there's three of us. We do all the farms way out, little hamlets, Hade Edge, Farnley Tyas, there's Tinker's Monument – that's not official that, everyone knows it as Tinker's Monument – Victoria, Hepworth, there's loads of little places. I'm driver loader which means if there's a driver or loader off, I'll take their place, so I move around from gang to gang. I like moving around although it's not always top money because you usually go where there's trouble, where they're lagging behind or something like that.

Today it was me and Barry and Frank. Frank's a mate of mine and Barry's a bit of a character, he's well known in this area, Barry Lee, ask anybody and they'll know Barry. So I've been talking to him, but we're behind on this round and I got stuck in the snow and we didn't get finished on time, so we're still behind for tomorrow. What else happened today... the dog tried to bite me, that's a constant problem, the women'll come out and say, 'It's all right, he won't bite you,' and you're trying to shake him off your leg.

I try and enjoy myself while I'm at work, you have to make the most of it. So I look around at all the beautiful things that are going on around me, and I like talking to people. I think about how long it's going to take us to do such a street and how long it's going to take me to get down to the bottom and all this, and then I think about my life, and I have a couple of mates, and we talk, we swap yarns about women and booze, you know.

They're fine lads. There are some characters. We're shouting and bawling at each other during the day because the pressure's on to get the work done, so we get a bit ratty sometimes, but then when the work's over we'll have a pint together, so it's nothing serious. It's the hardest job physically I've ever done. It keeps you fit, but if you're getting on a bit it doesn't do you any good.

If people all worked together I think it would be a lot nicer. They could help by putting the dustbin neat instead of overflowing it, and making it easier access. I had a syringe in my leg today! I picked a bag up and it swung, and this hypodermic syringe was sticking through, and I don't know what they used it for, it could be anything, could be AIDS, stuck right in, I'll have to put it in the Accident Book. I forgot all about it. But I'd say most people are considerate. If there's broken glass in the rubbish, they'll wait for you and say, 'There's some glass in there but I wrapped it up in paper,' and you say, 'Fair enough.' Most people give you a tip at Christmas time. You can make a nice bonus out of that. I'd say on the whole people do consider the dustbin men, it's just that when you're rushing about you don't want to get one that's overflowing.

I'll get shot for saying this, but there is one big perk. It's called tatting, it's like junk, what people throw out; all sorts of stuff, televisions, crockery, I got that clock there, that pewter mug, the coal scuttle, anything, books – I've got quite a lot of interesting books out of that. You get to know when you pick a bag up, you can feel if it's rubbish, or if there might be something in it. It does slow you down a little.

I go to night school. I'm studying art. Just passed my O-levels; I'm studying A-levels now. I really like Leonardo da Vinci. I think he had a brilliant mind, a beautiful mind, he was so intelligent. Not just an artist, inventor as well. He had style, didn't he?

I do a lot of portraits of the boys, and I do a lot of buildings, old buildings. Well, my line of work is excellent for having a look and seeing what'll make a good picture while I'm out on the job. The lads will say, 'There you are, Phil, there's a good one there.' It's great. And on the weekends or at night I'll go sketching. I look around the beautiful valley with the sun setting and that inspires me, and first thing in the morning, if we get up and stop for breakfast and it's a nice clear, crisp morning, and the sun's just coming out, that inspires me, plus we always see lots of squirrels, rabbits, foxes, hares, sheep, you know, things like that inspire me.

The lads do tend to tease me. They'll say, 'Hello, Picasso,' or they call me a piss artist. I get my leg pulled all the time – 'Do a drawing of this', and it's an old dustbin or something like that. They're always taking the

Mickey. But they are interested, they ask me a lot of questions, and if I get them on my own, we'll have a serious conversation about art.

I'd rather paint. I'd rather be an artist full time, it's what I want to do, I'd be more content if I was an artist. I could put in eight hours a day quite easily instead of putting in eight hours a day emptying dustbins.

I'm frustrated I haven't got the time to study. I mean an ordinary artist, he gets more practice in one day than I get in a couple of weeks. I know I could do better in my art if I had more time to study, but because I work hard physically, I get home, I don't feel like doing it sort of thing, so I do get frustrated.

I've done a lot of pen and ink sketching, I've done so many of them and sold so many, it's boring me now. So I'm starting on to colours, coloured pencils, oil paints, what I can afford. Coloured pencils are the cheapest so I'm into that now. I'm trying to improve my application of colour.

I can see myself being a fairly good artist after about another five years. Whether I'll make a living at it, I don't think I will, I think I'll remain a dustman. Or maybe try and work my way up in the dustbins, supervisor or something like that, but that takes a lot of concentration so I wouldn't be able to concentrate on my art then. I'm being realistic. I know what I want to be in the next five years, I want to be a full-time artist – but being realistic, I think I'll spend the next five years on the bins.

Maybe I am more optimistic than I'm letting on, it's funny, you don't want to reveal all your dreams to a stranger. You know, you dream about being famous – it just seems absolutely ridiculous, but it's not actually fame that I want to achieve, I want to give people a message. I can't communicate in words, as you can see, but I can do it through art. Peace, love, beauty, truth, that's what it's all about.

Employment Advisor
Amanda Maddock

Basically the main emphasis in this job is to get people into work or into rehabilitation schemes, depending on what they need. The people I deal with, many of them have been unemployed for at least six months, most of them a good deal more. It might be a simple retraining need, and as I am also training officer here I'm well placed to know about those – you know, adult training, further education, or whatever. Sometimes they have other problems as well. Usually their unemployment causes them to have depression, their previous job might have made them unhappy, they may have had an accident, or been in prison, there are myriads of reasons why people become unemployed, and then why they find it difficult to get back. Sometimes there just isn't the will to get back to work, after you have had so many rejections, you can't cope with any more.

You're always going to get your residue of lazy people who don't want to work. I quickly fathom them out and I don't bother with them, to be honest, because I haven't time. You get people who have had the sort of job that they then have to stop doing and they can't readjust to another form of work, and because they can't readjust they lose the will to try, they just can't imagine another life. The biggest problem with losing will are your middle-aged men who get made redundant and they can't understand why it happened to them. It's a funny thing, work, isn't it? It's the sort of central pivot that most of us that are in work live around, and we then make social pariahs out of people who don't work.

I wouldn't go so far as to say that it is morally wrong to be out of work, because there is an awful lot of people who are out of work through no fault of their own, but it is morally wrong to expect someone else to support you.

I always wanted to do this job, ever since I left school. But I was told that I would never get into it because of my eyesight and lots of other reasons that were never really clear to me. I went into an employment office in Kent when I left college and became unemployed. And the woman there would never speak to me directly, she spoke to my mother. You see I'm blind, and blindness is a problem that a lot of people seem to tie up and think, 'Well, if you're blind you've also got something wrong with your head.' So they scream at you in monosyllables and carry you off the bus, that kind of thing. Anyway, I had had a gutful of this one day and I said to her, 'Listen, why the hell can't you speak to *me*?' and she said, 'Well, all right, what do you want?' And I said, 'Your job, love, because I'm sure I could do it ten times better.' And from then on I decided that that was what I wanted to do. When I saw how incompetent this lady was, I decided that was the very job I wanted because I wanted to do it better than she did. It was the competitive instinct, you see.

I can't imagine me without a job. I live through my job, I'm sure I do. I work as hard as I can, not all the time, mind, nobody does. I mean I can be a right lazy pig, but I like to think that I'm a grafter, like my father always taught me I should be. I think work was bred into me through my family. I'm from a large family: there are eight of us, and I'm the last of eight. My father was a farmer, never had a day out of work until he was sick, then he had five weeks out of work and died. He taught me an awful lot about work, how important it was to be working. I always remember one instance when he and I fell out about me being out of work, and he said, 'I haven't been out of work in my whole life for as long as you have at the minute,' and that struck me hard.

I work on an appointment system so I have about five appointments a day, that's five forty-five-minute appointments. Then there is paper work to do, which takes a while, and there are people coming in off the street, although it's difficult really to say how many you'll get. Probably fourteen, fifteen a day. Sometimes they are terribly distressed, and then there goes your lunch break, or your tea break, or there goes five o'clock for the bus. I've know me for example when one particular young woman I had been dealing with and I wasn't aware of some problems in the family that there were, and I ended up saying to her, 'Look, here's thirty pence, come on the bus with me, and we'll talk about it,' and I took her as far as where she lived on the bus and then went home myself, because you can't say to someone, 'Look, turn your distress off, please, and come back tomorrow.'

I can't leave my work at work. I went home last night and felt as though I had been wrung out, you know, because when you put emotional effort into somebody, a lot of emotional effort, it becomes a physical thing as well and you actually feel drained by the time you have finished. A lot of the time you've got to motivate them, and that's really tiring, you've got to get them going. I mean if I've got someone going to an interview I like to see them in the morning before they are interviewed so I get them psyched up and relaxed. That's a contradiction in terms, I know, but it's not only to get them ready, but also to get them to feel, 'I can do it.' It's the reassurance that people need.

When you're sending someone along to something, you could change the pattern of their lives just by selecting a job, and that's a very onerous feeling. That's why I also insist that my people have got to come in and see me, so we can go through the vacancies together. There are boards with vacancies in the entrance and I tell them to arrive ten minutes early and to go round the boards and get an idea what there is, because basically it's got to be your choice, I tell them. I can push, but you have to actually jump.

Being blind, I have to have somebody work with me all the time which is a nuisance, because I'm a bit of a loner when it comes to work. I like being shut in this office, I don't take kindly to teamwork, because I like to take responsibility for what I do, and not what anybody else does. I work at a different speed and in a different way, and I find it difficult to have to cope with the way other people work.

I would be more fulfilled if I was allowed to do more. I still don't feel I'm allowed to do enough. I still don't feel that I can stretch my own net wide enough, but the sort of work I do really turns me on. Because when the people that I'm dealing with come in and they've actually got what you were trying to get for them, or better still, if you have encouraged them and they have got it themselves, it is fantastic.

I talk to my husband about my people, he listens and then we talk about something else, but he's interested because he knows it worries me so much. I try not to talk too much. I mean we have our half hour after supper when we both talk about our work, and that's the end of it.

My husband is blind too. He's a civil servant, he works for Health and Safety, he's a very good typist. His blindness has affected him in the way that he hasn't pushed for promotion, he's just sat back and let things happen which he wouldn't have done if he had been sighted. He wouldn't have ended up in an office at all if he had been sighted, I don't think. I tried pushing him but... well, I suppose one of us has to be sensible.

In the end, I think everyone will only be working half weeks, so we've got to get ourselves sorted out leisurewise. And that's where the jobs are going to come, in the leisure industries. I wish we would spend more money on the construction side because there are so many construction workers out of work, and they are not, a lot of them, the sort of fellows you could train to work computers or do video presentations or run leisure centres, and it's the construction workers who are my biggest problem. Anyway it would help us all, because look at the state we are in at the minute, look at the state of the roads, the state of housing, the state of the sewers, and now with our unemployment we have the ideal chance – why spend the money on unemployment when we could spend it on getting the unemployed to revitalize things, you know, giving people a purpose again, because that's what it is, you know, everybody has got to have a purpose of some sort.

I wouldn't like to earn less than I earn now, but the salary is not the first thing I look at in a job. It's important, because we like to go on our holidays. I like to go abroad once or twice a year and that's one of the reasons it's important. Also I have a large family, not children of my own, but I've a large family who I like to buy presents for, and that kind of thing. And it's important because I don't like to depend on anybody else for anything. But it's not important for its own sake, and I've never been in a family that's been living in the lap of luxury, and I think what you haven't had, you don't miss.

The best part of this job, apart from Christmas dinner, is the people, it's when you have a success, or when somebody is pleased with what you have done for them. A while ago I had a chap who hadn't worked for four years, and he had been addicted to tranquillizers, Valium I think it was, and he finally decided he'd got to pull himself together, and I got him on a community programme. He was like a dog with two tails because they gave him a jacket and a free pair of boots.

Hardly any of them bother to say thank you, that's why it's so good when the ones that do, do. Just occasionally you get a surprise, I mean I had a card and a bunch of flowers a while ago. It doesn't hurt me that people don't say thank you, I've got used to it. It hurts me when they don't turn up for interviews I've sent them on, or when they turn up and they make a mess of it, that hurts.

It's difficult to explain, but you get certain messages from the way people say things to you. You can tell, for a start, whether they are lying much more by the voice than you can by looking at someone, I think. And you can tell whether they are enthusiastic or whether they are unsure, and it's like vibrations, you get ideas about people from the voice and the whole way they behave, whether they are at ease or not, because you can't really hide it in a voice. There is only so long you can wear a facade, and if I think they are hiding something from me and I don't crack it the first time, I'll see them again, and I'll crack it the second time usually. You see it's not a game of them hiding something from me, and me having to find it, it's essential that I find it. Because usually if they are hiding something from me, it's a big something. Somebody who's been in hospital, who's been mentally ill or something like that, they don't want to tell you, but you can always tell. I had a chap once who had been a soldier in the Royal Engineers, and he'd been in an IRA bombing in a pub, and I knew there was something wrong and he wouldn't tell me what it was, that he'd been very seriously injured, and he kept going after training courses and not getting on the course he went for, and he really needed training. He told me eventually, it came out, and I said to him, if he had told me before we could have saved each other an awful lot of difficulty. But I got him sorted out, I mean he's running his own business now and that's fantastic. But people hide things from you because they think it's going to make their life more difficult, they think that every time you ask them something you are trying to catch them out, they are very suspicious.

It's not how they treat me as a blind person I'm getting at now, it's their whole manner, it's how they behave towards us as employment advisors. Some regard us as people in authority which I hate, because I'm not in authority, I'm there to help. Some are very obsequious towards us which embarrasses me, to see a middle-aged man tugging his forelock to me. And some are absolutely indifferent, and I know then that I can't do anything with them, because I can't get through to them. The most difficult ones are the people who just sit and won't answer, or just give yes and no answers.

It's the whole way people approach us, whether they take us seriously. Some of them come and regard it like a job interview, which is great, because that's really what it is in a way. But it is this whole business of how people sit, how they behave, what they say, how they say it, whether they sit and yawn, the same things that anybody sees but doesn't catalogue, things that may go unnoticed. But with me they go noticed because I haven't got the visual thing, I'm listening all the time, and when I shake hands with someone at the end of an interview I know then if it's gone well. It's the different handshakes. If I'm going to see someone again, I make a point of always saying goodbye and offering my hand at the end of an interview, and you gradually feel the confidence build in the handshake. And I always think, if someone comes in really distressed and unhappy, if I can make them laugh before they go, or at least make them feel a bit happier, then I've made the first tentative steps, because you've got to win their confidence before you start shoving them into jobs.

Farmer
Richard Pennink

I was going through a very frustrating period at work in that I'd been appointed export manager for the bulk packaging division of the group that I worked for, and I'd spent three years travelling around Europe drumming up sales. I built up quite a reasonable market for the product but I was having the usual battles with our factory in the UK because they couldn't make what I wanted on time, and the quality wasn't up to scratch, and I found that I was just going around from dissatisfied customer to dissatisfied customer and seeing the work that I'd put into it frittered away.

I was abroad at least two weeks out of every month. I had my American Express card and expense accounts and a reasonable car, all that sort of thing, so you could say I was quite well looked after. In fact I felt very privileged being able to go around Europe, eating in the best restaurants, and drinking the best wine, without having to pay for it myself.

I don't think I was quite into the male menopause or anything like that. But I suddenly realized in absolute horror that I was totally unqualified for anything other than another job with another large firm – more of the same, basically, and that didn't really appeal at all. It was making life difficult at home to the extent that I felt unfulfilled and frustrated, and that obviously rubs off on one's home life. I mean, so far as we've had a difficult stage in our relationship, Sarah and I, that was probably the worst time, you know, you could see everything was coming to a head, and something had to be done. It was no one factor, it was a combination of the frustration at work, and a dissatisfaction somehow, having arrived in a very nice house with a very nice garden, and very nice neighbours in a very nice neighbourhood... it just somehow wasn't enough.

Years and years ago, long before it ever became a practical reality, we'd been staying with some friends of Sarah's in Reading, and they left this book on self-sufficiency by the bedside, and Sarah I were both reading it – and that is absolutely, definitely, where the original idea came from. We read this book and we were both rather impressed by it. Actually, in retrospect, it was a very bad book, we get it out every now and again, and you could sue the author about some of the things he says. But it hit right at the romance of self-sufficiency, growing your own food and starting a smallholding, and that sort of thing. I suppose that was a good six or seven years before it became a practical possibility. But we were prepared for the change in a way, because we both wanted to do it.

We bought the farm and moved down here while I was still employed with the firm, and the idea was to build up the farming business whilst I was still enjoying a good salary, and then we could offset some of the tax losses on the farm. But the frustration built up to such an extent that the overlap period was far less. We imagined we'd be able to keep going about three or four years, and then gradually phase out of one and into the other, but, in fact, I just said one morning, 'Right, that's it, I'm not going in today,' and that was how it ended.

When I left, they wound up the whole export side of the business. In fact I made a very grave tactical error in leaving then, because had I stayed another two years I would have been made redundant. But I guess that's life. You can't win them all.

We're just beginning now, after five or six years of farming, to get into quite a comfortable routine, in that I'm doing what I really want to do, Sarah's doing what she wants to do, and actually, the two are becoming quite compatible. It's enabled Sarah to do what she wanted to do. She's a musician, she teaches in ten or twelve different schools on a peripatetic basis, and she has private pupils in the evening, none of which she would be able to do if I was doing a nine-to-five job, because although I'm reasonably fully employed on the farm, I'm here and I can take the kids to school, I can fetch them back, and get the supper on the go in the evenings.

Starting the farm was quite frightening, really, because although I'd done a correspondence course in farming, I basically knew nothing about it at all. I kept the course under my desk, and in between phone calls I'd be reading the books and writing the essays and posting it all off. That gave me the basic theoretical knowledge.

It's all very well reading books, but you wake up one morning and look out the window, and there are some cows out there, there's a tractor, there's a plough, and one hadn't a clue what to do, and we really have just sort of learned as we've gone along. Helpful neighbours, the farmers around here are so nice. I can remember the first time I went out to plough a field. I'd read what to do, but I couldn't get the thing working really well, and the neighbouring farmer, I could see him watching me over the fence, and to his everlasting credit, he didn't come and interrupt me in what I was doing, he just watched. I think if he'd come along in the middle I would have resented it, so he was very tactful. And he came over when I finished and he said, 'Well, you've done a pretty good job there, but if you'd done this, that, and the other, you could have done it a bit quicker, and it would've been a bit better.' I dare say that if I'd been completely ruining the field he would've come and said something. There's always a better way of doing something.

Another thing I did, I'd bought a brand new hay mower which has a latch on it which lets it ride over the contours of the land, and I used this thing for six months without releasing the latch, and wondered why it wouldn't cut very well. You know, every time it came to a bump, instead of sort of following the contour, it would just stay level, and of course, you'd get long bits and short bits. It didn't actually matter, but it probably wasted about ten per cent of the available grass, and eventually somebody came along: 'Oh, aren't you going to take the latch off?' and I said, 'What latch?'

Most farmers have started off either as farm workers and worked their way up into farm management, or they've started off working on the family farm, and learned from boyhood how to do these jobs properly. But I think if you start without the benefit of that type of experience, you're bound to make mistakes. I've been very lucky in that although I'm still making mistakes, nothing's actually ever cost me a lot of money.

It's complete chance that we're in East Sussex. When we went out to find a farm, we literally scoured the country. I imagined we'd go up to North Wales, and we looked at a lot of farms there and in the north of England, and the Midlands. But my family originally comes from this part of the world, my mother in fact lives in Frant, and my sister and her husband have a farm which is about ten miles away, and one day my brother-in-law rang me up and said, 'Come and have a look at this place.' We never really thought we'd be able to afford a farm in the south east because they seem to be disproportionately expensive to the quality of the land that you're getting, but this farm seemed just right. We're very near the garden of England, Kent, and the fruit-growing areas. This particular little patch is in pockets of clay and green sand, and we've got some good land and some difficult land.

We've got about 165 acres, and we carry roughly 140 head of stock. Breaking it down roughly, we've got a breeding herd of about 30 cows, and we have their calves from one year, and there are cows from the year before which are finished. It's a two-year cycle producing beef. So from those, we've got about sixty or seventy head of stock at any one time, and we also buy in calves which we rear artificially, bucket rear, and take those through again on a two-year cycle. There's an awful lot of mouths to feed, and we're farming all through the year in order to feed them during the winter.

My attitude towards the animals is that I look after them as well as I can and at the end of two years, apart from the breeding cows, they're off, they're meat. Boom. I don't kill them myself, but it doesn't worry me in the slightest. I don't have any sort of qualms about sending them off to market. I mean I would kill them myself if that was the way it was done. I'm far less sensitive now than I was when I lived further up the food chain where most people's idea of a cow is a shrink-wrapped steak in Safeway supermarket.

I feel I've developed an amazing adaptability. It's no good being a worrier, it's no good getting uptight about things, you know, spending your whole time worrying about whether it's going to rain when you're trying to make hay. The first two or three years, I was in absolute misery because I worried the whole time. I worried about whether my calf was going to die, I worried about whether it was going to rain, I worried about whether the grass was going to grow. And I've changed enormously, I'm far easier going now, I'm far less tense. I really don't worry too much, because I've come to terms with the fact that there's nothing you can do about it, you know, if you've got a crop of hay down and it rains for a week, you've had it. When I started I used to ring up the weather forecast two or three times a day, and I'd get a crick in my neck when I was out in the tractor, because I'd always be looking behind me in the direction the wind was coming from to see if there were big black clouds coming up. I was probably under more stress those first couple of years than I ever was in the office.

I feel far more at peace with myself. I used to hate being on my own, and now I absolutely love it because I think a lot more and I worry a lot less. I find a great sort of spiritual calm, being with the animals, and working a lot on my own as I inevitably do.

The things I can do now that I couldn't do when I started never cease to amaze me; I mean, I can lay bricks, I can plaster walls, I can put a new roof on the cow shed, all sorts of things, and if I could've pictured myself twenty years ago doing these things, I wouldn't have believed it.

I've grown a lot closer to my mother through being here, I've developed a relationship which I never really had before. It's probably proximity and change in personality, because one wouldn't have happened without the other, but I think it's largely because I've calmed down a lot since being on the farm.

The world as I knew it seems very remote. I mean, you go in the village pub, and you're talking about the potato crop, or how your best bull is doing, and this sort of thing. We don't talk much about politics. We still read papers and things, but summit meetings and invasions seem a million miles away. When we were living in town, for some reason one felt very much closer to it. I seem very rarely to make value judgements about anything now, I'm much more inclined to take things as they come. I'm far less opinionated. I used to have fairly strong views on what was right and wrong in a lot of spheres, and now, I've either revised my ideas or I'm not at all sure that I was right before.

It makes it sound terribly romantic, sitting outside in the meadow, you know, swigging your cider after having got in a successful crop of hay, and the animals are all munching away and everything's lovely. And it really isn't like that, because at the end of the day, you've got to make money out of it. If you've got a family, it just isn't possible to make the sort of money that you can in any other sphere of life, you've got to work very hard, not just at making stuff grow and feeding the animals etcetera, you've got to make sure you get in your subsidies, you've got to be switched on about doing your accounts, this sort of thing.

If you just took the complete book of self-sufficiency, and read that, and you thought, 'Great, I'll sell my nice little house in London, I'll buy a farm and I'll live happily ever afterwards,' you've got about a one in a hundred chance of making a go of it, I would say. We were very lucky. And not only that, but we had sufficient capital to see us through our mistakes. And we had another income as well, as Sarah built up her business.

The biggest stroke of luck we had was starting when we did, because I don't think it would be possible to start up now. For example, I'm getting the same price for my finished beef animals when I send them to market that I got six years ago when we started. Now all our inputs have gone up quite considerably since then, and I don't seem to remember being terribly excited about the price six years ago. You certainly couldn't build up a herd of cattle, such as we've got, from scratch, unless you had an enormous amount of capital. And if you had to borrow any significant proportion from the bank, you'd have no chance, because the return on capital invested in conventional farming is 1½ to 2½ per cent, if you do it really well, and to borrow the money you'll probably be having to pay 19 or 20 per cent. And the equation doesn't work.

Farming is really in the doldrums. The general view of non-farmers and town folk is that farmers are unbelievably wealthy, but to make a living on a small farm now is almost impossible. Whatever crop you're trying to produce is in surplus, or nobody wants it, and you're never properly paid for it. The support system is breaking down, and the Common Agricultural Policy is under fire left, right and centre, and the farming lobby in this country is insufficiently strong to do anything very much about it.

Like anybody else, we need enough to be reasonably comfortable, we need enough to buy the children's clothes, that sort of thing. We don't actually spend a lot of money; one of the advantages of being on a farm is that we do produce quite a lot of our own food; not by any means all – we still have tremendous bills from the supermarket – but we probably eat better, more cheaply, than most people.

All I had to do to get money before was to do my job and I'd get a cheque at the end of the month. Now I've got to do more than that; I've got to not only do the job, but I've got to manage the business as well, and if I don't do both effectively, we're not going to get paid. But I quite enjoy that. I feel that I've got more control over where my money comes from, which is more rewarding than just getting paid for a specific job.

It's probably the first time I've sat down and tried to compare life now with life before. And, you know, I've never felt dissatisfied; I've never been unhappy at making the change.

Film Director
Lewis Gilbert

I started directing films at twenty-four and I learnt very early on that the great thing is to pace yourself, otherwise you can head very quickly for a nervous breakdown as lots of directors do. It's very important to count ten and not lose your head, and if something goes wrong, to spend your energy in putting it right rather than holding inquests or accusations and things like that. I'm very calm on the set. I started as a child actor so I have great sympathy for actors because I can remember being shouted at at quite an early age, and it put me off terribly. So I never lose my cool unless an actor is being really stupid and wanting to do something in a certain way which is absolutely wrong.

In the old days you made two films in a year because it was all done in a studio. Now you're lucky to make one film in two years, because it's usually made in some exotic part of the world and it takes such a long time to set up; and because the money often comes from America, you're swanning around Los Angeles for quite a bit. It's not a nine-to-five job, it's a twenty-four-hours-a-day, two-year job.

If I'm spending a few hours with my grandchildren, nine tenths of my mind is playing with the grandchildren, but one tenth is always thinking of the project, you can never get it out of your mind. The business side you could almost make nine to five except for dreadful phone calls from Los Angeles where the time-change means that you're woken up at all hours of the night.

It is a very complicated and complex business and I think that everybody has their failures as well as their successes. At first, when I was young, I reacted pretty badly to failure, but as you get older you learn to take it in your stride. I mean, everybody has failures. Funnily enough I find success much harder to take. You are in so much demand, particularly in America where success means everything. Your phone never stops ringing. I think more people are ruined by success than failure, particularly in the film world, because really the success that we are talking about is out of all proportion to what it's for. I mean, a great brain surgeon doesn't have what a film director has to go through; when he's been eight hours operating on somebody's brain, he doesn't have every single paper and magazine in the land telling him what an idiot he is or what a great man he is, according to how the operation goes. After all, if the film is lousy, so what? You haven't killed your mother-in-law, you haven't murdered the Prime Minister. It isn't such a terrible thing if you think about it, but neither, if everybody thinks it's a great picture, is that so fantastic, because after all people are doing much more than making great pictures in the world. You know, they're curing leprosy or incredible things like that.

On the set you are the Field Marshal and as such you have tremendous power. Very rarely does anybody question a decision that you make, and that is not a good thing because you can be lulled into a very false sense of security. Even a great novelist like Somerset Maugham had an editor who worked with him to say, 'Now that's a lousy sentence,' or 'Shall we change it to this?'

It's a bit lonely. I've made many films at sea so I can make the comparison with the captain of a ship who doesn't eat with anybody else; he can't go into the wardroom unless he's invited, and he must invite officers to come and have dinner with him.

I sometimes feel it's not a job for a grown man. I remember once doing a Bond film with Sean Connery in Japan. It was about midnight and we were filming outside a hotel. I said to Sean, 'Now you get the gun, you come down this corner, and you pause behind the corner and you shoot, bang bang . . . ,' and I looked at him and I said, 'My God, I've done this before, I remember doing this when I was about eight years old,' because that's exactly what you do when you're a child, isn't it? And Sean said, 'For God's sake don't tell me that or I'll never act again.' I very often watch children play, and they order each other about in the way a film director orders his actors about. There is always a leader who says, 'Right, you six be the Indians, and you four be the Cowboys,' and they're inventing a whole scenario, which is what we do.

In fact the greatest thing about actors is their childlike quality, and you have to treat them as children. And I suppose because one is in a position of authority, you are the father figure on the film, and they tend to come to you with their troubles.

I know that acting in a studio is much more difficult than acting in the theatre, because you have a hostile audience on a film set. Everybody is doing a different job: the focus puller is measuring someone up thinking, 'Is he or she in focus?' And the hairdresser is thinking, 'Oh God, now they're clinching, it's going to mess up her hair.' They're all worrying about something, and for the actor there is no reaction to work off. The director is the only audience they have, and if he's sitting there shaking his head, it's going to be a very dampening experience for them. So you must behave like an audience for them, you must laugh if it's funny, and cry if it's sad, and help them in that sense.

It's the director's job to manipulate the actors, to get them to do what you want. You'll do anything to get a scene. I remember the only time in my life when it was beyond ruthless. There was a scene where the child in a film had to cry. He was a little Cockney kid of about three or four, and I said to his father, who was with him, 'I think I can talk to him about crying.' And he said, 'I'll make him cry – you just turn the camera.' So we turned the camera, and the father went up to the kid and put his hand in his pocket and pulled out a half-crown. 'Where did you get this from ... you bloody nicked it,' he said. And the kid said, 'No, dad, I didn't ... ' And the father said, 'I'm taking that aeroplane,' and he grabbed it and smashed it into little pieces. And this child started to cry. The entire unit must have thought I told the father to do it, and I could feel the hostility in the back of my neck. But it was fantastic, this kid really cried his heart out, and half of me wanted to go up to him and say, 'Don't cry,' but the other half was the film director thinking, 'Jesus, this is unbelievable, this is the most fantastic scene of a child crying I have ever seen,' and that I remember very clearly as of the split personality of the film director. I was shocked. I was very shocked, but I was unable to say, 'Cut.'

I've had films which I desperately wanted to do but if I can't get it going within a certain amount of time I will drop it and work on something else. I suppose I regard myself as a kind of professional film maker who has to supply the public with films, although that's a different thing now from what it was. Twenty years ago it was a steady diet, today the film audience only goes to something which is exceptionally good or exceptionally out of the ordinary, and so you had better be much more sure of it than you were twenty years ago.

In ninety-nine cases out of a hundred the film studios are wrong. Nearly all the films that are successful have been turned down by every single company, and it's invariably the obsessiveness of the director or the producer that makes the film in the end. I'm pretty obsessive in the sense that once I go for something, nothing stands in the way. I mean I will get on a plane tomorrow night, in ten minutes' time, if someone rang from America and said, 'We are interested in your subject.'

If we have to talk about money, I'd say one is overcompensated, really, but then that's the old capitalistic system, isn't it, supply and demand. I suppose there aren't so many film directors with a long track record, so therefore you tend to command high fees, the same way as a barrister who's now a QC gets terribly highly paid, and the lowly barrister doesn't get so much. How can you tell in the capitalist world who is overpaid and who isn't? I don't think I would ever accept a film just because there is money in it. I suppose it's easy for me to say that now because I'm not poor any longer, but when I was beginning I certainly took films on for money. After all, you've got to eat and pay the rent.

Looking back on all the films I've made there is a consensus of opinion. I mean, however good the film, you're bound to get a few bad notices, but in the main I've always found the critics fair: if the film is bad the majority will say that, if it's good they'll give you praise. I don't think they have any particular axe to grind in that sense.

The worst part of the job is showing the film – not necessarily to critics, but to an audience, because until that moment, you're living in a fool's paradise. You've worked on the screenplay, you've worked through six months of shooting day after day, you see the rushes over and over again, so you are physically incapable of saying whether it's a good film or a bad film.

The moment of truth comes with an ordinary audience, and that is the moment which every director fears and hates. I don't hate the audience, I hate the moment. I'm up for judgement like before the judge to see whether I'm going to be found guilty, or not guilty.

I could be flippant and say money was the best part of the job but I suppose really the best part is holding the end product, the satisfaction of knowing that you have taken nothing more than an idea, and you have managed to steer this craft home to safety. It is a very long and complicated job, and you never know whether you are going to dock into a safe harbour, or whether it is going to be total disaster. In the end you're left with just twelve tins of film of which the intrinsic value may be fifty pounds, and you've spent twenty-five million dollars on it. So it is in a sense something of pride just to get the craft there, never mind whether it is going to be successful or not.

Funeral Director
Ian Fraser

We were established in 1884. My grandfather, my father, myself and my nephew, who's my sister's boy, we've had four generations in this business now, and it gives me a certain pleasure and pride that we've been able to keep it in the family for so long. We have been approached on many occasions to sell out, but that's not on the cards, certainly not in my lifetime, and I hope for another generation after that we would still continue to remain independent. My nephew, he's a young lad you see, he's only thirty-three, so hopefully he's got another forty to forty-five years.

We are a household name in the north of Scotland, there are very few people who haven't heard of us, and we are proud of the service we give and the fact that it is still continuing under the name Fraser.

Well, we feel that we are giving the ultimate, a very top, professional service. It would perhaps be wrong of me to say that our service is better than others, but I think the increasing volume of business, and customer satisfaction, in the sense that they keep coming back, is a tribute to the fact that they are satisfied. We provide a service in the true sense, twenty-four hours a day, seven days a week, three hundred and sixty-five days of the year, and we also provide a personal service in the sense that with it being a family business, either myself or my nephew personally meet all the relatives, and personally attend all the funerals.

When a death takes place, the relatives or the next of kin contact us – we are usually one of the first people to be contacted – and from there we provide our full service and advise and help wherever possible; whatever the relatives want, we give it, a complete service. For example, if somebody wants to be embalmed, well, we can embalm the remains ourselves, as part of our service. My nephew does all the embalming, he's a qualified embalmer, and if the remains are being transported to England or abroad, it is compulsory that the remains be embalmed, and there is in fact an increasing call for embalming as a whole. There is no crematorium in the Highlands, so any cremations have got to go to Perth, which is about a hundred miles away. But there is not a big demand for cremations, because basically the Highlanders prefer to be interred, and the prices of plots are quite cheap here.

The Scottish, and particularly the Highlanders, are much more respectful and reverent and considerate of death. The funerals up here are very well attended, particularly in the country. In the small parishes, even if it's in a place where there are a thousand inhabitants, every house is represented at a funeral, and if your cortège is going along the road, the cars will stop and let you through, and people will doff their hats and stand at the side of the road, whereas in the busier places like London, you are just swept by.

One of the worst parts of the job is meeting people at a time when you must accept that you are inadequate, with what support or comfort or words that you can utter, to give any condolence to the bereaved. It is most difficult and trying to get things on a base for getting arrangements made, and at the same time not upsetting the family unduly, and a great deal of tact is required.

Death is a tremendous blow to a family, irrespective of the highest or the lowest in the land. To lose one's dear one, or somebody close to them, is a traumatic experience in one's life. We are not heartless, of course we have had our own personal bereavements and we have felt them deeply ourselves, and we try to assist people in cooperation with the Minister to minimize the grief wherever possible. And I think that's where an efficient service, carried out with dignity and reverence, plays no small part in assisting people at that time of grief. It doesn't actually bring them back but it allows them happy memories of the departed person.

Everybody reacts differently and therefore you have to assess each situation and see how you can handle this person. Sometimes the ones who are emotionless on the surface could be in the deepest distress, but people have different ways of showing emotion. I suppose women are more inclined to show their grief, being the so-called weaker sex. Men are more inclined to bottle it up or hide it behind something like drink, and I think at the average funeral you'd find the women would be perhaps less able to control themselves or be more hysterical or weeping than the men would be. But I don't look upon tears as a sign of weakness, I think tears are an expression of relief, it's trying to get rid of some of your tension.

One of the saddest things is to see somebody suffering and eventually dying from a lengthy illness. My own father died from cancer, and he was ill for a year before he died, and really and truly to see somebody suffering to such an extent, that's one of the tragedies of modern life when they can put people on the moon, but when an illness like cancer comes, man is completely lost, and I think more effort should be made to try and find a cure for cancer. When you see what they can do now with open heart surgery, for example, that's a tremendous benefit, and I know quite a few people personally who have had open heart surgery, and it has made new men of them.

If you talk about people suffering, this year alone we had a personal friend who died from cancer; he had an outstanding war record and got the Victoria Cross and a host of other decorations, and then he contracted cancer at the end of last year. We saw him in March, and I asked him what's been wrong, because he looked terrible, and he said, 'Good God, man, can't *you* see? I'm dying… ' and he came up and stayed with us in May with his wife for two nights, and eight weeks after, he was dead. And I think that is a sad thing, when somebody who gives wonderful service to his country, so brave, and has got such high honours and survived it all, and then died with such a horrible trouble.

I was very upset when my own mother died. She died in Spain on holiday. She sent me a postcard which arrived one morning to say that she was enjoying her holiday, and quarter of an hour after, the phone rang to say they had found her dead. It was quite a while before we were able to get her home, ten days, and we had a very emotional time of it, and I was very upset because I was very close to my mother, we were a very close family.

I am reminded every day of death. That makes one very humble in a sense, to realize that whatever one can have in life, whatever material things, the still most important thing in the world is to have your health.

I often think about the finality of death. I've been with quite a few people and they have spoken to me and then just died, and I think when one minute somebody is breathing and talking to you, and the next minute they are dead and gone, I think that is really so final in life it's quite frightening.

Well, you get one or two who try to be funny about your job when they find out what you do, but I think the majority of people realize that we are in a caring business, a business that everybody some time in their life has to deal with, and a lot of them have an experience of bereavement and they appreciate the essential service that is required, and they don't like to be too humorous or joke about it, because they don't know what tomorrow might bring.

You do get lighter moments. I remember a country funeral. The service was held at the house, and the Minister read quite a long prayer – I think it lasted about half an hour – and then he had the Benediction. There was a silence for a moment or two, and then a voice said, 'I'm not satisfied.' So everybody looked up, and there was the son-in-law.

And the Minister said, 'Mr So and So, what do you mean, you're not satisfied?'

'I'm not satisfied you've given my mother a good enough send-off,' he said. 'You're far too short, I want you to start again and don't be so short.'

And for the first time ever in my life, I was asked to extend a funeral service. So I gave him another half hour and I turned to him and said, 'Well, have you got your money's worth, are you satisfied now?'

And he said, 'Yes, that's OK.'

And that's a true story.

Going through life I think people should try to have a wee bit of consideration and understanding. The saddest thing in the world is to see where parents are put into homes and suchlike, where the families concerned are quite able financially and otherwise to look after them and don't do so. In this modern society people abdicate their responsibilities and leave it very much to the State, which I think is wrong. The fact is that in later years children should be prepared to consider their parents and look after them. Because I've seen older people, how lonely they are at the end, especially a widow or a widower on their own, they are very lonely and sad, and that is when they need their family about them more than anything else. You go to all the various homes when we have a death there, and they are looking around and wondering who's going to be next. They know their days are numbered because they are all so elderly.

Well, I'm getting older myself, and weary. I'm fifty-five. When you are younger you feel you will never die, but when you have lived a bit, and you have seen a bit of life, and you have seen a lot of good friends go, suddenly you start to think, 'Well, it's my generation next.' And there is not much you can do about that, I know.

Game Dealer
Nigel Harvey

The business started in 1924, here in Norwich, with my grandfather, and in those days the only products that we sold were wild rabbits, farm butter and honey, and that was it. Father came out of the war and took over what was not a thriving business, and the natural progression, especially when myxomatosis virtually wiped out the rabbit population, was to go into game.

People that buy from us? Everybody, right through the whole scale, from the little old lady in the council house down the road that will come up and buy one rabbit leg for her poodle, going through the middle and upper classes, who are now realizing that game is such good value, because it hasn't really gone up in price for the last ten years. The other end of our business is wholesale, and we supply people like Harrods and Fortnums, and we do some export customers as well.

Selling pheasants in Norfolk, certainly over the retail counter, is a bit like trying to sell coal in Newcastle. There are those that get it given to them free at source, friends of friends who've got shoots, or they get paid in game, like the local doctor who always gets pheasants. Because they are given birds in the feather, they bring them to me and we charge them a nominal amount, and we pluck and dress them. We charge 80 pence per bird, which for coming in with something like that, and going out with something ready for the oven, has got to be good value really.

I'm down the shop at 7 a.m.; we have five of us there. The staff are Jack-of-all-trades, and they have to be. They serve in the shop, they process the game, they do virtually everything. My main job is to get on the telephone and sell game which I know is coming in, perhaps it hasn't even been shot, but I know that there are estates shooting in the next two or three days. I have a rough idea, there might be three, four or five thousand pheasants that I'm going to have to turn over in the next week, so my job is hopefully to find customers and fix a price before the birds enter our premises. That's the difficulty. That's why there aren't more game dealers about. It's a fluctuating market for a start; you're dealing in fresh food, and because game is shot and not slaughtered like normal meats, you can't freeze it in the condition it is shot, i.e. leaving the feathers on and then deciding what you're going to do about it later. One has to process them as and when they are shot.

I didn't really have too much choice about going into the business. I went to school not two hundred yards away, King Edward School, and by the age of about fourteen or fifteen I was old enough to realize that my father was very ill. He had, well, he still has got Parkinson's disease, he's had it for thirty years. It was becoming more and more difficult for him to carry on with the day-to-day running of the shop. After having two brain operations, he had problems with his voice, but I could understand him, so I would be standing next to him acting as an interpreter.

I had to learn the business that much quicker. There was a lot to learn. For instance, guinea-fowl are hung up by their feet, and a pheasant is hung by its head. All game is hung up to retain the body fluids in the gut, for a period depending on whether it's warm or cold, whether it's humid or not, how old the animal is. An old red deer will want hanging for at least a fortnight in relatively cold weather. An old cock pheasant you could hang for two or three weeks in certain circumstances, but the criteria is how long game must hang to attain a certain flavour, and that flavour will also depend on what the bird has been eating.

I love work, I thrive on work. My wife will tell you that I'm a miserable toad in the summer because I'm bored. This is why I'm so much looking forward to this new shop I'm opening up in Grove Road. There's so much to organize and I shall love that. I hate kicking my heels, I'm sure that the staff are the same, I think that's mostly human nature.

My first wife could never really come to terms with what every farmer's wife has to put up with. You know, that there are busy times of the year, and business has to come first. If you are earning your main living from something which is essentially very busy for four months of the year, the social world has to come second. And because it's over the Christmas period, it didn't go down too well starting work at five in the morning and finishing perhaps ten o'clock at night. I'm lucky, my present wife, she was brought up in the farming fraternity where they have seasons like Harvest, and everybody has to muck in, and now she is taking the most active female role in the business since my grandmother was attached to it. I don't have to come home and explain why I'm completely pissed off or whatever; the chances are she's already heard about it during the day, and she does come up with some extremely good ideas. It's always very good to get somebody totally from outside to come in with new ideas. One tends to become very staid, with old, traditional family businesses, you tend to get in a rut, it's inevitable.

From March to August we have to fall back on more traditional-type foods. It's less interesting because everyone else is doing it. I mean there's no way that I can compete any more with the supermarkets selling things like fresh chickens. Ten years ago a fresh chicken was very much more difficult to get because it was the era of frozen foods, but people now are definitely going back to something that's fresh, and they will have frozen food as a standby.

All the game that I handle is shot by sportsmen. Nobody yet has successfully reared pheasants because of today's costs. A pheasant put in the air for shooting next season is going to cost a conscientious landowner, who doesn't skimp on the food and employs a gamekeeper, about £12 to £14 each. He is going to get back from me a maximum of £2 each. So he's going to lose on average about £10 per bird. Now when some of them rear 30–50,000 pheasants, well, it's not business because they don't expect to make money out of it. But at the same time they expect the best return that the market will allow from people like myself.

I get a great deal of satisfaction out of selling, and if I get one customer a week that I can convert to buying something he or she wouldn't normally buy, for someone to come back and say, 'That was super', that makes my day.

Partridge is probably the best of all. English partridge, mind you; there are two types of partridge, English and French, and a young English partridge is reckoned by the gourmet to be *la crème de la crème*. It's something which requires only twenty, twenty-five minutes roasting, and it literally melts in your mouth, it's superb.

I have one daughter, and she's nearly seven. Obviously she's had to come to terms with a lot of things which most seven-year-old young ladies wouldn't have seen, and it would probably turn over a lot of mummies' tummies too. She has to accept that animals are killed. She'll drag twenty dead rabbits in from the back of the van, and it's all part of her education. She may want an academic career, in which case I shall help her as much as I can if she's good enough to go to university; or hopefully, she'll marry the right guy and go off and have a family. But she will certainly not go into the business. My job is quite physically demanding. There's a hell of a lot of lifting and driving vans around at high speed, and it's long hours. I wouldn't want to wish that on my daughter. Certainly she will not go into the business, this lease on our new shop premises is going to see me out.

Gamekeeper
Andrew Seaman

My father was in forestry and as a boy I had two hundred acres to go and do what I liked in, really, and when I came home from school I'd make a little hide and I'd sit there until it was dark, watching the birds, and Ma can't relate to how I could want to do what I'm doing, which most people think is killing things the whole while, when I was such a nature boy, as she used to call me.

My beat is approximately three thousand acres. That's as big as they come. I ain't got to look for a job, there's always something to do somewhere around here.

Even though I live in the village, it might be a week before I talk to people, even the farm people, other than waving when they go past. It could be a lonely profession but I don't find it so.

I completely nurse the pheasants from the day-old eggs right on until they're shot, and then make sure there's enough left behind for stock for another year, and generally control the vermin that would prey on the wild birds. Really I'm a conservationist, with pheasants in mind more than anything else.

It's a complete loss for my guv'nor right from the word go, really and honestly. The only bonus he's got is that I'm able to keep the odd vermin down – you know, rats and rabbits. They say that every bird shot costs £10 and when it gets to Nigel the game dealer, Nigel probably pays maximum £5 a brace, well, if you get £5, that's top money, and sometimes they don't reach that. The only money to be made out of it are the estates that let days out – perhaps they'd have foreigners come and let a day out.

But that doesn't happen here. Simply, it's just a tradition that's gone on and that's their hobby, same as someone else's hobby is darts in the pub, you know, it's just the thing that's done. And my job when you boil it all down is to produce ten, fifteen days' shooting through the winter. I mean my whole year is based on that, really.

Until they started this driving towards them, they never really killed a great number of birds, and of course once they started, they got into competition with landowners round about to try and rear even more pheasants because Lord So and So wanted more pheasants in his woods than Lord Such and Such, and that's when the really big bags started. Of an average now it really does vary, we have several smaller days, more a fun day, where we'll perhaps have only ten beaters, and if we get 120 head, which is accounting for the odd woodcock and pigeon, perhaps seventy to eighty pheasants and a few bits and pieces to make it up to that, that's acceptable. When we start to do the woods, then really we're thinking about four to five hundred pheasants a day.

We have about thirty beaters a day which I have to organize and somehow get to synchronize so they come in the right place at the right time. We have thrcc, perhaps four pickers behind with the dogs that go right back behind for any runners, so we don't leave a lot behind by the time we're done.

The standard of gunnery here is very good indeed, you'd have a job to find anywhere where they have a better team of guns. Maybe it's hard for you to imagine, but it's an art form, really, to see them shooting. There's very few of them that get hurt, they're dead in the air before they even come down. You see the art is to hit the bird in the head, and our guns are good enough, they do enough shooting, so that's just what they do. There are very few guns that come here that can't shoot. If they come here and they don't shoot very well, my guv'nor don't have them again, and that's all there is to it.

As far as the traditions go, it's always been a tradition that the gentlemen give the keeper a tip on a shoot day, and it's tradition again that the gamekeeper takes the birds out for the tenants on the estate. They're just little things, but things you more or less take for granted, things that have been going on for over a hundred years or more.

The tenants that actually farm land that belongs to my guv'nor are obviously not allowed to shoot, but it's common courtesy really that when we shoot the pieces of land they farm on, they put out a piece of kale which is a crop they will grow for cattle food, but which we can also make a drive out of. That'll probably grow five or six foot tall, absolutely ideal game cover, so we get them to grow that on the top of a hill somewhere and the pheasants that come out of there are real screamers, you could say.

We try and make them into as good a sporting bird as we can. We improve the woods by cutting the front down so that they fly a bit higher, and the birds aren't so close to the guns when they take off. So they take off on a hill and they're probably forty yards higher and they make a really good shot.

And then of course we leave it nice and quiet and feed them up again. They're fed all during the winter on straw and we see what we've got and whether we can shoot again, decide whether perhaps there's too many cocks, and so then we'll only shoot them and leave the hens. It's very much 'make it up as you go along' through the shooting season. But if you want to have a stock at the end on a private estate like this, there's no pressure. If it was a shoot where they'd let all the days for X amount of pounds, the people who have already paid their money want their blood, don't they? They want their shooting, even if they have to shoot everything on the estate.

I've got a very good relationship with my employer. You know, he's the same age as me which I find quite helpful. Usually we see each other at least once a week. I think he's been quite a wild sort of chap in his time, agriculture college, all that sort of thing.

In a way I suppose it is quite feudal because the shoot actually holds back the farming for the tenants, because to do what we want for the birds means that some of the farm activities are going to be done slightly different. Mind you, it benefits all the rest of the wildlife as it means instead of coming in with a damn great sprayer, charging along spraying everything, we have to be careful about the hedges and things like that. And if they aren't being careful of the hedges I soon get my eye on to it and make sure they are. So really my guv'nor is the only one who benefits from it, and to everyone else it's just a damn nuisance.

There's general aggravation with the farmers in that we want things done how we want them done. I mean when you see someone driving down the farm track and they've got one wheel up on the verge where you've got nests, you're going to say, 'Come on, you've had one too many at dinnertime,' and they don't really like that. But you don't want the wheel there, and that's the sort of little thing that upsets someone for perhaps a couple, three years afore they forget it.

Personally I like the trapping part of it best, trapping the vermin and that. To me that's the most interesting thing. Really it's a matter of deciding which way your vermin is going to come from and making the relevant trap to catch it. I'll dig a hole right through the bank, what we call a through-hole, and we've got traps today which are a hell of an improvement on the ones of years gone by. Stoats, weasels, rats, foxes. Nine out of ten things are dead in the trap these days. Crushed and that's that. And of course, me being me and liking some of the old traditions, I actually hang all my vermin up on my vermin line, whereas the old keepers used to nail them all round their shed in the wood.

You've got to check the traps each day, which is the fun part, if you like. I try and run just about two hundred, which is quite a lot to look at each day spread over three thousand acres, and I concentrate on that for six to eight weeks. I have a man trapping session in the spring, and I say, 'Well, by the time I done that, what's left over deserve to be there, or there ain't enough to do you a lot of harm.' And by the next year there's just as many again, I catch just as many every year because it moves in, but at least it gives the birds a chance to get going once the pheasants and partridges get to, say, six or seven weeks old.

I did actually take another job before, just to appease mother, really. I took a job with a builder for a month, but I knew when I took it I shouldn't be there. You don't work gamekeeping round your life, you live it, and if you didn't you couldn't do it. There's plenty of times when I've been perhaps two days without sleep because there is things to do, the weather is such that you want to get on and make the most of the light, and you have something to do in the dark as well. You just have to sort of plod along. Luckily that don't affect me too much.

My wife's father was a gamekeeper, so she knows as much as me. If she wasn't I don't think she'd still be here, she'd be gone by now. And little boy Robert, he's now nine, and the other boy's only just over a year, but Robert being nine, he loves it, he'd far rather come with me than anything else. I don't want to push him either way, it's very tempting to get him to do what I'm doing, but I can see that my job has not got many years to go as I'm doing it now. I mean legislation is already coming on the Continent to restrict the rearing of pheasants, and if my guv'nor was not allowed to rear pheasants I don't think he'd particularly want a keeper. Full-time keepers are getting thinner and thinner, there's no doubt about that.

I don't meet up with other gamekeepers. I'm classed as unsociable in the gamekeeping world. The others get together but I don't have time, actually, I spend so much time at work, and the odd time that I do get off I try and put aside for my family rather than jigger off and yap about what I've been doing for the past umpteen weeks. It doesn't interest me what other people are doing on other estates.

I don't know how I'd stick a nine-to-five job, I don't know how I could get into such a rut; maybe I'm in a rut here, but I am my own employer. Really and honestly, I often look at my job, and I get more out of the three thousand acres that I look after for my guv'nor than he does himself. Far more. Don't put that in the book because he'll dock my wages!

I like my work, I do like my work. Sometimes I consider it work, but truthfully, if I had a nine-to-five job, I'd have to have a piece of part-time keepering to do, and I'm really being paid for what I'd be doing as a hobby.

Golf Professional
Chris Moody

You read about people who say when they were twelve years old they decided they were going to be... something or other. I always sort of thought I'd like to be a professional golfer but it was more a question of I couldn't really think of much else to do, to be honest.

I was keen to play golf for a living, and a chap that I used to give lessons to sponsored me for two years to go and give it a try. The first year I won something like £380 on the tour, and the second year I did quite a bit better, by no means making any money, but showing signs of getting somewhere. This chap sponsored me for about £5000 a year, which was ample to play the tour in those days – I wish it still was now. It meant you could go play and not have to worry from day to day about making a cheque. I didn't see my sponsor from one month to the next. It gave him a good interest, a bit like, I suppose, owning a share in a racehorse. He did it because he liked golf and presumably liked me, and to give me a chance to get going. It was all a bit... philanthropic I suppose is the right term.

When you say you're a professional golfer, people say, 'Oh, really, but what's your job?' And I say, 'That is my job.' Then they say, 'Really? Don't you work?' And I say, 'Well, that is my work.' 'That must be nice,' they say, 'playing a game for a living must be great fun.' Which of course it is, but at the same time it is very hard work. That seems to be the mental leap that most people can't make – that if you enjoy it, it can't be work.

It's very hard work. I mean, most people think it's the life of old Riley and every day's a holiday because we go where they go on holiday, Barcelona or Malaga, south of France, I keep going off to different places every week. I've just been to Rio. But you go there and you've got to work, because if you don't make any money, you won't be doing it for very long. Actually making money out of golf is quite tough to do. Unless you're incredibly talented you have to work hard at it. And really it is a seven-day-a-week job. You can never really stop working, you've always got to go and practise.

You've got to keep your game in shape all the time. Basically speaking, Monday's your travelling day; Tuesday you've got to play your practice round, and practise your game; Wednesday it's either the Pro-Am or it's another practice round - more practice. Then the tournament starts Thursday, finishes Sunday, and then you go to the next one and it's the same thing. And all that time, you're having to try and maintain your golf game at a standard to win money.

The golf game is a bit like a pendulum; your game swings from one side to the other, and you're trying to get it steady in the middle. You start to battle with one part of your game, be it your short game, or your putting, or your driving, or maybe you're battling a hook. You tend to concentrate very much on that aspect of your game which is letting you down, and then the pendulum starts to swing the other way because you've neglected another part of your game a little bit. So it's a constant swinging from one side to the other to try and keep it on the straight and narrow.

People do get obsessed with golf, in the sense that it is a permanent challenge, and you know you've got to keep grafting at it all the time, you have to practise continually, to fire on all four cylinders as it were.

A lot of people would hate the life, I think, it's just hotels and airports and golf courses. You get up, you fly from one airport to another airport, and the hotel, go to another golf course. I happen to enjoy travelling, and I think we're very lucky that we play lots of different countries because if you make an effort, you can get around and meet the local people and they'll take you around and show you things, and it can be quite interesting. But generally speaking, it's a pretty relentless slog, throughout the year; and you don't get the chance to see very much.

I think for me, I much prefer the uncertainty of playing the tour - even not really knowing whether you're going to make any money that week, but being very independent - than actually working for somebody else, and being answerable to their whims. You are your own boss in this life, and you can't fool yourself. There's no office politics. I mean you either shoot a good score or you don't. If you shoot a really bad score, well, there's nobody to take the blame, but if you shoot a very good score, there's no one else to take the credit either.

If affords me more freedom than a lot of people, but it means while having a lot of freedom, I have to be a lot more disciplined than a lot of people. You have to keep practising all the time. You have to stay relatively fit; you can go out and have a few beers, but if you tie one on right before the first round, it's gonna cost you. I mean a lot of people can go to the office with a hangover, and they put in a dismal day's work, but they still get paid, and they probably even have people to cover for them, but with golf, all your pleasures have to be slightly disciplined.

It's very difficult to analyse the way you play. I'm pretty erratic. My main asset, I suppose, is I've got quite a good mental approach to the game, I've got a reasonable ability to concentrate, and even when I'm playing badly, I get the ball around. I'm pretty good around the greens, my short game is pretty reliable, most of the time. I'm known as a pretty good putter, which is a big asset. You can't play golf if you can't putt, basically. Mind you, I would look at my sixty- and seventy-yard pitch shots and say they were pretty indifferent for a professional player.

When I'm playing well, most of the parts of my game are pretty good. I'm a lucky player, you know, I bounce off trees and land back in the fairways and things like that. It's always better to be lucky than talented.

'Professional' means you play for money. With four good rounds of golf you can earn as much as some people earn in a year. Even if you're not in the top two or three there is a lot of money to be won now in the tournament. I'm not a wealthy person as a result of playing golf, but I live very nicely: I won enough money to be able to buy a house, I live quite comfortably I suppose, you know, middle-class comfortable living. There are people who are making a great deal of money out of the game, which we all aspire to do.

Hitting balls doesn't guarantee you will get better, because obviously everyone would just be out there twenty-four hours a day and make fortunes. I think the best players, the top players on the tour, certainly work the hardest. The Sevvys and the Langers and the Faldos probably practise more than anyone else to keep their game up at the standard that they've got it. Anybody can have a set of clubs as good as the ones I've got, it's the man holding the other end; it's the puttee not the putter. You know, Sevvy has very, very good equipment, but give me Sevvy's clubs I won't become Sevvy – otherwise I would have stolen them long ago!

The difference between winning comfortable sums of money and quite substantial sums of money is a great big leap, and it is a difficult step to get on the next rung of the ladder. I don't know, maybe I'm over the hill now – I'm thirty-two – who knows? That's old for a sportsman. I mean in a lot of sports, people have retired long since – squash players and football players are considered well past it at thirty-two. If you're playing badly for a couple of months, you think there must be better ways of making a living.

My mother is actually now dead, but I always remember she used to say, 'Well, why don't you get a proper job?' when I said I wanted to play golf for a living. My parents were very disappointed I didn't go to university, because both my brothers work with computers and are doing quite well for themselves. They're both older than me and my parents obviously had visions of me doing something similar. In fact I'm the only person in my family who plays golf at all.

At the moment I'm trying to use the money that I'm making to give myself a sort of financial base, so that I won't starve to death if I suddenly stop playing terribly well. It never used to concern me at all. I suppose as I'm getting older I start thinking, 'Well, I might have to stop playing in X number of years – what am I going to do then?' I would say after ten years of playing tournaments you're almost unemployable in the normal sense of the word. Having been my own master completely for ten years, I would find it very difficult to try and settle into a routine job, and I want to have sufficient money behind me so I don't have to rush off to some dead-end job if I do decide to stop playing.

It's a very anti-social existence, really, because you're away most of the time. It makes any relationship very difficult. I don't know how golfers who are married cope; it must be very difficult for the wife. I'm thirty-two and still single. I know my girlfriends have always found it pretty difficult, and really, being frank about it, I suppose I've always put the golf ahead of the relationship.

One of the things that I've found with golf, I think it tends to dull your brain in that it makes you so inward-looking. It's such a selfish life, you spend half your day planning the next day, so that your schedules are correct; you do the right amount of practice, and then you've got your travelling, and then you've got to watch what you eat, watch what you drink, and you've got to do your jogging, and your exercises, and the whole thing is terribly self-orientated, and it's very easy to think and talk about nothing else but golf.

I took my new girlfriend to Monte Carlo and she spent the entire week on the beach, and as an afterthought last thing in the evening, she'd ask, 'Oh, what did you score today?' Which is fine, it doesn't bother me at all, I don't need her to be hanging on my every movement. It's quite refreshing, really, because if I start talking about how I duffed a chip into a bunker at the fourteenth, she hasn't got a clue what I'm talking about, so the conversation doesn't start.

I think I'm very fortunate to have been able to do what I've done, you know, and whatever humble achievements I may have had have given me a great deal of satisfaction. Obviously you feel disappointed that you haven't done more – I'm sure Sevvy feels disappointed that he hasn't won every British Open since 1979, and I feel comparatively disappointed that I haven't won a tournament in Europe. I've been second, but there's a big difference between coming second and winning. Well, we all have our disappointments, but you can't go through life kicking yourself for all the things you failed to achieve. So I'm very fortunate to have been able to have done what I've done, and at the same time see half the world.

I find it a little boring outside the tournaments now; if I stopped playing tournaments I doubt that I'd play a great deal of golf because for me the enjoyment and excitement of the game is the playing under tournament conditions and there is a world of difference between ordinary golf and tournament golf, which you can't appreciate unless you've ever tried making a living with a golf club in your hand.

Hairdresser
Richard Brockwell

I've been doing it since I was eighteen, I'm now twenty-five. It's something I've always wanted to do but where I come from you don't really get that many hairdressers, or I didn't know of many. I used to think it's only a job that women do, but a friend of mine worked in a salon in the West End, and she talked me into coming up for an interview, I got the job, and it went from there.

I don't know why I wanted to do it. At school I was worried sick about what I was going to do when I left, thinking I hadn't got anything I really wanted to do. I did day-release in a mental hospital and I thought I might want to be a male nurse, but I've always liked playing with hair, so after a couple of other jobs I went into it.

My father still thinks it's not hard work, it's not strenuous. I suppose my mum thinks it's glamorous, as people who don't have their hair done do. She thinks it's all glamour and nothing else. But I work very hard. It's mental and physical strain. If you've got a client every half an hour you don't want to be running late for the next woman because she'll be going mad. You've got to keep going, you've got to keep your stamina up, and if you're feeling low one day you can't let your hairdressing slack off, because it will show. You ignore the fact that your back aches and your legs ache. I notice I'm getting round-shouldered.

There's mental strain, too, dealing with each person, and having to stay happy and cheerful with them, even if you're really pissed off with listening to them.

I don't know why, but I can always remember the conversations we've had when I do their hair, they always say, 'How on earth do you remember?' Say they're moving or something, three months later they'll come back and I'll say, 'How did the move go?' And they are amazed that you can remember.

How interested I actually am depends on how much I like the client, I think. But to be cynical about it, you've got spring, summer, autumn, winter. In the summer you'll be saying, 'Are you going on holiday?' to every person that comes in. In the winter it's, 'What are you doing for Christmas?' or something, and you think, 'Oh God, I can hardly wait for the next season.'

Generally people are okay. Someone who's got an exceptional amount of money and comes in two or three times a week, they're usually well over the top. But I think the general public overall are very nice. They can be pretty shy when they come into a salon, especially the one I work in, because it's got a name and that sort of thing.

When I go out I'm pretty shy, I can't go up to someone and start making conversation. In work I have confidence in myself and that I will make people liven up and relax. I like dealing with people that are actually frightened of coming into a hairdressing salon, which is quite a lot, actually, and it makes you feel good if you start getting them chatting sort of thing if they're really nervous. Another reason people don't like going to a salon is that so many hairdressers are standoffish.

The upper-class person will treat you wonderfully if you do their hair well, but then after that you're just really like one of their little maids or whatever, and you're running around after them. You get treated a bit better with people with not so much money or not so much class, and someone from the working class like myself would think, 'I'm friendly with a hairdresser, isn't that good!'

You get lots of people that come in every week and you do get to know them, but you can never really say they're a true friend, because all it takes is for them not to like their hair once, and you've lost them, no matter how friendly you were with them.

If anything, if you know you've got a bitch sitting in front of you, you would actually put much more effort into it, because there's no way you're going to let her say, 'I don't like it,' but then no matter how much effort you put into it, you know she's going to say something. People actually get a real high out of being a bitch to a hairdresser or beautician. They like to be awkward, like they'll say, 'You didn't use that brush last week,' when you know you use the same one all the time. What the hell does it matter as long as you finish it right?

It can get you down. I've never felt like this, but at the moment I hate work. I love what I do but I hate work. I begrudge going into work, I begrudge being there, I actually think I'm becoming really pissed off with people, with the public. Okay, not all of them, you look forward to seeing some of them, and some you really get on with. I don't know why I'm pissed off, some people say it's the seven-year syndrome, which is fair enough, maybe, but I think – do I still want to be hairdressing, do I still want to be banging away behind a chair for the rest of my life? People think the money is brilliant, but it's not, you've got to work your guts out to get it, because in the West End you work on commission, and if you want to get a good wage, you've got to really go at it.

I get there at eight in the morning and I quite often have an eight-thirty client and then finish at six, and every half hour, every three quarters of an hour you're cutting a head of hair. You get 20 per cent commission on each one you do, that's about three or four quid you get for each client, so you'd have to do between fifteen and seventeen clients a day to earn any good money.

I'm not one of these hairdressers who think, 'That's so and so, she gave me a fiver, or she gave me a few quid, so I'll fit them in, or be particularly nice to them.' It doesn't matter if someone doesn't tip, I'll still fit them in if I get on with them.

I love cutting hair. I always look at people's hair, on the bus, walking along the street, I like to admire hair. I'm not one of those people who say, 'Who on earth cut your hair!' sort of thing. If someone has nice hair I'll ask where they got it done. I love the creative part, to see if you can actually do something different. I like someone to be pleased and happy with their hair. That's the ego-trip part, they're happy with their hair, so you get a boost, or whatever. But the longer you do it, the less the boost lasts, and it's not such a good high when you do it day in, day out: you say, 'Another one that's pleased, good, where's the next lady?'

I could open up my own salon, but there's so much hassle to own a salon. You're working four times harder than you would be working for someone else, although I suppose in the end maybe you reap the rewards. But I wouldn't like to settle for an average salon, I'd like the best salon …

If we had to take bets about what I'd be doing in five years' time I'd like to say I'd be really famous or something, but I have to say I'll probably still be slogging away behind a chair at someone's hair. I don't know, I'm at the stage where it's been bothering me for quite some time. But then you'll forget it for a little while, you get distracted. Unfortunately I don't see it leading to anything. I wish I could see some more future in it.

Kissagram
Stephanie Greenslade

I've always, I suppose, been the kind of person who has done strange and mad things when other people are looking – such as jumping into swimming pools topless and that sort of thing. I was working as a graphic designer and realized that I wanted to do something that was more flamboyant, because I've always believed that I'm a flamboyant person; and deciding that it was the nearest I would ever get to Hollywood, I hit the Kissagram lights.

I do lots of different things – naughty nuns, silly schoolgirls; I do a sadistogram, hair pulled back, the whip, leather. I charge into the restaurant and bash on the door and get my victim. I vary the acts that I do, and I actually develop and work on the character so that I know what that character would say in response to a question or a remark.

There are a lot of Kissagram agencies around that really serve nothing but titillation, and don't consider that there could be a more entertaining value in the Kissagrams. I suppose if I go in with a whip it is highly suggestive, but it has got to have that element of suggestion to make it an exciting event. Because, let's face it, for a lot of people that I do, this is the one show-bizzy thing that happens to them in their life. I mean I did a Kissagram on a chap who was sixty-five and who'd retired, and there was almost a tear in his eye because it was something that was totally unexpected and probably the only time he would experience somebody in fishnet tights and a G-string coming and making him feel like a special person.

It must be rather strange for Rebecca to see her mother leaving the house scantily clad; and apparently the neighbours are starting to talk. I wonder what must happen when she goes to school and says, 'My mummy went out today dressed with a whip and hardly any clothes on.' I wonder what kind of reaction her teachers have, but I don't worry about it. I came to the conclusion that I must do what I must do, is it really anyone else's business? I know what I'm doing, I've spoken to the teachers at her new school and told them what I do: I'm a Kissagram girl, I do Kissagrams.

Obviously the money is a consideration; not many people do things for nothing, and although that wasn't the prime motivation – the initial consideration was to do something that would be exciting for me and varied, and because I have the ability to chat and to make people laugh and I am a bit of a comedienne, you know – it was an opportunity to do all that and earn money as well. But I think, really, the most exciting part of it is being able to show off and to be enjoyed and to entertain. A lot of people possibly don't think of Kissagrams as a form of entertainment, but I make sure that people are actually getting about half an hour of theatre, instead of just someone who's rushing in in a scantily clad outfit reading a poem.

I sometimes get very profound about it and say that it stems from a desire to be loved by people. And a desire to be noticed and to be different. I find now when I go into a pub as I am, I just want to take all my clothes off, and I know it sounds really crazy, but I hate it when people don't notice me or don't look at me.

I've been told many times I live in a fantasy world. I suppose I do in a way. I'm a vain creature as you've probably gathered. I think I must get this or that to look right... hair, face, make-up. Even with housework and looking after my daughter, I'm constantly criticizing myself and wondering if I could do better at it. I'm fastidious – probably neurotic is a better word. It's important that everything works out just right. If I'm doing a Kissagram, I get very upset, I almost cry, if my hair isn't right. I'm having my teeth done, and my nose, and all the little bits and pieces to make things what I consider just right. I'm going to have cosmetic surgery, and I'll probably have the money to pay for it by the end of the year.

I mean, what is reality, anyway? Reality is only a product of fantasy, isn't it, to a degree? We think about something we want to happen, and the fantasy makes reality.

I think that if I were flippant about it then I would lose the sense that I was trying to make myself better each time, trying to make my act better. I think of it as hard work. There are lots of times when it's not fun or glamorous. If it wasn't work, why should I want to drive around in freezing temperatures in the middle of winter, to some fat spotty man and sit on his knee. I don't see how I could not think of it as work, really.

I had a dreadful call from the taxman – I nearly had a heart attack! He wanted to find out how much I was earning. So I sat down the other night and worked out how much it actually cost me to start up, and I've paid out much more than I've earned in total. I've spent a fortune. But I love my costumes! My costumes are little characters of me; they are little facets of my personality, all in my cupboard hanging up, ready for me to assume.

I suppose in some ways it is sexist. But I don't look on it like that. I consider myself to be an entertainer. I don't do topless, I don't do stripping, I don't consider myself to be exploited. I'm running the business myself and the takings are mine. How can someone that is attractive and funny be exploiting themselves? I don't really know. I can remember once there were three nurses in a pub who said that it was disgusting that I was going around dressed like this, and wasn't I harming the women's cause? And I said, 'Well, you know, I'm doing quite well out of it' – that was my only reply. It sounded awfully mercenary. But I don't see that it is sexist. To me it's dressing up. I don't think of myself as someone's sexual fantasy. Obviously I realize that I must look sexy, people tell me I look sexy, but it doesn't make me feel sexy.

I live with someone – that can be difficult, especially when he's chauffeuring me around. Just the other day we were out and we had a tremendous argument because we couldn't find the place. Also there are always stagedoor Johnnies, and that has to be faced. And obscene phone calls – hundreds of them – oh, horrible disgusting phone calls. So that can make things difficult. And obviously if I'm out on a Kissagram and somebody starts to chat me up, that can make things very difficult too. Problems of jealousy.

There are some nights, the kind of nights where I may have been pushed against a wall and offered a hundred pounds, and those are the dark nights. I try not to dwell too much on it. Occasionally, you'll get a guy who'll just pick you up and toss you on to the floor and kneel across your arms – and what do you do about it? You can't physically fight; you have to beat them with chat.

Sometimes after a very, very hard night, perhaps doing two, three, four 'grams, I can feel very lost when I come out. Because one minute you're in a pub being watched by everyone, and everyone is there and the focus is on you; and when you come out there is nothing... suddenly that tremendous rush of adrenalin that was present while you were doing the 'gram has gone and has nowhere to go. I suppose it's the same kind of thing that actors and actresses feel when they've performed for an hour. The work itself is very much an up-and-down syndrome, whereby I'm getting very excited, coming down, getting excited, coming down, getting excited, and when I get home I think, 'What can I do now?' And I tell my boyfriend, 'You're boring me! I want to do something exciting. You know I've just done *this* tonight and you expect me to watch the television?'

I've always hoped that there would be a pot of gold at the end of the rainbow, that I would swoop into Stringfellow's, someone would meet me and say, 'Goodness me, she'd look ever so good in the next episode of *Dallas*, or *Dynasty*,' or some strange fantasy like that. I've always hoped that I could just make it by being seen and by being me. I have met a few people but they've all been rogues. I don't think that it's going to happen that easily, which is sad. It's a sad part of my life. Very sad sometimes. I battle with the sadness. I've just recently met somebody that wants me to sing in their pop group, but everything is going very, very slowly at the moment. I'm getting downhearted because nothing is happening really. I suffer from depression a lot. So there are times of depression, but I snap out. Being an up-and-down person, because my highs are very high, I must expect my lows to be low.

I'm getting old. That's how I feel, I feel very upset about it. I'm twenty-three. I feel that I had so many opportunities when I was younger that I didn't take, that I should probably be further on in a career. I left school with O-levels, was going on to college to take A-levels; I wanted to go and study Fine Art, and I have a sense of regret that I didn't plant my feet firmly on the ground and embark on some fantastic career. I always wanted to be a psychiatrist, I just ended up on the wrong side of the couch. I'm thinking about going to drama school now. I just wonder if I can take myself seriously enough to learn a piece of Shakespeare and actually to bring it off properly. Each time I turn to something, I put everything into it. My all. So that's it, really, that's me.

Lexicographer
Robert Burchfield

The goal of finishing the Supplement to *The Oxford English Dictionary* has been the central part of my life for twenty-eight years. It's been my main consuming passion, to investigate how it was to be done and to set it in motion, and then to see it through to the end, and has occupied the time that I regard as my work time all these years. Once embarked, I was in some kind of very acceptable track with the end of the journey seeming a long way off with thc accumulation of new evidence, the discovery of new kinds of vocabulary, the remorseless rise of space science, space travel, the rise of computer technology, the distributional problems of American English, Australian English and all the other forms of English. One had no idea, to begin with, of the profundity of difference between these versions of English and British English, and you could never find out without elaborate analysis. The editing process itself is so complicated at this level of lexicography that it took me ages to find out how to control all the divisions and sub-divisions and types of defining and grouping of words, and how to cope with the frightful prefixes like 'un' and 'non' and 'pre' and 'pro' and 'post' and so forth. I'm talking about entries that run to thirty or forty pages, each with three columns of type. Words to me are messy objects, capable in a chameleon-like fashion of acting differently each time you grasp them.

If anyone sets out on a journey, they don't want to stop short, to return home with the job unfinished. Any athlete who sets out on a mile race likes to run a mile. I would have hated to let everyone down, that was the primary thing. Once started on a project where you yourself had set the rules of what was to be included and excluded, how ambitious the project was to be, it was a terrifying prospect that I would not finish the project, and the relief that one feels now is the disappearance of that fear.

I started work on the Supplement to the *OED* thinking I might do the job in one volume of about 1250 pages. It's ended up four volumes in over 6000 pages.

I don't separate my identity – career, work, identity – rough synonyms. Probably other people would say I was obsessive. I don't feel it to be obsessive in the least, it seems to me to be a natural thing. If I were a farmer I would be totally and utterly and completely a farmer – and extrapolate from that to any occupation you like. I could not abide an attitude of starting work on the dot of nine o'clock in a civil service way, and stopping at five o'clock and totally switching off. I don't understand how people can endure that as a way of life, where work is thought to be physical effort restricted within certain hours, and then the rest of one's life is not in any way connected to the nature of that work. My life is of a piece in that the work extends into the leisure, the leisure extends into the work.

I'm not elderly, I'm only sixty-two, but the first signs of conventional running down of the body machine have hit me this year. Whether it's connected with the completion of the Supplement or whether it would have happened whatever I would have done with my life, who knows? I've run up against that nasty beast called cholesterol, and am now on a diet as a result, nothing more than that, just first intimations that what people call elderliness is beginning to creep up. But feelings of mortality happen at my age in a completely natural way because your friends start to die – and they die aged sixty-two or younger.

In the nature of things lexicography is a sedentary occupation. When young I was an athlete, played rugby, ran at speed. But from the time I was thirty-four, when I started on the dictionary, until this time, my exercise has been gardening only, and so from time to time if I was looking a bit tired, somebody or other would make remarks about working too hard. Quite often you think you might not survive to see the end of it.

I find it difficult to imagine how I could exist without a project, and without a target. The pursuit of leisure as a way of life is to me almost wholly mysterious. Holidays have been taken in short bursts and they have had an object in mind, like taking the children on a camping holiday in France or Switzerland or Italy, and the enjoyment has been primarily that of the children, not of the parents. The whole aim and object of it was to allow the children to run free in foreign countries, and see strange objects, to eat strange foods, and so forth.

I see no connection at all between money and work. I know that society is split down the middle and the country is being pulled to pieces by people who want more money – teachers and miners and so forth. I don't know what it's all about: whatever they get, whether it's 4 per cent, 5 per cent, 15 per cent, the difference is imperceptible when the tax man has had his share, and when the expenses of life eat up whatever you get. I don't see the point of all these dreadful, splitting social arguments about money.

Life was very hard indeed when I had three children, on a very small salary, and decided to send them all through the public school system. It was a deadly combination, small salary, high school fees, so I was essentially living from hand to mouth until the last few years. When I remarried, two incomes were coming into a childless house with no more school fees. Since then things have been quite easy, and I find myself saying, 'What's money?' I travel on Concorde from time to time. I've discovered the deliciousness of the British Rail card and travel first class at half price, but money doesn't mean anything to me any more. I find that against perhaps my own expectations, I'm proving to be what people conventionally call generous, when for thirty years or so I had to be tight-fisted out of sheer necessity.

I don't honestly care too much about money. I worried about it when it was short, and I feel an absurd sense of security now that the worries are over.

In a quite hard-headed way, when you are sixty-two, you have reasonable expectation of eighteen years' day-to-day activity. In my case I will concentrate on grammar. Some people like to travel, other people like to garden, other people like just to visit or play cards or whatever. I don't play cards, I don't propose to learn how to play chess, I propose to go on with work.

I have made a start converting myself from being a lexicographer to being some kind of grammarian, but the time left to me is obviously not anything like as long as the time I've spent on lexicography, and so I must run with the speed of a sprinter in grammar, or it won't be done. But one cannot move with lightning speed in new, unfamiliar territory. Grammar, it may surprise you, is so distant from lexicography that one has only a layman's attitude towards primary rules of grammar, even after three decades of lexicography. I find myself floundering in the most primary things like grammatical concord, the gerund, the subjunctive and various other things where problems are lying strewn about.

When I was in the army, the commanding officer of my small unit had a habit of saying at the end of each day if he happened upon you: 'How have you justified your existence today, Gunner Burchfield?' That quite fundamental question I suppose has been pursuing me all my life. One's here for such a short time and one must justify one's talents, one's mere existence, by stretching oneself to the limit, I've always felt and still feel. Simply standing on the sideline of life is not attractive to me, I have always wanted to be involved in something that seemed to me to matter.

Life is full of illusions, and one of them is that you don't notice the passage of time. You make conventional jokes when you turn forty and then fifty, and then sixty, but you don't actually notice that you are growing a little older. You're totally unaware that your hair has turned grey until people tell you it's turned grey. You can't even see it in the mirror. You are totally unaware that your reactions have slowed down until you play in a cricket match against the young and discover that the ball which used to fall into your hands to be caught falls a yard behind you or a yard in front of you. Age seems to creep up in unexpected corners and in unexpected ways. You're not aware of it. The illusion is that you are still young, vibrant, reasonably good-looking, athletic, all that.

With my work I've been unaware of the passage of twenty-eight years, that's really what I'm trying to say, it seems to me to have been the twinkling of an eye. I started, I got into it, and now I've finished it... and I'm amazed, because I wasn't conscious of the passage of the years.

Literary Agent
Carol Smith

The nice thing about my life is that every day is different, and it's only structured in the fact that when the mail arrives I answer it and take the problems one by one. Every letter that comes in is answered that day, every manuscript that comes in is acknowledged, and all telephone calls are returned. We get an average of three hundred unsolicited manuscripts a year, I counted them up once. They are mainly first novels and wc look at every single one of them, and out of the three hundred, we take on about one a year.

Because I work for myself, I only take on writers that I can get on with, and sooner or later I part with the ones that I can't. I've got between forty and sixty clients, and I try to keep the agency as small as possible so that I can give time to each one, because I find that pays off in the long run. So I can truthfully say that all my authors have my equal attention. Maybe I could make more money if I took on more writers, but on the other hand if I gave each one less time, they might not do so well.

The relationship you build up with your client is so close that you have to put a barrier between you. It has a lot of the relationship between the psychiatrist and patient in it, because you really do get to know a writer very well, you know all their weaknesses, you know their depressions, you know their money problems. I've learnt over the years that you have to keep them at arm's length, however much you like them, because I don't think it would work if I let my clients into my life in the way they let me into theirs. Also my role is to talk about them , not for them to talk about me. I don't think they know me a fraction as well as I know them.

We have a very good relationship and they trust me, they trust my judgement and my advice. If any of my authors write something that I don't think is up to scratch I will send it back to them, I will not do what many agents do and just send it out to the publisher, so I do a lot of editorial work on all the things I handle.

Authors do need to have their hands held a lot, and the main reason is that writing is a lonely business, particularly fiction, because it's all coming out of your own mind.

Because an agent is usually the only contact between the writer and his livelihood, I think it's vital to be totally involved. If you are doing a bad job for an author you could be damaging his whole future. On the other hand, if you are doing a really good job, it works the other way.

Most of my clients are earning quite a lot of money. But truthfully, money is of no importance to me at all, I'm genuinely in this business because I enjoy what I do and I enjoy the game. So the only role that money plays is that that's the way the game is assessed. It's like playing cards. Every deal is a gamble in my agency, they are all new hands, and it's the way you play the cards, the way you call the shots, and when you do the deal. Before I became an agent I used to play bridge regularly. I gave it up because I get exactly the same thrill out of doing a deal.

Several years ago when I was much less experienced, one of my writers wrote a book and we auctioned it in the States, and we sold film rights, book club rights and paperback rights in one night from London, and we got a total of three quarters of a million dollars out of that. I went to New York and I got him a million dollars for his next book, without even a synopsis. And it worked. It was extremely frightening because when you are dealing with money that big, it's no longer a game because it's the author's livelihood.

I think I've had more reward and pleasure out of being an agent and dealing with and watching other people's careers grow than sitting at home and writing myself. It is tremendously exciting to be the first person to read the typescript of a talented person, even if it's flawed; to have the right to say, I love it, or I don't like this character or this ending or whatever… it's history in the making. It's the reason that people buy literary biographies and volumes of letters, and it's actually happening in my life, and I think that is very exciting.

There is always the dream that one day one of these writers will become truly great, and perhaps in thirty years' time I will be able to look back and say, 'I remember the first novel whoever wrote.'

Most writers aren't grateful. It isn't important, really, except it hurts when they are not. It is surprising the number of writers who take for granted things that I think it would be nice if they acknowledge, or the small number of clients who send Christmas presents or even Christmas cards. A lot of writers are rather self-absorbed and don't necessarily think of their agent. It is hurtful and if you have really done a lot for them and put a lot of energy and excitement into something and the author takes it without any comment, or worse still, isn't as pleased as they should be.

A lot of the social life I have centres round the work I do because it's a business in which I meet kindred souls. I find that nearly all my friends are in publishing in one way or another. We don't talk business all the time but we talk business quite a lot of the time, because that's the thing we have in common. There is almost no division between my leisure time and my working time because the two fit in so well together. I think of that as a privilege, that's the bit about my work I like best.

Everyone thinks they can write because most people were taught to put words on paper, whereas not everybody thinks they can paint, or play the violin. There is a lot of arrogance amongst writers who think they have something to say just because they were taught to put words on paper. I stop people introducing me as an agent because everybody has got something... they've nearly all got a half-finished manuscript, or they've got a wife who's written children's stories, or they always meant to write a book when they have the time, and everybody is fascinated by the whole subject – and they all think there is money in it, that it's a fast way to riches.

My father worked very hard, and I think it was the way I was brought up. For example, I'm never ill, I never take time off ever, and that's an echo of childhood in that my father was never ill. I only ever remember him missing about one day from work. My mother has never been ill. And my brother and I were never off school. And when I started work as a secretary, I always worked hard, and I often didn't take my full holiday allowance.

So I work hard but that's my nature, and I feel guilty if I take time off, even though I'm the boss. The reward is that it is all tremendously interesting, much more interesting than most people's jobs, and it has this endless variety. Theoretically any person in the world can write, and so you never know from one day to the next what's going to come through the door. If life is a little flat, suddenly the phone rings and it's another exciting thing.

I don't think I'm so obsessive that it's unhealthy. I sometimes think I should develop other interests because it is probably fairly tunnelled to always be thinking about fiction, so lately I've been taking on a lot of non-fiction. I don't have any hobbies, but that's because the thing I'm interested in is writing and reading, so my relaxation is I'll read a lot outside of what I have to read.

When I step out of the world I'm used to, I find that the attitude of men to women is different, and I get a tremendous surprise when I go to, say, a dinner party, and find that the men dominate the conversation and are inclined to think that women should be passive. I'm astonished at the pig-like behaviour of men who aren't in publishing.

I've never been married, and one of the things that people constantly ask me is, 'Why aren't you married?' And there isn't any easy reason, because I've always had good relationships with men. I really believe that because I have a genuinely fulfilled life, I don't need to get married. Nowadays it's even more so, because I can afford to live well on my own without another salary coming in. And I have enough to occupy my life that I think a permanent live-in other person would actually get in the way. I mean I have the luxury of being able to work all the time because I'm on my own. For example, I can watch breakfast television when I'm having my breakfast, and I can fill up all the social gaps with reading manuscripts and so forth and get through a lot more work as a result than if I had to be polite to another body. I think that most people who aren't terribly happy in their jobs would be lost without someone to share their life with, but I really believe my work does fill in that sort of gap of another person.

The women I know of my age who are manless through divorce or just being in my situation are inclined to be much more anxious about it than I am. If I get bored, if I get depressed, I can get on a plane this afternoon and go to America. I can do anything I like, and I do. When I'm fed up, I go to New York for a bit, and I go to the West Indies for my holidays. I have a wide circle of good friends and I think that is more rewarding than having just one person to share all your *angst* with. The other thing is that most people find themselves set in a career, and that's it for the rest of their life. The nice thing about what I do is that it does evolve and change, and anyway, I don't want to be an agent forever, I don't want to do anything forever.

Monk
Father Paul

It was just a feeling, a conviction that came over me to call me to this life. I was about nineteen when I first thought that God wanted me to join this monastery, to be a monk.

That was many years ago, of course. My parents never put any obstacles in my way, though I think they might have liked it better if I had done some active religious work, but they wanted me to do what I thought God wanted me to do.

When I say 'active religious work', I mean going to God through serving other people, serving the sick or working in a parish. But I regard what I do here as serving God more directly through worshipping at the services in the church, and, as it were, consecrating my whole life to Him in a more hidden kind of way. An imitation of Christ praying on the mountainside, if you like, rather than healing the sick.

We get up at three-fifteen. Our first service of Vigils in the church is at three-thirty. That lasts for about three quarters of an hour, then we are free until seven to give ourselves to private prayer and study. Then at seven we have the second service of the day which is Lords, morning prayer. That lasts for about half an hour, then there is an interval for about half an hour when we do the vegetables for the day. At eight there is the Community Eucharist. From nine till twelve there is the first period of work, then at twelve-fifteen there is a short service before dinner. We have reading during the dinner, and we are free then until quarter past two. There is another short service, and then follows the second period of work at two-thirty, which can go on until five-thirty when it's Vespers. Supper is at six and we are free until half past seven. Sometimes we have a community meeting or a discussion with an outside speaker, and then at half past seven we have Complin, which are night prayers, and we go to bed just before eight.

There is a Strict Silence from the time we get up until after the community Mass, so that's from quarter past three until quarter to nine.

Then there's a Strict Silence of the Night from the time we go to bed until we get up again.

We like it when it's quiet, it means that there are no distractions and that one can apply oneself more easily then to prayer or study.

Because one is in church for so many hours a day, trying to give oneself to the praises of God and singing, it does demand a certain amount of mental energy and a certain concentration, and I think Saint Benedict was right when he called it the *work* of God. It is demanding.

In Genesis, work is a part of man's penance for his rebellion against God – 'Thou should earn thy bread by the sweat of thy brow' – so that there is this penitential aspect of work, which is an important part of the monk's regard for work.

Well, the life is made up of three main elements, prayer, reading or study, and work. But you can, I think, call the whole monastic life the monk's work. Trying to form himself into the kind of person that God wants him to be is a life's work. It should be real work, work by which we earn our own living and have something over to give to the poor as alms. We live a simple, frugal kind of life, not necessarily a life of destitution, but we have sufficient and give what is superfluous over to the poor.

If one of our chores is a bit unpleasant, one can offer it up as part of the sacrifices that are part of our life. Work could be hard work on the farm, or there are the chores that have to be done in the house. One can be on a particular job, not a very interesting job, for quite a number of years. One might, say, be working on the orchard for about fourteen years, or something like that, and one would perhaps like a change. But somebody has to work in the laundry, somebody has to do the ordinary household jobs, keeping the refectory clean and things like that. We try and give people jobs that fit in with their particular talents and skills.

I have great sympathy for those whose work is oppressive, or exploited. Some people have work which is degrading, and my whole being goes out to people like that. We often pray at Mass for those people whose work is hard and unrewarding, and yet they may have very creative aspirations, and none of this part of their personality can be developed because they have to do this drudgery to earn their living or those they support.

I think a lot of people don't fully understand the reasons why a man wants to become a monk, and they may not appreciate it's simply a personal conviction that one has, that this is valid for you. It's between oneself and God, one can't really prove the value of a life of prayer.

I would say that the standards of judgement of success are perhaps different here, because the monk's life is a life of faith, and you have to take it on faith that what you are doing has a value, that your prayers for other people, for the third world, for instance, for the sick, for the dying, for the oppressed, for those in labour camps, the praises you give to God, this demands faith that it is of value. You can't weigh it out and at the end of one's life actually see any results. It is a life of faith.

God is the whole meaning of our existence as monks, and Christ is one's personal friend. This means everything. Even though at times He may seem to hide Himself, I think trusting in Him, putting, as it were, all one's eggs in His basket, one is so dependent on Him, but I think when one does that, one finds a peace and also a freedom because one's whole life is in wiser and safer hands than one's own.

Of course it doesn't only apply to monks; but I think to anyone who has reached 'the end of the road', the point where we can do no more on our own and a new Power must enter in. The alcoholic would understand this, or the incurably sick, perhaps too an aged community with no novices, or someone entangled in some unwanted sin. Their hope, their meaning, their very salvation lies outside of themselves.

There's an old monastic adage, 'To work is to pray, and to pray is to work,' and for many monks, especially those who aren't drawn to a lot of study, manual work is a form of prayer offering their talents, their skills, their energies to God through their work. Some monks do see manual work as a particular form of offering their life to God. I think perhaps monks may feel happier when they're working, that might be the happiest part of their day.

We can deal with the unruly elements in our personalities to a certain extent by the penitential aspect of our work. For instance impatience, anger, intolerance, criticism, resentfulness, all these kinds of things I think can be helped by work, and it's amazing that after a couple of hours of manual work, one goes in the church to pray, then it's often said that some form of contemplation will follow that work, a sense of being with God or in His presence, or compunction, a sense of sorrow for sin.

I suppose the most self-indulgent thing I do is some forms of reading. I like reading Dickens. I like biographies, I like novels that teach you about life, about character, about personality. I think quite a lot of spirituality can come over through drama, I think the philosophers these days do a lot of their teaching through plays. Just recently I learnt quite a bit through Oscar Wilde writing about good and evil, I thought he was saying almost the same as Solzhenitsyn. I'm interested in all these kind of things. My favourite authors are St John's Gospel, Plato, I think, and P.G. Wodehouse.

I would say that living in a monastery, one's imagination is perhaps more sensitive, more easily stimulated than if one were living outside. I think that living outside one gets a skin over one's imagination, one becomes hardened to things like advertisements, and I suppose much of what one hears on the radio or television. But I notice when I go out, say to the dentist, or shopping, I'm very much hit by advertisements.

We don't reject the world at all, or the people in the world, we want to help them, that's why we come apart from them. But there are certain things which you might say are worldly in the wrong sense, and I think that sometimes one can be hit rather strongly by these worldly attitudes, and these very often come across to one through advertisements, the emphasis on the material, the secular, the importance of money, for instance.

And the same with reading. I suppose that reading an ordinary novel, which perhaps wouldn't worry someone else, I find that for myself it could stimulate my imagination in a way that I could find upsetting, and it wouldn't do me any good. I find that I get distractions far more at prayer time, and so I know that there are certain kinds of books I have to leave on one side.

I don't feel out of touch actually. On some areas my knowledge of technology is far less than a boy of twelve or even younger, but sometimes, talking to people who come here, I'm surprised that I've had more experience of people than they have. For instance I've had dealings with Alcoholics Anonymous which widens one's scope, drug addicts that have come to the guest house, sometimes people come and they want to talk about their marriage problems. So there are areas where one doesn't feel so much out of touch really.

I often listen to the six o'clock news on the wireless. But I'm not up on television. We discussed it in the community and we decided that we wouldn't have a television set. But we do hire one for special occasions, for instance when the Pope came to England, and then we had one for the moon landing, I recall.

I don't get paid a salary. If I want to spend money, I have to go to the bursar. If I go to town I have to get money from the bursar. If I'm given money to go and see my sister, for instance, he'll give me so much to cover the cost of transport, buying a meal, and so on, and he'll expect me to use my common sense, to use the money responsibly. My sister hasn't been well lately and I asked if I could take her something on my last trip. If I want to buy a book I have to go and ask him; for my hobby, gardening, if I want to buy some chrysanthemum plants, I go and ask him. So although we don't individually pay rates and rent and so forth, we can't just go and spend money as we like. Obviously in this world, you have to have money to live, but you have to use it responsibly. Money mustn't become an end.

When I was running the farm, it was part of our way of earning our living, and we had to make it pay. We had to produce our milk at a competitive price in the same kind of way as other farmers. We fed our pigs for pork, so we had to cost our feed, we had to take account of the fact that people wanted lean meat, that our pigs had to be graded. So we're not an island, we are affected by the EEC and the milk quotas and so on, so that money does come into it, even for us. We have to balance our books.

We're given our food and clothing, and somehow we do get the hundredfold, God does look after one. And it's surprising some of the things He provides. Like a trip to America I made about thirty years ago to give a talk about the English Cistercians. It's part of the hundredfold. Somehow it's almost that God seems to know what you would like on a material level. I had a chance to go to the Holy Land only last year. The abbot had the offer of a cheap ticket and he put some names in a box, and my name happened to come out of it, and it was rather extraordinary, I thought, because travel must be one of the greatest things that I've given up, and yet, since I've been here, I've had quite a number of opportunities that have come right out of the blue.

I hope I will do this for the rest of my life. One of the vows that we take is a vow of stability, that is, to live with the same community, normally in the same monastery, so one hopes that one would persevere. There is no profession that I'd rather practise than the monastic one.

I'm over sixty now, and I don't work as hard as I used to, there are things I can't do now. I still try to be conscientious and do what I can. Every so often I look at myself and make sure I'm using my time to the best of its ability. Sometimes, if one feels that one is slackening off, you can look around to see if you should volunteer for anything particular.

I hope I've become more open, less narrow, and more tolerant, more trusting in God, more relying on Him, more aware of His mercy, more thankful and more grateful for what He has done for me. I hope I've grown to be more Christ-like. This is the great thing – that one has actually followed Christ to some small degree.

Musician
Peter Hanson

It used to upset me when people say things to me like, 'You're lucky to be a musician, it's not work when you're doing something you like.' My reaction was, 'You have no idea how hard we work.' People think that you stand on the stage and play just for fun, and then go off and do an ordinary job. Lots of people have no idea of the skills that are required, that in order to be a violinist you have to study for such a long time, and practise and practise, and even then you may not achieve what you're looking for. So in no way can it be regarded as frivolous. But the hard work isn't really in the actual playing; it's to do with the quantity of playing and the travelling to get to places to play. That's where the hardness comes in. Constant movement and constant playing is physically and mentally very demanding. I try not to overwork but it's very difficult to avoid. There seem to be so many things to do, so many things to organize just to keep the whole business going. Because at the same time as being a musician I've got to be a businessman, an accountant, father, husband. There's no such thing as weekends. You don't have any days off.

I think that it's necessary for a freelance musician to have a wife who understands, because your hours are so varied. Every day is completely different. Some days I will rehearse from ten until one in north London, and two till six-thirty in south London. Today I've got a rehearsal from two till about nine. Tomorrow I'm going off to Wolverhampton. I'll stay overnight, do another concert on Sunday night near Manchester, drive straight home and arrive back about three in the morning. Then I have a rehearsal all day Monday. I find it increasingly difficult to find time to practise and accomplish everything else. So you just have to try and desperately find the time to do it. I don't practise much more than half an hour a day. Sometimes I don't practise at all.

If you're not careful you become a bit removed from everyday life because you can spend all your time travelling, meeting other musicians, and playing music and literally doing nothing else. You have to be careful that you don't get cut off, and I take great pride in the friends I have who are non-musicians.

I'm from Halifax, and to be stuck in the north of England would mean a limited supply of orchestras and people to play with. London is the best place to be, there's just so much music going on, classical music as well as all other types of music. Because everybody who studies a musical instrument usually ends up in London, you're also meeting musically more interesting people than you might if you were in the north. I've decided to give it ten years in London. I've got plans to take back with me what I've learned – though the more you stay in London, the more difficult it is to move out.

What I'm looking for is a kind of self-expression which doesn't require a solo career, because I'm not really up to a solo career. Because nowadays if you're going to be a soloist at all, you've got to be a prodigy, a child prodigy. I should have started learning the violin when I was seven and been touring the world at the age of thirteen.

I come from a musical family. I loved it. I played every instrument, and then suddenly it became obvious that I was going to play nothing but the violin. As simple as that, really. And when I was about seventeen, it was either university or music college, and I decided to plump for music college. And once you have spent your three or four years' grant on a music college, there's no going back, really, it's very difficult to change.

What I do is freelance. I play with all sorts of different people. I play with orchestras, I play chamber music. I have my own chamber group, a string quartet. My priorities have got to be with the string quartet in which I play first violin. If you play the violin you can either be a soloist, in which case you have to learn by memory lots of big concertos and play them pretty loud and big and massive. Or you can be an orchestral player, in which case no one ever hears you. You just play away and your own conscience is the one that's telling you whether you're playing well or not. Plus the people around you. There's a high standard in the orchestras. A very high standard.

This is what I want to do more than anything else. Some of the best music is written for string quartets, and we're four people who work together, grow together, play together and learn together. It's very, very interesting to do, it's a terrific challenge, so I put that as my priority. So if some other work comes up, which may even be paying more, I will dismiss that for the quartet. At the same time I do jingles, sittings, commercials, TV, orchestral playing. It could be anything, it could be an album for a pop group – and that pays very well, and it's terribly easy to play.

I suppose the highest paid music is the easiest to do, and the reason is that you have to pay people a lot to get them to do it, because it's such a dreadful job. For instance, session music. You turn up for a jingle and go... dum, dum, dinker dum, dum, dum, bom, bom. And that's all you have to do. And you've spent four years at music college and you've studied and practised for years, and you can play the most intricate Beethoven string quartet, and yet you find you are paid much more for doing something very simple. But to be quite frank, I feel a boring job needs more financial reward, and an interesting job in some respects doesn't need as much incentive.

I must admit my finances are pretty chaotic. I'm vastly overdrawn and all the rest of it, but so's a lot of people. I just try and balance it out. I don't like to get too involved with money, so long as it's just not getting ridiculously out of hand.

Because you're always travelling to different places, the expenses are very high. I imagine someone working in an office every day would work out the cheapest and the best and most efficient way of getting there and back, but that's impossible to do if you're at different venues all the time. And you've got to get there. If a recording studio is paying forty people to be there at a certain time, you can't afford to be late, otherwise you're holding up everybody else. So you often have to shell out for taxis.

Well, I suppose everybody has the grudge that they are not sufficiently compensated for the work they do. The attitude to a musician in America is that he is a skilled craftsman and should be rewarded as such. The attitude in Europe is the same. But in this country, which everybody knows has the cheapest musicians in the world, hence all the big films are done here because it's about a third of the price of anywhere else, the attitude is: 'You're a musician, you're lucky to be doing something you enjoy,' rather than, 'Oh, you're a skilled person – you ought to be rewarded for your skill.'

I hesitate to say I should have more money because I see so many people around me with absolutely no money at all, and so many people with absolutely pots of money, that really I find this society very confusing indeed. I could do with a bit more money. Life would be easier, and I wouldn't have to work so hard to earn the little money I do. I really think that a musician works just as hard as anybody else but doesn't get anything like the financial rewards. But I have to admit a musician has the reward of doing something that he loves doing, something that in lots of ways is incredibly satisfying.

I'm the sort of person who tends to make life into a struggle. I mean I could have easily had a very cushy life by joining an orchestra. I could have easily got a job with an orchestra which would require far less effort than I'm subjecting myself to, and far more money as well. So I've opted in a way for a difficult life, so I ought not to grumble.

I'm ambitious in that I'd like my quartet and my life to be a success. But I'm not ambitious in that I'm prepared to drop everything to get that success. I very much believe in letting things come to me rather than me going out to get them. I feel if someone doesn't phone you up and say, 'Please try for this job,' then I don't believe you're going to get it. You've got to be asked to do things, really.

If you are a professional it is very difficult to maintain the spark of inspiration, joy, and the love for music, but it's important to try and maintain that innocence. You work at choosing things so that the spark isn't lost. For instance, I like to escape out of London to the country to regulate my life a bit, so it doesn't get too frenetic. I just try and do things so I have time... to play around with time.

I hate travelling. I mean it's so difficult to get in a car and drive like a maniac through the streets of London, get out, sit down and play serene music. You find you have to almost pretend moods sometimes in order to cope with it. You get out of the car, you go into the rehearsal and you know deep inside that you're absolutely all over the place, your mind's buzzing around from all the horns blasting, dust, filth, fumes everywhere, and to calm down quickly is a difficult thing to do.

Audiences always have a completely different atmosphere. Each audience is different. Some audiences look as if they're a bit sleepy. Some audiences look as if they're bursting with life and energy. It does affect you very strongly as you sit on the stage. People see music in different ways, some people go out to concerts for a nice night out and want to sit there, relax and enjoy themselves. Some people want to go and be inspired, or affected by the music.

I think music does all sorts of different things to different people.

There are symbols in music which represent personal aspirations, hopes, losses and feelings in everybody. There's also sheer joy in music. There's intellectual fascination in music. There's physical sensation in music. Everybody can enjoy it on a different level. There's the sensual experience where you're being caressed with music. If you go and hear a string quartet, you've got to remain very still and very calm for the music to flow through you.

It's very different from area to area. The audiences very much reflect the area. In London, string quartet audiences are full of eccentric enthusiasts. Marvellous, fantastic. They really know their stuff, they come along with the scores, and they know the pieces and know them well. Just about every music club, there's always a few people who are really knowledgeable. They spend their whole lives studying string quartets, even though they don't perhaps play. Up in the north of England where I come from, the audiences are very warm, very cheery and enthusiastic. Somewhere like Banbury, Coventry or Cheltenham, they all seem to be pretty sleepy, and also there's a certain element of going to concerts to be seen to be going to concerts.

The violin I've got is a beautiful instrument, old, Italian, a Pressenda, 1847. It belongs to the Royal Academy of Music where I was a student, and it's on loan to me at the moment. It's a wonderful instrument, and I need it because of the string quartet. If I was playing in an orchestra, perhaps I wouldn't need such a lovely violin, although some people in orchestras do have beautiful instruments. But I do feel that I ought to have my own instrument at some stage and I'm hoping that my flat, which I think was quite a good investment, might prove useful in that respect when I come to sell it. I'll be able to get hold of some money then. But violins are just so expensive. I mean it's £40,000, this one, and if I wanted to get something similar, that's the cost of my flat. Even with a violin worth £10,000 you can really hear the difference. Anything under £10,000, then you'd might as well not bother, really. I don't like saying that because there's a lot of very good instruments around for a thousand pounds that new English makers have made, but they lack the maturity that comes with age, and the feeling for wood that some of these Italian masters had. It's like if you were going round a painting exhibition. You might see some of the modern paintings and say, 'Well, that's a very good one.' And then you see the greats, the Leonardos and the Botticellis and you think, 'Well…' you know.

You do fall in love with your instrument. It becomes part of you. It's the most distressing thing to see a damaged violin. It's extraordinary how people get affected by it. It's because you've played a violin for years, every day at least four or five hours a day. And also, it's because the violin is such a great work of art in itself, just the making of it. It requires tremendous skills to get all the angles and the weights of the woods right. And you can never get bored with a good violin because it's always coming up with new sounds if you care to find them. So it really is like a love affair, and that's why people do get very attached to their instruments.

I haven't insured myself. Some violinists insure their fingers. Well, I thought if I had a hand cut off by accident, I'd have to do something else instead. I don't want to pay money now just in case that happens. I like to take life as it takes me. I'm not very keen on insurance. There's something spooky about insurance.

I think you've got to consider music as something that you could give up. I see it as a kind of security that I have the willingness to attempt to do something else, that I'm not frightened by the fact I can only play the violin. Of course it would be a great test if I had to do something else. But it gives you a certain freedom to know that you're prepared if something horrendous did happen.

I don't feel fulfilled particularly, but I feel as if I'm on the right path to being fulfilled. I suppose that's the best way of putting it. I suppose I get fulfilment from the fact that I'm rushing around, creating things, and I know if I do get to the age of fifty I'll be able to look back and say, yes, I did this, this and that, I did things. I have got a quartet. We have been going for many years, we have done interesting things, met a lot of people, and travelled a lot. So there's a sort of spiritual fulfilment, if not a musical one. It's still evolving, I wouldn't say I was there.

Out-of-work Actress
Victoria Wilmington

It's really important to get up early because if you lie in bed you feel a real slob, so I get up about seven or seven-thirty every day. Then I go for a swim, do my lengths, up and down; otherwise you get a bit vacant. And then on the way back - cycle back, cycle everywhere - buy *The Times* every morning, or if it's Monday get the *Guardian* - creative ads, of course, see what's going there - and I have my boogie pack, my Sony Walkman everywhere I go. Exercise keeps your mind going and you feel you're being positive and doing something, in fact exercise plays a huge part in being out of work because otherwise you just lie about and get more and more lethargic and tired and start sitting around for hours. I know it could happen, I know I could lie in bed until 10 or 11 and then get up and just wander around, so that's why I have to get up early and go for a hard swim.

I come back and immediately check the mail. As soon as I get back there's one thing on my mind - are there going to be any letters or replies, auditions or interviews? Usually it's disappointment. I check the post and hide any brown envelopes or windowed envelopes into the drawer, just can't face those at all, and then starts the phoning, phone, phone, phone, and letter writing, maniacal phoning, and I know it's the most expensive time to call but it's important to get it all done in the morning. Arranging auditions, setting up interviews with directors and producers, anyone I can think of, anyone at all who could be helpful.

Then I have to look at my diary because I have about five different part-time jobs on the go, and it's terribly complicated to know which day is which part-time job. It can be anything from working in a shop (antique shop this week), typing, being a nanny, doing research, anything at all. And if I'm not doing that I start writing something, just spend the morning being inside hoping the phone will go. I've done some fun jobs, like pretending to be a customer in a shop for a week. They actually pay you to be a customer if times are a bit slack. I sometimes think these jobs I take on are a bit of a giggle. I sold soap at Barker's and was really bossed about by officious manageresses, and I often think to myself, 'One day you'll wish you hadn't said that to me...' I love doing market research because I can practise my acting. I pretend I'm interviewing them on live television when I go up to people in the street and talk to them. It all goes into the CV slightly glossed up.

And then in the afternoon it's voice class which I have twice a week to get my accent down, to stop sounding so upper class. If I'm not going to a voice class then it's going to be an interview, and sometimes that means travelling to different TV companies, Yorkshire, Granada, TVS, Thames – either they've invited me or I've invited myself to just go and talk to them. If I haven't got anything on like that I go to an exhibition and try and make the most of the afternoon, or I go and see a matinee and try and catch up. If you're on the dole you can always get in half price. I went to have an interview with Michael Parkinson for TV-am very early on when I was starting out, and he said, 'What do you do?' And I said, 'I see a lot of theatre,' and then I couldn't think of one thing I'd seen, so I swore I'd keep up from that day on. He was nice about it but he kept on saying, 'Have you seen this? Have you seen that?' and it was 'No, no,' and I thought, 'I'm not going to be caught out like that again.' If you say you keep up with current plays you've got to be able to do it. Because if you want to be connected with the arts you have to see exhibitions and plays, it might spark off an idea.

And when I come back in the afternoon, I go for my run, more of this routine thing. It will only be very short bursts of exercise but they're important. I go for a run around Kensington Pond. Not the Serpentine, the Serpentine's huge, it would be impossible to run round that.

Being out of work I find I make a lot of friends, like at the market in North End Road, I know them all there and they shout, 'Hello, Blondie!' and things.

In the launderette I was feeling rather low one day, and I saw a picture of a film star on the wall and I thought, 'Well, I'm jolly well going to put mine up, too,' so I gave a picture of myself to the man who owns the launderette and signed it 'Lots of love from Victoria', and he stuck it up. So he knows me now and every time I walk in he always asks how the parts are going. It just makes you feel, well I am someone, I am supposed to be an actress, or something.

My moods vacillate tremendously. I think on the surface it looks as if

I'm terribly optimistic about it but inside I always know what the truth is. It's very easy to say to everyone, 'Oh, there are lots of irons in the fire', or 'Everything's coming along nicely', or 'Yes, I'm waiting to hear on this', and I always do have something on the go. So if someone knows I've been up for an interview and asks if I got it, I'll say no, but then I can always say – 'but I'm waiting to hear on something else'. It's forget one, go on to the other. There's never any time to mope around on one failure, you just immediately go on to the next one.

I suppose I never want to show that I'm feeling really down about it. I don't think I could do it if I wasn't an optimist. I'm depressed if I thought I could have got a job and didn't. The lowest ebb of all was when I was told I had to change my accent, because I thought, my voice is my tool, my craft, and if I have to change it that's a pretty major thing to change, and I was seriously worried at that stage. A director recently told me I was up for a film part, but he said, 'You look great, everything's great, but we can't have your voice.' And that was a real 'Look you're hopeless' assessment, because your voice is everything, isn't it, if you're going to be on television or on the radio.

It's very hard if you have a day when you wake up and think, 'I feel absolutely bloody today.' You still have to ring up as if you're full of confidence and you're the only person worth seeing that day, and to put on such a show, such a charade. If you're feeling really down it's incredibly difficult, and often you know you don't have anything worth telling them, but you've just got to get them to see you at all costs.

I always get people to see me. A lot of people say I wouldn't have seen you if you hadn't sent your photograph in. Because I've done so many jobs my CV is extraordinary enough that it catches people's eyes, and also I'm afraid the fact that I'm a girl and blonde does give me an advantage. But if it gets me to see them then I'm glad, because I want to get into that room – although it may take me five minutes longer to prove that I have got something to say and that I am serious.

I might travel four hours on a train journey, and it's nothing to the director. He'll see you for half an hour and you're prepared to travel all that way in the hope that he may, when he's looking for someone, think, 'Oh, yes, THAT girl...' But they just love it, you come in, you're completely at their mercy and you know they haven't got any job to offer, they can just click their fingers and you'll go because you know you can't afford to turn down anything.

I used to go up for television commercials, and you'd walk in and there would be ten other girls with blonde hair and a fringe, and you know you'd have to go in and smile and flirt with real creeps. It made me feel sick having to do that.

It must be fairly nice for them, a lot of pretty girls coming in and being charming to them, bending over backwards to be nice. I've even had to put up with these creeps chasing you around the desk, it happens all the time. There's an art. You have to flirt just enough to keep them liking you and be interested in you, and yet not enough to get any kind of lead. It's such a fine line and I hate myself, I know I have to do this vaguely flirtatious act, otherwise if you go in there and grit your teeth and look bolshy, they think, well there are plenty of other people who want to see me. You can't walk in being pessimistic, you have to walk in thinking, 'I *have* got something to offer.' If you walk in pessimistic you've lost, you might as well not have stepped out the front door.

The casting director can't say yes right away, hence that awful agony of waiting. Then the worst thing is people asking if you've got work because everyone finds it so interesting. It all sounds so exciting to them. You get fed up at making excuses for yourself, saying you're terribly busy doing this and that.

When you're famous you're recognized the whole time, you can't walk down the street without people recognizing you, that's the first thing that I eventually will have to come to terms with. I don't want people knowing all about my personal life, but unfortunately that does go with the job.

I couldn't go on if I wasn't convinced I was going to make it, I might as well give up tomorrow, this minute. What's the point of going on putting so much time, money, effort, thought, energy into something if you think you might not make it? It's a totally all-consuming preoccupation and passion. Every day is angled towards making it, every single thing I do. It's a goal, it's what I get up every morning to do, it's what I want to do, and I've never thought of doing anything else. My parents are happy I've found what I want to do, a lot of people just haven't got a clue what they want to do.

Oxford Don
Christopher Tyerman

In this university, Modern History starts at AD 285, because it is designed to distinguish it from Ancient History. But I have taught various subjects, English and foreign history from shall we say the seventh century AD and the break-up of the Roman Empire to the sixteenth-century Reformation, as well as some nineteenth-century constitutional theory.

If you're clever you lecture on things that you're actually researching on. I am at the moment writing a book on England and the Crusades over a period of four hundred years. There's a vast amount of material and therefore to help me organize it in my own mind I give lectures on it and see if I can make sense or shape of various themes. In Oxford the bulk of the teaching is not done by lectures; it is done in tutorials.

The point of teaching history is not actually to pump people full of information about the past, it's whether they can appreciate the workings of certain historical phenomena; social organization and political action, warfare and the economy, social class and things like that. It doesn't really matter whether someone's writing an essay on the ninth or the nineteenth century, the phenomena are there in different forms, in different guises, in different stages of development. We want people to be able to think, arrange material relevantly around topics that, as they applied to read history, one assumes they might be interested in.

Obviously there are some tutors who go out of their way to impress their personalities on the undergraduates, and that can be a function of personal inadequacy on the don's part. Some undergraduates will like you, some won't. You will like some undergraduates and detest others and be irritated by some and bored by some, and some you become very friendly with. It can depend on what year they're in; first year, nervous, shy, writing juvenile essays, or third year when you're teaching them more detailed subjects they'd be more interested in, and they'd be much more mature.

I've found over the years that I've taught a significant change. Ten years ago undergraduates were much more intellectually irreverent and questioning, now they sit in tutorials and take notes of what one says and they're much more deferential, respectful, worried about their careers.

The public image of Oxford, the sort of Brideshead image, is inevitable because how can you portray in an interesting way chaps sitting in chairs reading books? That's what most people spend a lot of their time doing. Working. And that is bad television, therefore anybody who comes to make a film about Oxford finds a party or a lunatic society or something because that's good entertainment; or they and we can give them news like not giving Mrs Thatcher an honorary degree, but most undergraduates spend most of their time being fairly ordinary people like the rest of us.

I'm accused of living in the past or living in an ivory tower. I'm an historian and I happen to be a medievalist but I'm equally interested in the present and the recent past, and have the same curiosity about the future as anybody else. One reads the newspaper, one listens to the radio, takes a part in matters, one does all the normal things that people do like buying houses and educating children, and failing to buy what you want in the shops and not having enough money and those sort of things. The idea that because you're, say, a commodity broker, in some sense you're more plugged into modern reality is misleading; their views on real life, whatever that means, can be just as blinkered, obscure, out of date and downright odd as any don's. I'm a modern person studying the past.

I'm very much in the Oxford tradition of historians in the sense that I'm an empiricist. It seems to me to be entirely bogus to impose a modern theory on your understanding of evidence of the past if the evidence doesn't fit that theory. You've got to try and understand what the charter or chronicle meant then, how much you can trust it: you must never be bamboozled into using evidence merely because it's convenient.

A good historian is one that is honest and discriminating about his sources. Honesty in an historian is the great thing. Instead of saying, 'Right, I want to take a view that's going to be appealing to people,' you ask, 'What does the evidence tell me of what view I can take?'

Obviously historians in one sense are going to end up knowing more about certain things than contemporaries did, and also less because one isn't there, so one is always looking for the truth; what does this mean, what is this document I've got, not only physically, where does it come from, who made it, etc., but having established that it's genuine, what are the layers within that private or public document? It is important to study the past for its own sake and on its own terms, not ours.

The physical process of doing research can be grindingly tedious. You plough through some illegible documents in bad Latin or bad French, hoping to find something and you never do because what you hoped was there simply is not, and that's boring, but equally, the other day, for example, I was in the British Museum to read a fourteenth-century manuscript, partly burned in the eighteenth century, and it told the story of an individual who had a remarkable career as a crusader in the late thirteenth century, early fourteenth century. His career hasn't been covered, perhaps because the manuscript is so illegible and people have probably said, 'Well, life's too short.' There's a physical excitement of trying to decipher it and a physical regret that one's palaeographic skills are not greater, but the excitement of reading about this chap is genuinely stimulating. His career illustrates and confirms much wider theories of what people were doing at the time, how people viewed the world and what people were saying to politicians in the early fourteenth century. So the excitement isn't simply about this chap's life, although that was exciting enough. He was an English Hospitaller who had fought at Louis IX's last crusade at Tunis in 1270; he fought in Palestine and was at the fall of Acre in 1291 when the Egyptian Sultan threw the crusaders out of the mainland of Palestine for good, he was then captured and spent twenty years in an Egyptian prison before he came back to Yorkshire to raise his ransom. At the end of his life, when he was about eighty, he wrote this book for Edward III, advising him the best means of how to conquer the Holy Land, and he prefaces it by saying, 'My credentials are…' and narrates the story of his life. Roger of Stanegrave. That's fun.

You can't build up a reputation without publishing anything, and in the end you've got to put something down for all the world to see, and that's when the emperor either has or hasn't got clothes on. And being solitary, being presumably reasonably intelligent with reasonably active brains, we therefore have a lot of time to think, and if you have time to think, if you've got any imagination at all, you do quite a lot of worrying.

You've got to be prepared to be your own man and that sometimes means periods of solitariness and being able to stand up to other people. This is why dons get involved in rows with other academics, because you are a pedagogue, not simply in your teaching but also in your academic work and your research and your writing. It's Tyerman's book, it's not the University of Oxford's book, it's not the firm's book, it's your view. I think I have always been something of a pedagogue so in that sense I've found a suitable career for me.

I think the measure of success would be to write a great book, a great book not necessarily in the sense that millions of people read it, but that your peers in the profession said, 'This is a great book.' That presumably is the highest achievement, to become an acknowledged expert and writer of good books that one's colleagues admire. It's a fairly self-regarding exercise within a small world.

But the worst part of my job is finding oneself unable to achieve that through a mixture of technical and intellectual deficiencies. I find the margin between elation and despair is very narrow. If you're trying to write something subtle and you actually write superficial, misleading or obscure rubbish, which happens to us all, that's the worst part, the consciousness of one's own intellectual inadequacies on many occasions. A number of my colleagues give a fairly arrogant, self-assured exterior, but many of the historians I know best are riddled with self-doubt and have moments of depression and despair when they fail to do what they want with the material. It's an intellectual problem. Why isn't this better? Why is this shabby?

I think that institutional philistinism has long been the rule in this country – academic cleverness has always been frowned upon. There's never been the cult of the intellectual as there is, say, on the Continent, which I think on the whole is perhaps a good thing, but the spin-off is that they treat apparently irrelevant subjects like medieval history with contempt. One is always asked to justify why one is doing medieval history. Well, one can, but it's that sort of attitude and philistinism that one would have hoped that educated people don't have. If they can't see the use of people doing higher research in higher educational establishments, there seems to me to be a problem.

If there were no historians at all, nobody studying history, that would probably be a symptom of a totalitarian state, either left or right, it doesn't matter, because the study of history has always been part of man's curiosity and it's been a feature in this country, an important reflection of liberty and democracy. The fact that you get the history wrong doesn't matter provided you keep on discussing history and looking at it and seeing what went on, because it breeds an accurate mind. You can see through the lies, the cheats of any government, you can see their mistakes, you can see them with their trousers down, and if you don't want people who see that wandering around, then you stop them. But the attitude of mind, the cynicism if you like – or one might put it more politely, the critical faculty, the refusal to believe just simply because one is told to believe – must be a good thing for a healthy society, and if you don't have that, it must be a symptom that something's gone very badly and oppressively wrong.

I think the point about being an academic, the great charm and the reason why people do it for so little money in this country, is that it is part of your life and that you're in control of your own time. This is sometimes a good thing, sometimes a bad thing, sometimes you wish you had someone to tell you what to do next, but therefore it is impossible really to separate out private and professional life. Obviously when one is bathing the children one is not being an academic, but there isn't a sharp divide between work and home.

Quite honestly, I don't feel sufficiently compensated. In real terms academic income over the last twenty years has decreased enormously. It's all very well, you say, you lead a comfortable life and lots of people want to become academics, therefore we can exploit the fact that it's a buyers' market and pay the buggers nothing. If you do that it says a lot about what value you put on higher education, and this society is putting less and less value on higher education. It's depressing.

I think the basic point about university life, and what the outside world doesn't appreciate, is the hours of tedium involved in simply reading books that both dons and their pupils go through. It's not a life of wine and roses, but equally it's a very pleasant life, one wouldn't deny that, and it would be foolish to be self-pitying. Sitting in a room with a view like this, it's indecent to complain overmuch.

Palaeontologist
Richard Fortey

My job is to do research on fossil animals, and in particular, things called *trilobites*, which are now completely extinct, but they were the dominant form of animal life about five hundred million years ago. They're extraordinarily interesting, because they were diverse in the way that insects are now diverse, except they lived in the sea, of course. Not only that, but they're important for dating the rocks in which they occur, and for inferring things about the environments of the past. There are an enormous number of them; that's one thing people don't realize, that fossils are in fact extremely common, and if you know where to go you can collect them in great quantity.

Well, if you're a natural historian by nature, which I was, almost since I can remember, you start off with birds, like most boys, and then you get interested in wild flowers, and fungi, which I still am. And then at some stage, I think it was on holiday in Dorset, I picked up my first fossils, and thought these were really rather interesting, and by the time I'd reached the sixth form, collecting these things and finding out about them had become something of a passion, so you could say I was pre-conditioned to it from an early age.

I work almost entirely on my own, and I would guess compared with most people my time-scale is completely different. The end-products of my work are scholarly monographs which can take several years to produce. I've been working on a piece of work on the rocks and fossils of Wales, which has taken me literally a decade. Eventually it will be published and will stand as the definitive work.

Providing you do a little bit of work on the collections, and generally broaden your level of expertise, it's perfectly possible to survive here, at the Natural History Museum, for years even, showing no visible signs of your activity. The motivation has to be to continue to write on the interesting things you've found out. And that's an entirely solitary occupation. Sometimes it's lonely. You're sustained almost entirely by your internal motivation to get a piece of work done.

Almost more than anybody I know, I have complete self-determination, so that nobody knows if I get up in a slightly depressed state and do nothing all day; it has no repercussions whatsoever. I can determine both what I do short term and what I do long term. I have very few what you might call formal obligations to carry out. So I have total academic freedom.

Just today I've been looking at a particular kind of *trilobite* that lived five hundred million years ago, a thing called a *symphysurus*, with a view to working out what its life habits were. One thing that interests me is the methods that you use to infer how extinct animals lived. Quite a lot of the time if you look at popular books, you see dinosaurs gaily wading through swamps – how do people know that they waded through swamps? Quite often these things, although they're portrayed as facts, are actually only mountains of inference. I've been looking for structures on this particular animal and comparing them with the kind of structures that you might find on animals that are still living, and seeing if I could infer things about comparable structures having a comparable function. This particular animal, the *symphysurus*, was able to enroll, just like a woodlouse, for example, and by studying and looking at the animal in great detail. I've identified little locking devices, very precise, which enabled the tail to join up with the head and securely lock the thing into position when it was rolled up.

I find it interesting; that's all I can say. I write it up for a paper; other *trilobite* people around the world also find it interesting, hopefully, and it adds to my scientific lustre. If you wish for me to say, does it have any other spin-offs, the answer has to be no, any more than, let's say, finding Etruscan vases has any other spin-offs. You can't claim very easily that these kind of studies have any relevance to finding mineral deposits or oil deposits: they don't. You just have to be interested in the thing for its own sake, very much 'knowledge for its own sake', and the whole thing is predicated on the assumption that it's a good idea to have scholars in society pursuing this kind of esoteric pursuit – which I believe it is.

I think that a particular kind of curious person, if they're lucky, can be gainfully employed in doing things which just satisfy their curiosity. Against that, you have to accept the fact that it's not remarkably well paid, but then why should you be particularly well paid for something which is essentially what many people do simply for pleasure. For most academic types, of which I'm one, of course, the academic prestige is far more important than money.

One of the things that you most have to consider is the worthwhileness of what you do, and sometimes, of course, that is a problem when you're involved in something which has very little connection with late twentieth-century activities, like getting a newspaper out, or putting a building up, or curing somebody's sickness. I suppose inevitably, if you're working on things that have been extinct for five hundred million years, you tend to regard short-term historical perturbations a little sceptically. I have had a reaction against it on one or two occasions, thought that it was far too introverted, far too navel-gazing.

But I'm as committed as I can be. The terrible thing to happen, and it does happen, would be to lose your interest in the thing you're studying. That's absolutely fatal. Because here you are, you have no pressure on you from anybody else; you're simply left to get on with it. I'm seen by my superior officer, of whom there is one, once a year, and the interview is run something like this:

'Oh, sit down ... how's it going then?'

'Pretty satisfactory I'd say, all around ... '

'Jolly good, well see you next year.'

Now, I know people that work in other fields for whom every day is a more or less continuous battering from one direction or another to get something done: the phone rings, there are deadlines to be met, all that kind of thing. If I feel a generalized sense of *ennui*, I can sit with my feet on the desk, picking up a piece of paper and putting it down again, and doing no work at all, although one never feels that is a satisfactory way of spending the day. For me there are no deadlines, no pressures ... virtually no inducement, either. I'd earn the same money if I do nothing or if I work hard – which I do. So, it's a curious existence.

There are a number of cases of people here who have simply gone bananas. And it is an environment which fosters eccentricities, as you can imagine. If you have a peculiarity, the chances are that given the chance to grow alone in a greenhouse, the peculiarity gets worse and worse. In fact, I designated this some years ago as Mattingley's Syndrome, after somebody who worked in the Entomology Department. Of course, if you think more about some group of insects, or the past, exclusively, or a lot of the time, it's bound to make you slightly odd. The first result is that you become extremely absent-minded and start to talk to yourself. That's what I call Primary Mattingley Syndrome. That doesn't matter because we all do that; if you come in here silently, you would find me mumbling to myself down the microscope. That's all right, nothing to worry about; that's only primary symptoms. At that stage you usually talk to yourself quite politely. The secondary symptoms set in when you begin abusing yourself roundly in a loud voice. When you start getting extremely bad, you cannot switch off thinking about your mosquitoes in his case, or your *trilobites* in my case. And there are famous instances of Tertiary Mattingley's – when Mattingley himself remarked to a colleague, 'You know, the most extraordinary thing, they seem to have taken the urinals out of the gentlemen's toilet,' and the colleague wondered what on earth he was talking about, and then saw him going into the Ladies', and they had apparently moved the Gents' five years previously to another place, and he'd gone into the Ladies' which was right next door without even noticing. Now that's Tertiary Mattingley's – which I haven't yet started manifesting any symptoms. But of course another symptom of being in the Tertiary phase is that you cease to worry about getting Mattingley's Syndrome.

You have to be pretty obsessive to get things done. When you publish large monographs you are building some kind of monument to yourself. It's selfish. Three or four years ago, I was sufficiently obsessed not to realize that that's what I was doing. You become a world authority, you see, and there's something terribly appealing if you're a young scholarly type to the mere phrase 'world authority'. It's only when you start getting there, which I suppose I am now, that you might question the motivation more. The personal monument may not seem so important if you think that there's only you and two other people in China to admire it. So to that extent there is a certain amount of self-doubt these days.

Perhaps I'm more impatient, a bit crotchetier, but that's probably just the early symptoms of Mattingley's Syndrome. Earlier on I might have spent longer finding out about some small fact that I wasn't satisfied with, and now I might hurry it up a bit. You know, my goodness, I've been five years writing this thing up, I must get it done.

There's always the banker who feels trapped by a nine-to-five job who when I describe what I do, his eyes grow misty and he says, 'Oh – that sounds absolutely wonderful. I've always wanted to do something like that.' You'd be surprised how many people have wanted, or think they want, to do the kind of thing that I do – a surprisingly large number of people. Then I get the, 'What use is it anyway?' reaction which I find extremely hard to cope with, mainly because, of course, you can't actually defend it in the kind of line which is spun these days, that every piece of research has to have its immediate spin-off which will produce pounds or dollars. So then I find myself using slightly intellectually arrogant lines of arguments which are always guaranteed to get up the nose of the person I am talking to.

Everybody likes to be thanked for the work they do. This again goes back to the solitary life and the internal motivation. What you get are never thanks, all you get is disagreement. So you work several years on a large piece of work that you then publish, and the next thing you hear is some bloke in Czechoslovakia disagreeing with you. That's one of the tougher aspects of it, really. Just occasionally you'll get the annual pat on the back from the head of the department if you're doing all right. And once every decade you might get a promotion.

I'm all for work if it's enjoyable. Some people can achieve satisfaction from almost anything. And just as the banker might think my work is ideal, and a lot of the time it is enjoyable, in the strictest sense of the word, just pottering around doing the thing you like, it's also possible to have dark nights of the soul about it.

They say work has its own reward. I don't know. I want to feel that I'm doing really good stuff, and on occasions, when I doubt it, that's when you need someone to rush in through the door and say, 'Don't doubt it, you are.' Of course that doesn't happen very much in academic life.

Peer of the Realm
Lord Brocket

I never know, when I'm filling out forms, what to put down under 'occupation'. In the old days, they always used to put 'Peer of the Realm', which I don't know if it's supposed to represent status or whether it's supposed to represent a job. Technically it is a job because it means you have a seat in the House of Lords, but even if I was a full-time member of the House of Lords, sitting every day – which I don't, I go about once a week – I'd still be terribly reluctant to put that down as a job. But I bloody well work, unlike some aristocrats that don't work.

My mother always said that I was born to be a bricky or a labourer. She's right, because I adore doing things with my hands. I mean yesterday, for example, I was up to my neck in shit as the plumbing went wrong in the basement, and I was shovelling sewerage and other things – very nice! A job had to be done, I don't mind doing it. I'll never forget when I was about twelve, my mother caught me painting the stones around the drive white, and she said, 'You ought to be in a three-piece suit and somebody else should be painting that, because it's wrong for your image.' I said, 'Bugger my image. The job needs doing, and I enjoy painting the stones!' But just because I actually like doing things with my hands, I very often have to stop and remind myself, I say, 'Look, Brocket, you could be in your office making decisions, important decisions which in themselves are worth more than, say, if I'm cleaning sewerage.' Now a man who's cleaning sewerage will probably be paid about £4 an hour, so why am I doing an hour's work at four quid, when I could earn for the business more than four quid by sitting at my desk, ringing a few companies, telling them about Brocket Hall?

I inherited the title age fifteen from my grandfather. I didn't understand what it meant; I only met my grandfather twice in my entire life, and therefore I didn't know what Brocket Hall entailed. I know my name changed, which was a bit odd, I thought, but the impact of having a few thousand acres and a big house really didn't come to me at all. To be absolutely honest, the estate was virtually bankrupt, it had been grossly mismanaged before I got here by somebody who was not a realist about the way that society was going, and how you had to adapt the estate. In the old days, farm rents and income would be such that it would maintain the big house and the big lifestyle. Of course, things changed, and I don't think my grandfather saw the change coming. The cost of living went up, the cost of maintenance soared at places like this, and taxes went up. So I took this place over, and I had a very simple decision: flog it or keep it. And of course it is very easy to take the money and run. There are quite a few people who have done that, Lord Jermyn for example. I was offered at one stage about seven million for the estate as it stood – and the house was in a very bad state. Now to any person seven million is a hell of a lot of money. It certainly was to me, twelve years ago when I was twenty-one.

I'd never had money in my life up until I got this place, never, but I decided what the hell's the point of living in Monte Carlo with a few birds hanging on your arms, living it up? You can't have any self-respect, you can't. You must do something. And so I decided to take this place on. It was basically bankrupt, so I did some neat tax avoidance by leaving the country for three years and joining the army, which got me off a lot of tax when we sold some building land, and then after that I came back to England. The place still wasn't making money, and everyone, especially the banks, kept telling me I should sell it.

Meanwhile, it was considered by my family that if you run an estate, you want to go to Cirencester where you learn estate management. Of course, a more stupid idea I simply can't imagine. It couldn't be further removed from the actual problem. The problem is not how you grow crops and keep the woods looking nice, the problem is how you turn an eighty-five thousand square feet hunk of bricks and mortar into a profit-making enterprise. Bugger the land, that will sort itself out later. The rents wash themselves on the land, so at least they'll keep the roofs watertight, and keep the place looking reasonable. So that will break even. The building's the big drain, and you want a course in business management; you don't want to go near a place like Cirencester.

So I went to the States, got some creative thinking under my belt, came back with the firm idea that conferences was the answer. Then I needed money, and the funny thing was I went to a lot of English banks, I wanted half a million. I didn't have it, of course, I had an overdraft.

And they said they wanted it secured by more than a hundred per cent, to which I said, 'Look, do you think I am cuckoo? If I had that sort of security, why should I want to borrow the money?' Typical sort of English situation. And they wouldn't lend. So then I went to the Americans. Now the Americans have a different idea of banking. They say, 'We take some risks, you take some risks, if we make money, that's great.' The English banks have a totally different crazy idea of how to make money, and if the so-called working class (which is a word I hate) want a gripe about capitalists making money, there's their best gripe, why the hell should bankers make money when they don't take much risk? Anyway, eventually an American bank gave me the money with virtually no security. I put some cars that I had and a few other bits like that, even my family tiara, I put in as a bit of security – and that was enough. Within eighteen months, out of profits, I paid back that money.

My father died before my grandfather, so the title went straight to me – which with all due respect to my father, who I didn't know very well, because I was seven when he died, I think was probably the life-saver of this place. Because what happens is, there's a problem with the roof, it needs replacing, damp, dry rot or something. The owner says, 'Well, I'm seventy, I can't stand the major upheaval to get it all right, I'll leave it to son.' Son is meanwhile coming up to fifty. When father dies, son thinks, 'Well, hang on, that's two hundred thousand or something that I've got to spend' – nearly all the major expenditures are about that amount. Now either he thinks he's too old to do it; or he'll leave it to his son. He thinks, 'Sod it, I'm not going to spend two hundred grand, 'cause I've got better things to do with the money.' And so it goes on and on – the problem never gets dealt with until the house is in such a bad state of repair, either the local authority takes it on or they start squealing, saying, 'We're impoverished poor people with a lovely house, why doesn't the government help us out?' Or else you suddenly put your foot down and say, 'No, this problem's got to be dealt with.' And I was young and daft enough to live in a house with no floorboards, and I used to sit frying eggs on a camping stove and I had to put some planks across so we didn't fall through into the entrance hallway, camping amongst all the rubble for nearly two years until I got the house into shape.

As my mother said, I should have been a bricky – I mean I actually love bricklaying – but no doubt, like for the poor sod who does it all his life, the novelty would wear off if I did it as a full-time job. But I love building work, I love carpentry, and I like working with my hands. If I had my way, I would never come to my office, I'd never make a telephone call. Unless my wife gets irate with me, I'll be building a cupboard, painting, or something until say two, three in the morning – and that's often happened.

There was a hell of a battle with the family because they thought that I was taking leave of my senses in commercializing this estate. I got a broadside from all directions, I was almost a vandal with what I was doing. But I knew that it had to be. What was I going to do, dig a hole and find oil in the back garden? It had to be commercialized, and the only way to do it was the way I did it.

The whole estate itself is five thousand acres. But the estate side of it is just making sure it's tidy, well kept, well looked after, repair problems with buildings, repair liabilities, roofs, burst pipes, all this sort of thing we have to keep on top of and keep maintained, and the estate's water supply usually causes us problems. The core of the estate without a doubt is the building, Brocket Hall itself. It's a reasonably big house, five floors, thirty-five bedrooms and bathrooms, and the most important thing is to keep it running smoothly, keep it maintained, and of course on the marketing side, keeping it full. Also there are fifty-five staff to look after and make sure they're happy and are functioning properly. We had a sous-chef walk out yesterday, and we have a housekeeper who's gone into hospital for an emergency operation.

When people wander into the house and see it for the first time, they're amazed or dazzled by the architecture and the history, although inevitably, living here, you do tend to take it for granted.

It has a very strange history. Very briefly, in 1230 the Brockets bought the house and land and built on it. They lived here until 1760. In 1760 they sold it, and history doesn't tell us why they sold it; I wish I could find out. A gentleman called Sir Matthew Lamb bought it; he built this new house, demolished the old one, and died the year it was finished. His son had a wife who had a relationship with the Prince Regent, hence the racecourse which was built on the estate for the Prince Regent. The next son was Lord Melbourne the Prime Minister, his wife was Caroline Lamb, who had an affair with Byron.

Queen Victoria was here on a monthly basis, and sometimes more. She only used one room in the house; I don't think it's the nicest room by any means, but it was her favourite room and she always used that room. We've restored some of the fabrics. The watercolours on the walls she had commissioned for herself; views of the lake. Then another Prime Minister, Lord Palmerston, lived here because he married Melbourne's sister and inherited the house. He died in the Billiard Room. Then after Lord Palmerston died, there was a succession of tenants, and then in 1923 my great-grandfather bought the house back into the family.

It's one of the finest examples of pure Georgian house in the country. I take fantastic pride in the possessions, I absolutely love restoring them and looking after them. Inevitably we have a lot of valuable things, there are some excellent pictures here. There's a Joshua Reynolds, we've got a very good Coates called 'The Cricketing Boy' which is very famous, we've got some Van Dycks, Murillo, 'The Immaculate Conception' is a very well known picture, we've got van der Veldts, we've got Hopners, Landseers… All the furniture in the saloon, nearly all of that was made by Chippendale, even the pelmets, the mirrors, the lot, and the largest suite of furniture he ever built in his lifetime. Chippendale made the bookcases in the library, they're the only bookcases he made, I don't know why but they were. But all these things have to be looked after and maintained, and I adore doing it.

As and when damage crops up we repair it immediately. As we have odd bits of money to spare we restore another piece of furniture. There's always a programme, priorities of what's next on the list. If the next on the list happens to be something costing a hell of a lot of money, we go to the one above it; it's a constant programme of restoration, and once it's restored keeping it in good condition. Just painting the house – we have decorators in the house literally every month, a team of three or four people, and they just go round touching up little knocks, whatever it is, wallpaper scratched, they re-wallpaper, and they spend a week at a time every four weeks. It's a bit like the Forth Road Bridge, but that's the only way to keep a house like this in perfect condition. Because we have seventy people sleeping in this house at any one time, seventy people day after day after day, it would get knocked to hell, it would look like a scruffy old house, after a bit. All I am, and a lot of aristocrats who live in a big house like this, we're caretakers.

The responsibility doesn't weigh upon me at all. People always ask me that, as if they think it should, but it's a *fait accompli*, I've got it so what the hell's the point in arguing about it. I always remember when my father died, and my brother cried at the time, he's a year younger than me, and I said, 'It's no good crying over spilt milk.' I mean it's happened so it's happened. Of course I was seven and the full impact didn't come to me then, and with this place I was given it, there's no point in saying, 'Oh my God, woe is unto me,' the fact is you've got it and you might as well get on with it, and make a good job of it.

If I had my way I would like people to think that I live in a little cottage somewhere and I'm just manager of this place, and as the Americans would say, I'm a regular guy. I do sometimes feel as if I'm trying to compensate for having this place, not by working extra hard because I would do that regardless, but I find that I'm trying to pretend that it's nothing special having this place, if they had it they would do exactly what I'm doing, they would work to keep it going and it's just a job.

I constantly tell people I'm very lucky to have it – look at the view. I mean, Christ, even out of a basement window in the office you can see the lake with all the ducks on it, and the land opening out in front of you, I mean one is very lucky to have it.

English people, depending on background, react in two ways when they come to this house. It's bound to be different from the house they live in, or pretty well bound to be, because they live in sensible houses that are easy to heat, and so they either say, 'This is amazing,' or it's an inverted snobbery, they'll turn round and try and pretend it's nothing and take no notice of it and put their feet up on the furniture, you know: 'This guy's got this swell house, it's nothing, who does he think he is?' They don't want to show that they're impressed, it's a funny social thing. Americans are always totally open, they say, 'This is wonderful, tell us all about it.'

My wife's American. She has to be part of the business and show an interest and make sure the guests are okay and make them feel at home as well. One of the most important aspects of this particular business is to make people feel they're staying in our home, and we don't want to be like many stately homes which are now hotels.

My little boy, he's a year and a half. He, whether he likes it or not, will be the next Lord Brocket. If he doesn't like it he can get rid of it but then it goes on to the next son. No way would I ever push any son of mine into what he should do, but I suspect he's going to be rather like me, in that he's already shown he loves pulling things apart and doing things, and I think if he's creative, this whole set-up will interest him.

I'll certainly help him, but I'll never force him. I got that, and that's why I'm aware of it. They attempted to push me in all directions, particularly Cirencester, I had a gun practically put to my head about Cirencester, which is a typical upper-class way of thinking; and having to go to Eton, that was a mistake. I don't think I'll send my son to Eton. I'm not sure he'll even go to a public school.

I think generally the young modern aristocrats work very hard. We are much more with it. Gerald Grosvenor, for instance; mind you, he bloody well has to work hard. He has a huge empire to run and if he doesn't it'll fall apart around him. He's been dropped right into the shit, whether he likes it or not. Roxburghe, he's got a big estate to run; he's one of our wealthiest ones; he's a year younger than me. He has very much the same sort of life as me, but he's got a bigger empire to run; I mean I haven't got an empire, I've just got a sort of pad plonked in the middle of Hertfordshire. He's got hundreds of thousands of acres and a big house.

I am constantly ashamed if I come across aristocrats that don't work properly, and I'm suspicious of people who work in the City and sit there coining in millions.

It's extraordinary people's preconceived ideas of not only how wealthy someone is if they've got a title, but their lifestyle and their age. I mean why has a peer got to be rich, living a fantastic lifestyle and decrepit? A lot of people when they come in, they're flabbergasted by the fact that I'm young, they expect me to be an old man. It shows how stereotyped people's vision is, particularly in this country. And it's all to do with the bloody class problem this country has. America's got a lot to teach us on that, an awful lot. One is a party system that isn't us and them, Labour and Conservative, which actually categorizes political feelings in such a damaging way in this country. If we could just have Democrats and Republicans. And the other thing is this bloody accent problem. I mean I speak the way I do; I can't help that, it was just the way I was brought up.

People who read my interview, they'll probably read with interest what I do because they have these preconceived ideas. Having read what I do, they will go back to their preconceived idea and say, 'Well, bully for him, but the guy is still a lord, and a lord is a lord.' So it probably won't alter what their initial impression was before they read this. It's inevitable, the title is there, that's one thing, you add to that an Eton education and you add a big house, and I am what I am. It's no good a geranium trying to pretend it's a dandelion.

I think they might believe I work hard but they'll say, 'Okay, that's fine, the guy works hard, but he doesn't have to work hard,' so the point at the back of their mind will always be – 'but he doesn't have to, does he?' And the guy up north digging the hole will be saying, 'I work hard because if I don't, I starve. That guy Brocket works hard because it's fun, it tickles him.'

Anyway, the fact is that being a lord is something that one has to be responsible about, and it is just an accident of birth. As I happen to be born into that slot, then one might as well be responsible and in some way or another try and contribute to the country. I know that sounds like I read it straight out of a book. But that's how I feel.

Physiotherapist
Angela Bridcut

I wanted to do something with my hands, a practical job, I didn't want to sit behind a desk being a secretary. My mother actually looked through the career books for me.

It's very much stressed that people going into physiotherapy actually go round a hospital to see if they like it. Because a lot of physiotherapy stuff is pretty horrible. You're dealing a lot with sputum and all that sort of thing, that's expectorated material of mucus and saliva. And phlegm. You get it up off people's chests and you get them to do deep breathing exercises; usually they lie on top of the bed while you give their chest a shake, and that helps to loosen it, and you also do a technique called percussion, where you bang on their chest and that helps to loosen it so they can cough it up.

I remember, when I was a student, the first patient who made me nearly faint. I was walking along the ward and being shown somebody with a swelling in her arm and I keeled over because it was so swollen. Five or six times the normal size. I think she had had a break of her upper arm, and the nerve had gone and the hand was swollen too and she couldn't use her fingers. But that was the only thing that has ever made me faint, apart from going into theatre as a student and you see all the blood and all the chopping about. That sort of thing makes anyone faint.

I look after people who have undergone an amputation, after diabetes, or peripheral vascular disease, which is when your arteries harden up so the blood can't travel through. It's not like when they've had it off in a car crash and they come into hospital and their legs are completely mashed up and the surgeon must remove it straight away. With my people, once the decision has been made to have their leg off, they try and give them two or three days before they have the operation, so that we, as physiotherapists, can go and assess them and explain everything, because it's our job to explain the rehabilitation process to them after the operation. We let them practise in a wheelchair, which they can use immediately after the operation, until they are able to walk on a false leg, and make sure they realize they need the leg off, which is another important thing. Because often, although the leg might be discoloured and blue, they may not have a lot of pain. You need a lot of pain to convince somebody that they really need their leg off.

At the same time, you have to be aware of the patients who see the leg is blue and say, 'All right, that's got to come off.' I've got this lady at the moment who says, 'Have it off,' but I feel she needs to be a bit calmer. It's very easy to say, 'Yes, I'll have it off straight away,' but there's a great psychological crisis once you've had it off.

You have to learn to stand aloof from it emotionally, you have to. If somebody dies you're upset, and you think, 'Oh, what a shame,' and sometimes you say, 'Oh, what a relief.' But you soon learn to adapt and just not think too much about it.

The age range is between sixty and eighty-five. Of course it's much worse for people of that age because they've got all sorts of additional problems, the rest of their body is usually not in very good health. They might have bad arthritis, they might be deaf. Some of them are blind before their amputation, or they have their amputation, and their sight gradually gets worse. It's very disabling for them because of all the stiffness that occurs in other joints.

You must do the amputation within a week of when it's decided, because the patient can get very toxic, and if gangrene sets in, it could become infected. The patient can feel very ill and confused before the operation; you tell them things which they don't remember because they're so distraught and then you have to explain everything to them all over again afterwards because they haven't absorbed anything you've told them before. So it's very important to explain it to the family, if they've got any family, and you can get their support.

You really need two or three days for them to settle down after the operation, they can still be feeling quite confused, they're under a lot of pain killers, and you can get what's called phantom pain after your operation, when you think your leg is still there, and of course it's not, it's been cut off below the knee. Once they're up and about on the second day, they start work, facing life without their leg. And once they can walk confidently on their new leg with whatever walking aid they require, then they can go home. We do lots of visits at their home, check they can manage in their house with a wheelchair, and check all the facilities.

On the one hand you have to be very involved with the patients. You have to know the ins and outs of their lives in order to work out what's best for them and how they're going to manage at home. You do get to know them really well, because you're fitting their legs for them, you're handling a lot of their body for them, sorting them out a lot. You can't be stand-offish. You get to know them very well because you're with them for about four or six weeks after their amputation and you see them twice a day at their home.

On the other hand, you learn not to get too involved. I mean, if somebody has an amputation and the wound doesn't heal, and they go for a further one and then eventually they die, then you're very upset, but you can't be involved. You just can't get too emotional. It's the same as if a patient is dying of cancer. You know they're going to die, and with these amputees, after they have had one amputation, they're likely to have a second within five years of their first amputation, and then there's very limited expectation after that. It all sounds so ghastly to you, doesn't it?

I have fun. I really enjoy it, because I much prefer treating the elderly patients to the young. They've got a lot to tell you about life, they're all people who've been through the war, been through a different era to myself. And the people I see now, they've got so much wrong with them, and that's why I like looking after them. Most of them are alone, or if they've got a husband or a wife, they might be crippled as well.

There's a lot of people you can't help because they're going to die, and you have to recognize that, you have to decide, right, with that person I'm not going to be able to achieve what I hoped, so you set your sights a bit lower and work at that. You're always wanting to get the best you can for your patient.

As long as you can get them home, even if it's just for a month or a few weeks and then they die, they still have gone home and they've left hospital, and their family, if they've got families, are delighted to see them home.

You hear that they've died, and you do feel sorry, but if you burst into tears over every patient who died you couldn't do the job, you just couldn't.

The job's made me hard. You can be very unsympathetic and that reflects in my social life as well. Friends' predicaments don't move you, you hear someone has just broken up with their boyfriend, and their problems seem so small. Someone said to me yesterday, 'Don't you have any feelings?' It doesn't spill over into my social life. Work's work, and when I'm at work I don't usually think of my social life, and when I leave work I don't really think about work. Occasionally, say you're on holiday, you might wonder how so-and-so is getting on. It's very important to cut yourself off. I just don't take work home with me; I mean there's nothing you can do for the patient while you're not there.

You come home feeling very tired, you are literally hauling people around all day. You have to grab them out of a chair, and make them walk, and if a physiotherapist doesn't do it, nobody else will – and that physically is very exhausting. This job is exhausting mentally too, but we're a fit breed compared to say secretaries sitting on their bums all day typing.

I don't think we're paid enough. We're paid slightly more than nurses because we are entirely responsible for what we do, we make our own decisions, whereas nurses act much more under the role of the doctor. We go through a much heavier training. But we don't earn anything during our training which nurses do, so you have to be able to support yourself on a grant.

I've been doing my Senior One job for three years, and I get my next increment in June, and after that, that's it. My salary is stuck then. At the level I'm at now, I've got no further to go except into administration. Instead of looking after one or two staff, I'd be looking after a whole department of up to fifteen, and for all that additional responsibility, the money's not worth it. I already have to supplement my income by doing private work at a different hospital at weekends. There's lots of physiotherapists who do other work, they might do physiotherapy, they might do waitressing, anything to supplement their income. We should get enough money to be able to live.

At the age of thirty you ought not to have come to the end of your career structure salary wise. I do feel bitter, we're way behind what we should be getting.

Playwright
Alan Ayckbourn

To start with, the theatre is such an anti-social profession you tend to work while other people are playing, and the very time people are getting ready to go out to dinner, you're getting ready to go to work, and then because you can start work a little later in the morning, it makes for a peculiar closed circuit of friends, you know, either other people in the theatre or insomniacs.

I suppose work is 90 per cent of my life really, and particularly when one is a director or a writer, where your hours are not so defined, I think you tend to carry it away with you into the night.

There's a certain puritanical streak in me which tells me, 'You've been very lucky to be a successful playwright, people do come and see your plays, and you really ought to keep working at it.' The fact that the play is successful and one can afford a holiday, or one can afford to have some very good dinners, is great, but the main thing is to keep working. It's a nasty little habit, the work ethic.

Writing is lonely, that's why I do it so fast. I tend to take at the maximum a month off my directing work, and for three weeks of that I wander around just sifting ideas that have been fermenting. Then in the last week I actually throw myself into the business of writing and that is usually a very quick process, anything up to three or four days. Then that will immediately follow into the directing and the first day of rehearsal.

The slowest link in the whole chain is the publicity, you need to have the posters printed weeks and weeks before I have even thought of the next play or started writing. So because I have to at least give an indication of what the play is about, sometimes titles become desperately vague: 'Time and Time Again' which is safe... you could write anything about that.

I think because I put so much into that short period, one is being generated by a fair degree of panic. There is a sort of increasing exhilaration as it gets near finishing, followed by the deflating moment soon after it's finished. And between the two there is a fair tension. And a fair anti-socialness creeps over me and I don't talk to people very much, I can't communicate with anyone, and I nibble all the time on biscuits, sandwiches and live with the characters in the play which can mean one has a sense of splitting oneself into seven or eight characters – so you have a series of multiple personalities wandering around the house.

I've changed my working style a bit of late thanks to 'the brave new world'. I've got a word processor. So I type the whole thing out myself, which is my longhand draft, and I then correct it, and correct it again, and then get someone to read it, just to check the rest. And it saves hours, which is smashing. Though I know many people curse word processors, they are perfect vehicles for playwrights because they enable you to shunt your text around, and I work that way all the time now. Anyway, the last two plays seem to have worked out quite well.

One has been so lucky calling the tune for all these years, I could actually be working for someone whose tune I did not care to dance to and was compelled to for financial reasons. I could probably adjust to working in a vast office, processing insurance claims, say; after a bit you would just do it, think of something else and long for the time to go home. I would hate doing something that was purely destructive, I mean at least one has the hope in your heart when you are writing plays that you are doing something that might bring a little light into the world. I suppose if you were screwing on the end of a machine gun barrel all day or something, you might feel that you weren't actually doing anything much to help the world, and that I would find depressing. But my idea of hell would be to become involved in something you love and do it less well than you would want to do it, like directing plays for an inferior producer in perpetuity.

The thing I have to keep remembering, which is very difficult for people who do make a success out of originating things, is not to become totally involved in promoting the thing and appearing in Pro-Am golf tournaments or popping up on *What's My Line*? or something. My job is writing plays, and I always think people should ask themselves, 'What's the one thing that nobody else can do that I can do?'

The thing about being well known is you become public domain in that your name bounces around a lot in columns, and you are referred to by people whom you have never met, but who speak of you as if they have. It's a little strange occasionally. I have tended to keep rather a low profile. And I keep off those chat shows where you are invited to perform, because I don't think I'm awfully good at that.

There is always the possibility of the Muse drying up, and the problem that the more you write, the less there is in your own scope to explore. I suppose the things that one is aware of are repetition of theme, although I think every artist, whether they be musical, painter or playwright, tends to have a particular theme they come back to, and I think that is perfectly fair, after all most of us are finite. But there is always a worry that you're not doing anything better in what you're saying, just repeating a theme for the sake of repeating it… doing another play. At the moment, touch wood, ideas just pop out, as soon as I get one out, another one arrives, so that is nice, but there is always the fear that it won't happen, that there will be The Blank Sheet of Paper. I've come pretty close occasionally and one had the metaphorical sweat running down the brow… wondering whether it is going to happen.

I don't go to road accidents and stuff for material, things just sort of happen around me, I'm very much a lover of being on the fringes of things. I do wander around a lot on my own, the proverbial man on the street, but I pick things up second hand, from people sitting in the row behind me, at the table beside me. But I don't deliberately expose myself to life in the attempt to get something back from it.

I tend not to tell people I'm a writer, very much because they either get madly self-conscious and attempt to get themselves into your play by some devious trick of personality, or else they clam up completely and look extremely sheepish.

When something doesn't work, when your play is not firing on all cylinders, it's like when everybody leaves your party – or doesn't come. But the best part of my work is not the clapping, it's the feeling at the end of the evening, if things are going well, that you have given the most wonderful party, with no drinks, well only the ones they got at the bar, but those three hundred, five hundred, a thousand strangers who come in are leaving better, I mean whether they are better people or just feeling better, I don't know, but they are sort of unified into a whole and that is marvellous. That's really like shutting the door on a good party and thinking – that went well!

Plumber
Steve Harman

It is varied, the places that you work, some would be derelict, some would be ground work for the council where the properties are very run down with old ladies or old gentlemen living in them, you know, they've lived there all their life, and they've only got an outside loo, and we go and put in the basic amenities like inside toilet or bathroom, things like that.

Sometimes these old houses are in a very bad state of repair. I mean you wouldn't believe some of the things that actually happen in this day and age. There's one place that we're working at the moment which belongs to an old lady of eighty, and there's a toilet in a lean-to, and when she flushes the toilet, the sewerage comes up and through the back inlet gully in the back yard, and floods all over the place, and the smell is something else.

There are people living in houses which have no hot water, and eventually, either through complaints to the council or something, the landlords are forced to put hot water in. And the old folk just can't believe it, you know, like for forty years they've been filling the bath with cold water and bringing down kettles of boiling water to heat it up, and it gives me great satisfaction just to see them enjoying something that we take as a necessity.

You can tell a lot just by people's addresses. I find that at the more up-market addresses, people are very class-conscious, and if there was any possible chance of them getting you to come in through a basement door or a back door, they would rather you did that than actually walking through the front door. And yet they don't seem to realize that you're there to do them a favour if something has gone wrong with their plumbing or central heating, or something like that.

It's a funny relationship. The people look down on you, and yet they don't take any notice of the trouble that is in the drains is actually of their doing, and they try and put on this superior act: you know, 'Well, you're only here to clean the drains,' and I'm looking at them thinking, 'But it's you that caused it.'

Sometimes you feel like turning round at the door and saying, well, it's your drain that's blocked, up yours and off... I'm leaving. I find the posher the houses the more you are looked down on.

I was down in Hammersmith all day yesterday on an emergency for someone; he was a computer expert, the big house, an *au pair* girl to look after the children, and a servant, and they were really upset because the three radiators on the top floor of the house weren't working, and they were the kids' rooms. And we were there from eight o'clock in the morning to eight o'clock at night when we eventually got them to work, and we never got one offer of a cup of tea or anything while we were there, it was amazing.

I like it when people say thank you, you feel that you have achieved something. I just think it's nice to get the occasional pat on the back, it makes you feel that it has been worthwhile, that people appreciate what you're doing.

I think as regards to social status, the plumber is very far down the list. He has a cloth-cap image, you know, Andy Capp type of thing, but it has changed from where it was only a matter of cold water supplied to the house and the sewerage taken away, and that was it. Now there is a fair bit of technology to it, you have all new gadgets, water softeners, a lot of things that the plumber of years ago didn't have then like central heating, etc. so it does have a challenge to it.

Mostly it's about six days a week. You get a sudden rush of work, and then you're belting through the whole lot of it, you know, because when people want something done they want it done *now*, they've eventually decided to have the central heating done, so when they ring you they would like you to start immediately. But of course, you're already working on a job, so you have to try and race through that one to try and not leave these people too long.

I enjoy the rest if I don't have any jobs on. I like to sit back and take stock of what's happened say in the past few weeks and try and think of ways of getting things done better or quicker. I often think about whether I should employ people. It's at the stage where there's too much work for one person, possibly not enough for two, or there would be enough work for two, but then you'd have to get somebody that you can trust. I mean if he causes a leak or something like that and damages people's property it's down to you then, you know.

I would say that overall, plumbers do tend to be slightly dishonest. A lot of them overcharge for work that they do. If they are doing basic work, then everything is fine... it's the emergency calls they tend to give a bit of a hammering. Because you normally find when you answer the phone and it's an emergency, you get this garbled woman who's really frightened out of her skin because the water is coming through the ceiling, and they're thinking of all sorts, what's going to happen? Is the ceiling going to fall down? So you have that person at your mercy, you know, you could go in and say, 'Right, that's going to cost you one hundred pounds,' and I mean you're standing there in your Wellingtons while the water is coming up, and obviously they would pay anything you've asked as long as you stop the leak, so they do tend in that situation to overcharge, to let greed come into it.

Well, I would think that all you can base your charge on is time and the inconvenience to yourself. Usually the emergency happens on a Sunday. Mostly it's the do-it-yourselfer at home over the weekend who lifts a floorboard for some reason, nails it down, and of course nails the central heating at the same time. And he notices a drip, or he might notice a bit of a damp patch, he goes upstairs and pulls the board up, pulling the nail out of the pipe, and that causes a flood. They don't even have the sense to put the nail back in, you know, to keep the leak down to its barest minimum. Well, I have a basic call-out charge of £30 and then I use my discretion. Sometimes I don't charge them that, sometimes I charge less, you know. If I went out to an old person to do something like that I wouldn't charge them £30, I might only charge them a fiver or a tenner.

Nearly all plumbers suffer from housemaid's knee, because we are constantly kneeling all the time, the elbows suffer as well a bit. You get a lot of burns, like if you have to do lead work, which is soldering lead pipes above you: nearly always molten lead will hit you somewhere on the arms or on the hand, and they are extremely painful. I suppose it's the heat of the metal, it's around 600 degrees or something, so they say. Most of the fluxes we use are acid-based, so if you get the flux on you, as well as the feeling of the burning sensation you get a stinging one as well. About two weeks ago I nearly broke my back. I fell backwards off a pair of steps, you know the type where there's a rope that holds the two legs from spreading apart, and the rope broke and I went backwards and, you wouldn't believe it, I landed on a saucepan, which was on the gas cooker at the time. I broke it when I hit it with my elbow on the way down, and the saucepan just caved in. Mind you, the people were more worried about me than they were about the saucepan.

I need work to fill my day. I would think that if I spent too long just sitting about it would drive me crazy. You don't have anything to balance the good times on. I mean to know something is sweet, you always have to eat something that is sour first.

I enjoy work and I enjoy going out and meeting people, it's the way my life is organized. My brother-in-law is often involved on the building side, plastering and things like that, and we have a good time, you know, in fact the day goes very very quickly because we can have a laugh and a joke, and it just makes it nice to get out and to be at work, because we have some good fun during the day. So I never find it depressing, I never have the urge to say, 'I won't go to work today, I think I'll stay at home.' Even if it's raining or cold, eight o'clock comes, you're up, you're on the road, even though you might be scraping frost off the window or whatever, you still go to work. We meet up and go into these cafés first thing in the morning, and we have a gigantic big breakfast and a laugh.

My father was a policeman, and my mother was a schoolteacher. The drive was always there to get yourself a better education. I think in one respect they were a bit disappointed in me, because they thought I would have gone to university like my brother did. He went to university and qualified as a dentist. So they obviously thought that I would go along the same, and it took some years for them to realize that I wasn't university material. I could never make up my mind. If I did go to university, what would I do? You know like you get some people who from a very early age say, 'Yes, I'll be a doctor,' and then they work towards that end. I could never actually see myself as anything; I couldn't see myself as a journalist, I couldn't see myself as an engineer, or a doctor, or a dentist, none of those sort of things appealed to me, so I never strove to get the education to go to university. So I sort of drifted away and just bettered myself from there.

I have five children. I wouldn't mind if they wanted to follow my profession, but I would try and get them to strive for something better, the same as I'm trying to do. I shall obviously continue doing central heating and plumbing, but I do have the urge to do something like property development or something like that. I see the distinct possibility of being able to make something of myself, or something more than just being a plumber, you know.

As it happens, me and the nextdoor neighbour, we have just started a firm, and we are intent on buying properties and doing them up and selling them again.

The first bank manager that I went to try and borrow money to buy a house, it was: 'Do you know what you are getting into? Do you know how much the purchase price is? Do you know how much interest that's going to cost and all the work that you have to do... ? Where is all that money going to come from?' And he was totally condescending in his attitude. I would say being a plumber counted against me quite a lot at the bank, because he tended to talk to me like I was an imbecile, you know, anything over £200 was about as far as he reckoned I could count, and I would have difficulty managing that. Or I would think I was a millionaire and go off and spend two days in the pub instead of getting on with the work. Probably the fact I didn't have anything written down, and I didn't speak with a posh accent; if I had done, I think I'd have got it all right.

It was the difference between Andrew, the bloke that I do the work with, and myself. He knows nothing about the building business, nothing at all, and yet he can raise finance easily because he's a university graduate. And yet I do all the work. So you see the difference? I do all the practical things and he can't do anything other than wheel wheelbarrows and demolition. He can knock things down, but he can't build anything back up, and to me it's incongruous that life should be like that, that he should find it easy to raise money – and yet if he didn't have me he wouldn't be able to do it.

I think there is definitely a major injustice. I mean basically the way I look at it is that the people who hold the wealth hang on to it, and they keep it going in their circle, and if they ever lend it to people outside the circle it brings more money back in, so they are constantly getting richer and richer, and it is very difficult to actually come up to their level unless you're a genius or you invent something that sells millions.

It was purely and simply a stroke of luck that I did a job for somebody. There was quite a lot of work involved, and I got to know the person quite well, and I was telling him about the way banks seem to treat people and he actually gave me an introduction to his bank manager, and it sprang from there.

With the first loan I bought my house, which was derelict, and when I had done it up and the bank was paid off, the balance of it was transferred to a mortgage company so the second time when we did number three down the road, it was much easier.

From now on I think this will open up any other ideas that I might have for business. I think that I would find it easy to raise capital and I should have a lot more money myself, so it is not always going completely cap-in-hand to the bank, and not being able to put up anything. I've found that once you've made the start it makes a tremendous difference. I suppose the banks are using that as collateral, but it certainly makes it a lot easier to borrow money.

Our third property, the one that we are involved with at the moment, has cost us over £60,000, so now we are going into large sums of money. It doesn't seem to bother me, whereas it did at the beginning, I was always worried that I wouldn't be able to make the payments and that I would have bailiffs and all sorts of people hammering on the door, or the bank foreclosing, you know.

If it is a big job, it gives you a slight headache and a fluttering in the chest that you're getting too big for your boots and you have bitten off more than you can actually chew, but then once you get over that you find that you become, not blasé, but you begin to find that you look for bigger projects, you take them on and you find that the level of fear and panic drops away and is not quite so bad the next time. I suppose the next step for me, the next time I would feel panic would be to buy, say, a terrace of two or three houses all together, and involving a large sum of money. Then I would start to panic and say, 'Oh dear, I've gone a bit far this time.'

It's not to become a millionaire or anything like that, I think it's just comfort, you know, to make sure that my old age is taken care of, more than anything else: the fact that I haven't got any insurance policies, I've nothing to look forward to other than possibly the state pension, and I suppose there's a lot of years that I missed paying stamps, you know, so it would be of the very basic if I do get anything at all, so I really have to provide for myself and the wife. Mind you, I intend to outlive her anyway, I want to be the one that's left to spend the money.

Definitely life was simpler when I was less ambitious. But then when you look around and think of the things that you have been able to accomplish, I mean the freedom, number one, not just the fact of having money, but the things you can do with it. Like it's easy now if I wanted to go home, you know, if I ever want to nip across to Ireland, I could go twice a week if I was that way inclined, whereas before it would be dodgy, to say the least. But like my wife's mother is quite old, and my mother is quite old, so if ever there is a crisis at home you can just drop things, and it gives you that sort of freedom.

I think when you have nothing, and you do get a chance, it's easy to take it, because they can't get blood out of a stone. The first manager that loaned me the money actually went out on a limb, I should think, because he wanted to know whether I had insurance policies, or what I could put up as collateral, and I couldn't put up anything. And he took a chance which I think in retrospect he possibly shouldn't have, but that was *my* chance and I took it.

I'm trying to better myself all the time. Education gives you a better understanding of just how things, and people, work. It's like an adult and a child watching a film on television. If the film is adult-orientated – you know, say it's got a moral point to it like *Citizen Kane* or something like that – you are sitting there watching it and you can see the child's interest fall away because it's not educated sufficiently to understand what's going on. And I often find myself in that sort of situation, where the person you are talking to is highly educated and you can see that you're not actually communicating with him, and there is a lack there somewhere, and it always tends to be on my side; so I am trying to get a broader outlook.

I read quite a lot, I've got a schoolteacher friend who gave me the book *The Lord of the Rings*. Well, I've read it about six times, and every time I read it it's still difficult for me, I still don't understand it, but I'm getting there. And I tell you another thing. The missus buys the *Mirror*, but every Sunday, religiously, I read the *Sunday Times*, not because it's a status symbol, but it's just that I read the *Mirror* during the week, as it's the only paper that's in, but the *Sunday Times* gives you like the whole week's news decently, and you can read the *Mirror* and get absolutely no understanding of what is happening in the world.

And all this does open doors, definitely. I mean it's really self-confidence, because I can actually talk to people now. You know, like say meeting architects or quantity surveyors on the site, you can talk to them a lot better, whereas the lack of education always makes people like me look like they have a surly attitude, like it's always 'Yeah... no... okay'. Architects and surveyors, they can push because they have a better confidence of life. But now I find I'm able to hold my argument, as often as not I can change the quantity surveyor's mind or the architect's mind, and get things done according to the way *I* want to do them, rather than let them dictate to me all the time.

I'm definitely at a crossroads. If things could go on in the same vein as they are now, I could accumulate a lot of wealth in a very short time. Instead of me going for things, now I'm actually being pushed. It seems to have turned around. It's like I pushed the rock right up to the top of the hill and now it's gaining momentum of its own and it's going ahead and it's dragging me along with it. And I'm sure that next time, it's going to be a bigger house, and the one after that is going to be bigger... and I can see the situation if it follows along as it's going now, it's an XJ6, and a suit and tie, and me giving the orders.

Press Photographer
Bob Stanniforth

Originally when I left school, I had an idea that I would like to be a metallurgist, you see. I went to Sheffield University to study metallurgy, but I wasn't clever enough for that because it involved chemistry, physics and maths, and I've never been any good at maths. Anyway, during that time I became interested in a branch of metallurgy – metallography – which involves microscopic examination of bits of steel, and I became interested in photography through that, and decided to go into photography instead. I was probably more artistic than academic.

At that time it was difficult to say what my actual aspirations were. I think I tended to take things as they came. Times were slightly different, the war was on for one thing and I was due to be called up, and so you tended in those circumstances not to have as many ambitions as perhaps kids have today. I'm not so sure that isn't such a bad idea really in the long run. I don't think I would have liked to be a metallurgist at all, because I'm not that sort of person. I'm far happier meeting people and getting about taking photographs than I would be stuck in a laboratory analysing little bits of steel, which is what metallurgy is all about.

When I left the army I worked for a photographer. I enjoyed that very much. But after I was there for two years, I decided that I might as well be working for myself, and so I started a business in a little village outside Huddersfield called Holmfirth and opened a shop there and carried on with more commercial photography and the occasional press work, although in Holmfirth at that time there was not a lot of call for press photography as such, I mean nothing of a sort of national nature happens in Holmfirth. And so I did quite a lot of weddings, babies – you know, the usual stuff that commercial photographers do.

I was on my own at that time, I couldn't afford to employ anyone at first, although I did later on, and I was doing everything myself, from sweeping the floor, washing the darkrooms, doing the book keeping, as well as doing the photography. But I enjoyed it, I mean I'm not saying there weren't times I got fed up of it, but that applies to any job, I think. It was very hard work, up at four in the morning, and working till eleven at night, sometimes. I wouldn't have missed that for the world. I would advise anybody to go into business on their own, it lets them know what earning money is all about.

But jumping on a while, I was forty, you see, and I began to think to myself, 'I'm either going to close the shop and get a job, or stay here for the rest of my life.' Well, after forty it's not as easy to get a job, is it? At the same time this job at the *Huddersfield Daily Examiner* became vacant and I was approached by the chief photographer, who I had known for some years, if I wanted the job or not, and I gave it some thought and felt I'd been in business long enough, so I decided to pack it in and come to the *Examiner*, and I haven't regretted that either. I've been at the *Examiner* for seventeen years.

Although I enjoyed running my own business, it is much easier really to work for someone else, where you know how much money you've got at the end of the month, you know when your day off is, which you never do in business, and there are a lot of things to be said for working for someone else. On the other hand I miss the decision-making, if that doesn't sound too silly, I miss the sort of freedom that being your own boss gives... and yet it isn't freedom because you are tied to your business.

It's exciting all the time now, because one is constantly meeting new people, even on unexciting jobs. I mean we come to the George Hotel to photograph the B and P women's lunch – the business and professional women's lunch – they have every month. Now you could say that may not be exciting but nevertheless it's always different, so at least it's never boring. There are varying degrees of excitement, aren't there?

I'm never bored, I'm not a bored sort of person. Obviously one likes some jobs and not others. If you get too much repetition of one type of job, then it becomes slightly boring: if you do weddings, say, every week for six months and nothing else. But there are six photographers at the *Examiner*, you see, and we tend to run the department in a way which gives everybody a change, and that is essential, I think.

The best type of assignment for me are unexpected news jobs like fires, accidents, murders, anything that happens suddenly and where the conditions are uncontrollable. A fire perhaps occurring somewhere way out on the moors in the middle of winter, and you have to walk half a mile to get there – and although it's difficult, it's more exciting than wandering across to the Town Hall and photographing the mayor, it is a more worthy news job, in my opinion.

Most assignments you go on, the people you are going to see have a fixed idea of the sort of picture they want you to take, which is entirely different from your idea, and so you have to somehow convince them that your idea is the best way. Now a lot of photographers I know have fallen out with one or two people, but I can honestly say I have never fallen out with anyone, because I always take the picture that they want me to take. It's hardly ever the one that appears in the *Examiner*, because having done what they want you to do, you can then do whatever you like. It's a psychological thing in a way, you have to be able to deal with people.

A provincial newspaper photographer is very different, I would say, from a Fleet Street photographer. Most of the people we deal with we have to meet again and again and again, so we can't fall out with them, because that would make our job much harder. I think the Fleet Street photographers are bullies to some extent, because they want to get a certain picture, and they're not bothered if they fall out with anyone. I wouldn't want to be a Fleet Street photographer, I like to go along with people rather than against them.

I think if I could manage to earn a living doing artistic photographs, a good living I mean, I probably would have a go. I'd like to try landscapes, really. They're superb around here, I've done quite a few of them. The whole of the Huddersfield area is picturesque, but there are two valleys which run out from Huddersfield called the Holme Valley and the Colne Valley, and although they are very close together, they have very different characteristics: one is an industrial type of valley and the other is a very rural, farming type of valley, and you can get entirely different pictures from each one.

I suppose if I'm honest, work of itself is not that important. I suppose I am working for money really, although it isn't quite as simple as that, because I could have a worse job for more money, I could go and work on an oil rig which I would not enjoy, but which would bring me more money. I think if I was a man of means I probably wouldn't work at all, and I don't think I'd be at the *Examiner*. But that doesn't mean I'd be relaxing in some chair watching television or something like that. I'd want to keep busy. But I would like to have enough money to do exactly as I wanted all the time, that's a dream I'm sure everybody has, and not peculiar to me.

In the general scheme of things Huddersfield is a very small insignificant little town, and from a news point of view Huddersfield is hardly ever in the centre of things. It's a very parochial sort of place. On the other hand, there are some very fine people in Huddersfield. I've got my roots in Huddersfield and therefore I wouldn't dream of moving. Maybe earlier on in life I would have perhaps wanted to move, but not any more.

Prison Officer
Peter Dawson

I joined the prison service twenty-five years ago. I had just completed an apprenticeship as a tool maker in the north of the country, and as now, there wasn't much going on at all in the way of engineering. I think I saw it as an opportunity to get away from the Lancashire area, and indeed we moved south. The money offered then was £1000 a year, which was good money.

This is a maximum security prison. I enjoy it because you are working with people, with all the anxieties and problems that this throws up, not machines which you switch off. It is a twenty-four-hour-a-day job, same as nursing.

You think of a type of crime, and we will have that person in the prison, no matter what it is. I mean out of 1300 prisoners, they cover every type of crime, from terrorists to armed bank robbers to murderers and child molesters, forgers, con men, they are all here.

They all have problems. In a prison like ours where we are locking up so many men, you haven't got enough hours in the day to get round all of them. So you only deal with those who bring their problems to you. For example, an inmate may knock on the door and say, 'I have a domestic problem,' and you try and solve that. You may be able to do something about it but you're only touching the surface because these chaps are very secretive, they'll only tell you what they want you to know, or what they think you should know.

Your approach to the prisoner is very much based on his approach to you. So for instance, if he is a roughy-toughy aggressive, you've got to be a roughy-toughy aggressive; if he is a con man, then you have to con him the same. Because you're in an artificial world where you're trying to get people to do things which they don't want to do, the only way you can get them to do it is either by very rigid discipline, or by persuading them. And that is the art of the job, really.

If you imagine, the prisoner is locked up in a cell and he cuts his finger, he wants an elastoplast to put over it. He cannot get that without seeing me. That applies to everything. Whatever he wants during the day must go through an officer. He can't even clean up his cell unless an officer opens his door, he can't go for his meal unless an officer is there, he can't go to the toilet, or go and wash unless a member of staff allows him to do it, so in a lot of respects we are quite powerful people.

It's comforting to know you've got power, but you use it within the workings of the system, so if the prisoner is well behaved you open all the doors, if he is very badly behaved then the system allows us to close the doors, and that is a comfort to you. If a prisoner is not settling in too well you will have words with him, and if he doesn't improve then you can restrict his movements. You are training him to behave himself. The problem, of course, is when he is discharged, he goes out into the street exactly the same as he came in, because we are not really improving him for society in this particular prison because it is not a training prison. I don't feel we're contributing anything to them, all we are doing here is locking them up.

Prison officers are called 'screws'. This is an old Edwardian term which originates from when inmates worked in their cells and used to crank an anvil called a screw. That was their work, they used to turn this thing so many revolutions a day, and by a device on the side, the warder could make it hard or easy to turn – and that's where our name comes from. Well, in the old days the Protestant ethic was hard work and you'll get to heaven. Turning this thing all day was classed as hard work, but can you imagine such pointless labour?

We should be looking at the criminal's individual needs and sentence him accordingly, and we don't do that. A typical example has been the latest riots at football crowds. There have been the big headlines, 'Flog Them', 'Thrash Them', and all this type of thing, and when the poor lad who may never have been in trouble before suddenly appears in front of the magistrate, the magistrate is swayed by this so-called public opinion and sends the chap down for six months. He'll almost certainly lose his job, he loses his family life, it puts him back perhaps three or four years, you know, for probably swearing at a policeman. What they should have done was looked at that individual as an individual and said, 'Right, the thing to do is give you a fine,' and he would have kept his job, he would have kept his status, and he probably would never have offended again.

The whole criminal system wants reviewing and looking at. I don't think the court system that we have at the moment is just. It's not a court of truth. All right, you have twelve good men and true, and I think that the jury system is quite good, but the prosecutor or the defence counsel will only put to the jury that evidence which they feel will help their client, which may not necessarily be the truth, so really it is not a perfect system.

You don't build up friendships as we would understand friendships, but you build up a relationship which is based on trust. He trusts you, you trust him, but there is always a barrier, there is always a line that we never cross, because you are the discipline officer in uniform and he is the prisoner. But you'll go a long way to bending that line. You may even call him by his Christian name, in certain circumstances he will call you by your Christian name. If you are working with him on a personal project, for example you might be folding Christmas cards for the Church, and you ask a prisoner to help you work on it in his own time. You might be doing it in the privacy of your office or a small workshop. There becomes a close relationship where you can talk naturally to him, he will tell you his problems, you tell him your problems. The danger of course is that after a period of time he knows more about you than you know about him.

It doesn't matter what he's in for, whether it's the most horrible child abuse or robbing a bank. To a prison officer they must all be treated exactly the same.

But the law of the jungle rules amongst the prisoners. Popular belief is that if a person came into prison for child abuse, he'd have to go on to prison rule 43, this is where we segregate him for his own safety because the other prisoners will take the law into their own hands and beat him up. But if that prisoner is a strong-willed type person, then he will just go into the normal system with every other prisoner, and they leave him alone. It's if there is a weak character that we have to look after him and segregate him, so it really depends on the individual coming in. If he can look after himself, he can survive in the law of the jungle, and he just mixes in with the rest of the crowd.

Prisoners are no different than you and I: there by the grace of God it is, really. You could be driving down the road this evening, go through the lights at red, and finish up in front of a magistrate who didn't have his breakfast – and you could be inside, simple as that, and you would be coming to this prison as a 'remand and trial'. So they are no different to us, except the one difference, that a lot of them, the majority of them, earn their living by crime. A lot of them blame it on their upbringing or circumstances, but this is not necessarily true. Some of them, if not most of them, enjoy crime, they see it as a way of life and they make a reasonable living at it.

Because prisons are shrouded with this secrecy, the general public are very naive about what goes on in prisons – probably, I think, they still imagine the inmates walk around with ball and chains. They have funny ideas, the public. Many think that we beat the prisoners up, or that we torture them. But prison officers are just normal people doing sometimes a difficult job.

It affects you in how you select your friends and you tend to look at people and say, 'Hmm, I won't trust him,' or by having a few words of conversation with someone you can tell whether they're criminally bent or not, and it becomes a natural barrier.

It must be terrible to be locked up in that cell. Even the thought of being arrested sometimes gives me nightmares, not because I'm a prison officer, I mean that would be terrible in itself, but I couldn't imagine it. I would not like to be in their position, and though this becomes a way of life for a lot of them, they all regret coming inside, and they are all waiting for a date to be released, because no matter how nice the picture looks with all the facilities they have, they are still locked up.

Probation Officer
Deirdre Ashdown

I'm a senior probation officer, relatively recently promoted, and I'm in charge of a team of five officers and an auxiliary assistant information officer, working in the East End of inner London. Deep, deepest Hackney. It's a very – deprived, I suppose, is a word people usually use – deprived area, in the sense that it's poor, and the quality of housing's bad, very few jobs, and lots of unemployed black kids. But it's not a bad area, not as bad as people make out. It's a field office where the officers in my team supervise a broad range of offenders in the community, people on probation, people on parole licence.

There are different kinds of probation orders. The probation order plain and simple is an agreement which must be entered into by the defendant – has to agree to it in open court that he or she will receive visits from a probation officer, go to see the probation officer in his or her office, be of good behaviour, and lead an industrious life, a rather kind of Victorian way of wording things, but it's the framework on which the probation officer builds the relationship with the offender.

But basically, we're there to help an offender look at his offending, and why he's doing it, and get to grips with it. Now, that obviously means that you've got to have someone who's motivated, and none of us would pretend that there aren't people who agree to being placed on probation just to get off the hook, and then fail totally to make any efforts afterwards. It's also people who, with the best will in the world, can't sustain a great deal of effort. The majority of our clients are inadequate, not specifically very skilled or bright, many of them. They've often come from the whole round of social deprivation that you find in inner city areas. Many have been in care, or in and out of institutions, and so you're dealing with people who are not ready material for concerted, self-willed, self-disciplined effort. So you find you might have to work with somebody a very long time.

I have a small caseload because I'm a senior, and my energies have to go into making sure the officers in my team are happy, and are working to the best of their capacities. So I have only six clients. Of those, one is a man who I first met and became his probation officer ten years ago when he was sentenced to life imprisonment, and I have seen him regularly, constantly, throughout that entire period. He has had very little in his life but the probation service, because his family practically abandoned him, and he has now just been released on licence to me, and I've continued that contact, and it's seen him through a lot of very sticky patches in prison.

Another is a young man who is serving a much shorter sentence for a property offence. It's his first sentence, he's very distressed by it, he's very distressed at being away from the community for the first time in his life, and he's not coping with it at all well. He's not a particularly mature person, and in working with him, my role, I feel, is to combine supporting him and showing that I do understand how he feels, with also trying to get him to be realistic and not make so many demands on the prison authorities that they ship him out from what is a relatively pleasant establishment, where he is at the moment, back to much more closed conditions. He's expecting to be allowed to be sick all the time, and to go to hospital, and to have lots of visits that he's not entitled to. He doesn't understand what's going on; he doesn't understand that he's being such a nuisance, that they will get shot of him somewhere else, somewhere less pleasant, if he's not careful. The other thing is that he only has a relatively short period to go before he's released, and if you were to talk to him, you'd think he was going to be in prison for the next ten years, instead of in fact six months. He doesn't seem to be able to think that come June he's not actually going to be in there any more.

I have a lady on probation to me, who got into dire debt, as a result of her husband spending all the money, basically, and then leaving her for someone else, and leaving her with huge debts. And she defrauded the social security – of not a huge amount of money, but enough for it to be significant; she was placed on probation, and in fact she has now sorted out most of the problems that got her into court in the first place.

Then I have another girl on probation who's very much younger, a heroin addict and a glue-sniffer, and a waif; seventeen, no family, wandering around London, very much at risk. I'm finding it very difficult to get her to report regularly, and in fact, if she doesn't start coming to see me more regularly, she will be in danger of being brought back to court because she's unsupervisable. But I'm very loath to take action of that kind because I'm conscious of the fact that she is at sixes and sevens, and she's only seventeen, and I want to see her settled. I want to see her actually stick at a drug rehabilitation hostel, and do something about her heroin problem, which she doesn't take very seriously at the moment. So I'm unlikely to take her back to court, but if she doesn't make more of an effort, I would in fact find it difficult not to.

If somebody doesn't keep to the terms of their probation order, then you should breach them. And if you don't, of course, in the long term, the probation has no value in the eyes of the court. On the other hand, you don't want to breach people for technical, petty, silly-minded things, like, you know, just not turning up for a couple of weeks or whatever. If people leave their address without telling you, that's different; I can usually find no reason for not breaching someone who's just cleared off, because that's obviously quite deliberate. But somebody like this girl, I don't want to bring her back to court unless I've absolutely got to, because she is young, she is immature, she's not used to having any demands made on her; she's been used to running around and doing whatever she wanted for the last four or five years, and so, I want her to make the effort for me, rather than me being another person who says to her, 'You failed again,' and taking her back to court.

That's four. I then have a young man of eighteen who was on licence to me from a detention centre, who I've only met very intermittently, when he's either rung me up or come into the office to explain why he couldn't keep the last appointment. I'm very puzzled by him. He's a young man who practically sent himself to detention centre. Yet he wouldn't come to see me, except to make excuses, to say, 'Oh, I'll be in next week,' and he's a very presentable boy with considerable artistic talent, I have discovered, and obviously not stupid or without abilities.

I then have a young man who's serving ten years for two very unpleasant rapes. He's nineteen, and he is appealing against his conviction and against his sentence.

There are people who make you despair, because it appears that nothing you say or do has any effect, or you can't understand really what the problem is, and those people can absolutely grind you down if you have too many of them on your caseload. The really difficult people are the people in the middle, where you can't quite quantify what you're doing, where you think that the importance of the relationship with you, the support you offer, the criticism you offer, you think that is helping, but you're not sure, and you're not sure how much you impinge on a huge, ever-widening circle of other influences for good or bad that the client has. With those people you just have to have faith in your own ability, and carry on offering the service you feel is important. Sometimes I find that the longer you're in the service, the more of these people you see resolve into some kind of clarity for you. If you've only been an officer for three or four years, you can get quite depressed. You see yourself working in an inner city area where problems abound, and government doesn't seem to be doing very much, and the housing is all miserable and ghastly, and there's no jobs and all the rest of it, and after three years you haven't had enough clients come out of that and perhaps make something of themselves, you know, make something of their innate abilities or their own skills. But after you've been around five or six years, you do, because people come back and they'll knock on your door at Christmas or some time, and say, 'Remember me, it's Charlie, I never thought I would stop, but I have stopped – I don't do burglaries any more,' and something you'd said, or something you'd done or some support you've given has made a difference.

It's not just the job that motivates me. I really do like people, I am really interested in them. I have an enormous amount of faith in them. I know that I'm right about that. I know that everybody has skills, talents, abilities, stamina, drive, persistence that they don't know they have. It's only a matter of channelling it. Sometimes it's a matter of getting them to believe it, and sometimes you can't – I'm the perfect realist. Sometimes people also have a vested interest in being failures, it's easier to be a failure than a success, once you've got the hang of it, it's dead simple, much easier than taking the risk of succeeding, of taking up challenges again, of making a fool of yourself, etcetera, etcetera. And a good many of the people we deal with have got the hang of being failures and they're comfortable with it.

The majority of people the probation officer sees are not the high-flying criminal. They're not the people who get away with it, the people who do big bank jobs, they are the 97 per cent of people who are bumbling con men, or inept burglars, or inept something-or-others. They're the people who cannot aspire to very much in the criminal world anyway, and they're the people who have very low opinions of themselves and don't think they can succeed. People like the great train robbers or any other successful team of villains you might name are in a completely different category to the kind of people I'm dealing with.

The people I work with best are the people I feel I can give the most to. Definitely. But that doesn't preclude, and that's part of the profession, working with people who you do not find particularly engaging or interesting. You still ought to be able to apply yourself to the problems in hand, regardless of what you feel for somebody. I wish it were that simple; I'm giving a theory. There are always people that you don't particularly like to work with. Most people find it very difficult to work with, say, persistent sex-offenders, or very violent people, people who have committed rapes and things.

I find blackmail difficult to handle, personally, because of the element of premeditation and cunning and preying on people who are helpless. I find violence not too difficult to understand, but I don't find persistent offences against children, particularly when threats or coercion has been used, any easier to deal with than anyone else.

I do see it very personally; it matters to me what contribution I make to somebody's life, if I can make one. It matters profoundly to me what somebody else does that affects their lives and the lives of other people in their families, I do care. If somebody is offending, and offending, and offending, I get cross about it if I think that this person I'm supervising has had a sufficiently trusting relationship with me, that he or she ought to have been able to tell me about the problems that led to that, whether it be money, or temptation, or greed. And, I'm quite prepared to get angry, I don't want to see people ruin their lives – especially young people.

I've never seen this as a job. I don't want you to get me wrong. There's nothing pious about that. I'm never quite sure of the meaning of the word 'vocation', but if it doesn't have to have a religious overtone, then I suppose it is a vocation for me. It's something that I enjoy doing so much, that I feel is so much part of the way I spend my time, that there are times when I wonder why they pay me for it, because I'd do it anyway, if there was a way of making a living. It is something I feel I am very privileged to be allowed to do, when I might be in the position where I have to spend my time doing something I hated, stabbing people in the back, or filing bits of paper from one office to another. I actually spend my time doing what I like best.

How I got into this profession was when I finished my degree, I did think I might do an MA, but I didn't really know, and I wasn't at all sure I wanted an academic life. I was working as a temp in my holidays while I thought about what I was going to do, and I was sent to all manner of places – as you do as a temporary secretary – and they sent me to the probation service for several weeks. I had never heard of the probation service, I confess, I knew nothing of what it did, and I found myself typing reports, the day-to-day diaries on clients that probation officers keep, and I was fascinated. Not only was I intrigued, but it struck me fairly soon that it was the one job I'd ever come across in my life where you would never really and truly know from one day to the next how good you were at it, because each person you'd be dealing with would be different and would present a new problem. I thought it would be an eternal challenge. I thought it was the one job you could never get complacent about.

Hardly anyone knows what the probation service does. I say that with absolute certainty. It appals me. What people do know, they usually have got wrong, and they polarize you. Either you are long-haired, sandal-wearing leftie, you know, along with the social workers, who is there to get them all off and generally waste the taxpayers' money. That's the view that really annoys me. Or they say, as if you're a police officer, 'Oh, I'd better watch my Ps and Qs in front of you, or you'll have me up before the beak – ha, ha.'

My work does affect my outside relationships. There's time, for one thing. You have to stay at the office sometimes when you weren't expecting to because there's an emergency, a non-accidental injury of a child may come up, or somebody may need help, an officer may need help, or sometimes you have to cover for somebody who is ill, something like that. But because you're doing a very demanding, very professional, caring sort of job, you can't always be home when you say you're going to be home. The other thing is that of course you are working with lots of people who you're sharing yourself with all the time, and that can be very difficult for other people to cope with – particularly if you've got a boyfriend who doesn't feel he has a very interesting job himself. I've never had a boyfriend who was unsympathetic to my work, in the sense that he couldn't understand something of what I was talking about, in my work. But you do feel pulled a lot of ways sometimes, and I certainly couldn't be doing with anyone who said, 'I've got to come first all the time, why aren't you here cooking my dinner,' you know, that kind of thing.

I have heard it said that it's got more dangerous. And there's certainly a lot of concern amongst the management in the inner London service, which is the biggest in the country, about the number of seriously violent people who are coming out to us on parole. It's also the case that burglaries and assaults on probation offices have increased, at least in the inner London area. You go to most probation offices now, and you will find there are things like safety doors, electronic doors. But I myself have not actually seen any real increase in dangerousness, and I think it can be a symptom more of the anxiety and pressure of the job. When I hear officers complain about certain estates, or wanting grids or alarm bells, I think it's more to do with the fact that increasingly we have higher caseloads, the Home Office gives us more and more to do with no increase in money or establishment, and officers are hard-pressed now, in a way that I don't remember them being five years ago. I think it's a reflection of the fact that our officers are just working very, very hard, and are stretched terribly.

I've lost a great deal of my moral certainty, such as it was, as I've gone on. I just find it very hard now to make definite divisions between right or wrong, except in the most obvious cases. It's obviously wrong to inflict violence on people gratuitously, or without provocation – you'd have a hard job, I think, saying that was right – but the more you see of people's behaviour, you can see reasons for why people explode when you perhaps couldn't before. But, when it comes to offences, relatively minor ones like property offences, which is what we mostly deal with, then all sorts of things do come into play, like social conditions, like how much tolerance you can expect somebody to have of their conditions when they're living on twenty pounds a week, and have done ever since they can remember, and the shops are full of invitations for you to live on interest, and have things on credit card. I, and most other probation officers, believe very much in the fact that people do or can determine their future, but at the same time, one isn't blind to the fact that many people are adversely influenced to an extent that makes you feel very distressed sometimes. You see people appearing in courts for shoplifting or defrauding social security, and you know perfectly well that the flat that you just visited has mushrooms growing up the walls and you think, 'Well, how on earth would I manage?' I worked for three years at the

Old Bailey and there was hardly a day when I didn't go into court and I didn't hear some judge saying – and I have a great deal of time for judges, I might say, I think they're on the whole very humane and very sensible people about sentencing – but I don't think there ever was a day when I didn't hear a judge say, 'Well, you just have to learn to live on £18 a week, or £24 a week,' and you think, 'God, I bet there's no one in this court that's going to go home to dinner with a bottle of claret costing less than £10,' you know, it just seems to be so absurd sometimes to be giving directions to people that everyone in the court – barristers, solicitors, probation officers, judges – wouldn't have the faintest intention of trying to live with, and couldn't if they tried. I sometimes feel that that is very frustrating to work with those kinds of concepts.

It's a bit dramatic to say that one mistake can ruin your life, but it very often can. For instance, it is not too difficult to lose your temper badly with somebody that you love, or don't love any more, and that can then result in imprisonment, it can result in losing a job, your home, as well as devastating you psychologically because you've severely injured somebody, or whatever. Crime, in fact, frightens me from that point of view, because I've seen so much of what happens to people who commit it that I no longer have any imagination left over it; I know what can happen. I also know that people can get away with it for long periods of time and I have recurring nightmares in which I'm the person in the dock, I'm the person who has done something terrible; and the whole weight and wrath of the world is on me and the shame, and people saying, 'Deirdre, how could you? You've been handing out this advice to people for years, and here you are!' I live in great fear of something like that happening to me, but I suppose that as long as I am in fear of it, it won't really happen.

You can care deeply about people. I mean, I care deeply about some people in a way that if you met them at a party, or on a street, or any other situation, you would care about them, they would be entertaining, interesting people. And, I know people who have long since ceased to offend, and have gotten themselves straightened out, who have become friends, who have come to dinner, or go for a walk in Kew Gardens, or out to the pictures with. I mean one of the things that always troubles me about social work generally is the notion that it can be very much them and us. And you can go through all sorts of things with people that do make it, I suppose, rather romantic. I've got somebody who I've seen through all manner of deaths in his family, through a marriage, through births of children, and there's an awful lot of history there, and people say to me, 'Do you remember when …' and that's romantic, if you like. You can become very important to someone, and that person can become very important to you.

I have seen so much that is good in people and relatively little that is really bad. I've seen a lot of muddles and misguided, unthinking cruelty; I've seen a lot of that, but by and large I think that the human spirit is very, very courageous, and if it can get into the right gear, it can achieve wonders, really, absolute wonders.

Prostitute
Sonya

I certainly consider it a job. Absolutely, it's work. It's a business deal that's made between two people. It's dinner, dance or gambling, the screw comes last for a sum of money, and that's a business deal, it's a job. And it's a lot of work.

I have some regular clients now, some guys who call me at home, and there is a regular kind of evening, usually dinner or dancing. They aren't sugar daddies, because sugar daddies are more permanent. I also work for an agency where I call in and say, 'Hi, you know I'm working tonight,' and when someone rings through there, the agency will call me at home, then I go out and meet the guy, or group of guys, it depends what the scene is for the night.

We go out to a restaurant and have champagne and dinner and dancing, and there is a lot of chatting and smiling and kind of acting stupid. They really like you to act stupid, you know, giggling and fooling around, because it's more fun. It's also because they have this kind of control over you.

My price, what I charge, varies from, say, £200 upwards. I've got £500 a night, that was a great one, a real good job. If it's my own job through my regular guys then I don't have to give a cut to the agency. If it's from the agency I could be taking home anywhere from £150 to £300, depends on how it goes. I think work is underpaid generally, and I also think this job is underpaid, because it's been the same price for the last four years, and the same money four years ago is totally different to now.

It's so superficial, some of them want to tell you about their problems with their wives, or their work, and this and that, and really, some of the work is like being a counsellor: 'Oh yes, you poor thing,' 'It'll be all right.' They go on and on. Usually I have to drink champagne and chit-chat. Sometimes it's not so tense, you might talk about holidays or your car that didn't start, and you can have a giggle, a laugh.

The food is disgusting in these very rich hotels, it's very bad standard. If I work a lot I have to watch my weight. And they want you to drink all the time. I may not want to, but you've got to drink, there's a lot of things you've got to do that you don't want to do; you don't want to drink every night because it's a killer. There's so much champagne around. I drink it with orange juice sometimes.

A lot of the work is getting ready beforehand. I mean you have to have a good hour or two hours to get ready, so that's a whole chunk of the day, then you need half a day to get over the night, because I could come home at four or five in the morning, and that's as tough as shift-work, to give you a comparison. I know I'm going to be shattered and I have to put a smile on for up to seven or eight hours – it's hard work, it really is.

It's a bit like working on a factory line too, the predictability and the boredom, and you always know what they're going to say next.

Okay, some of the people are interesting, but there's a set run on how the evening's going to go and what kind of things may come up and what may happen. 'Where are you from?' 'How long are you in town for?' Then I know that life, I know that series of conversations.

Some people I warm to more than others. Some people are very decent, they treat you as a human being, and some of the clients are really quite disgusting. They think because they're paying for it... they treat you like the management, you're just one of their workers: 'Do this for me, get this, get that.' I'm not a piece of shit – so don't treat me like that. I get very angry. I get pissed off, but it's like I've got to pay my bills, and like any other job, I've got to finish the week through. I make a business deal, so I stick to it, unless if I think, for some reason, this smells... and then I'll walk out. I'm not going to sit there and put up with someone who's going to push me around or anything like that, no way. A lot of girls make stands, which is one way of making a fight in terms of your working conditions.

When I was nursing, the money was atrocious. I mean, thinking back on it now, I must have been mad to do it. I mean it was about £25 for a forty-hour week, and it was working really hard as well. But I used to have boyfriends, and they'd take me out for a meal, and I knew this was a way of topping up my money. And these blokes would always come round to take the nurses out because the nurses didn't have any money, and I used to think I was working as a hooker even then. They might buy me a jumper, for instance, and then I knew I'd have to sleep with them; it was like an unspoken deal.

I'm not cynical, I just realized what was going on. You think, 'I haven't any money, I wish so and so would call up and he'll take me out for a nice meal,' and a lot of the nurses were like that. It's basically a financial transaction. I'm not unique, a lot of girls think that way. My mother would say to me, 'Go and find yourself a rich man.' It's common knowledge there's very little money around for women – I knew that from nursing. There's very few opportunities, so women go on the game. There's nothing wrong with wanting nice jewellery, nice clothes, nice wages, and when I moved down to London it hit me how much money there was, and I thought, 'I'll have some of that – why not?' Some people say it's bad to want money or to believe in a nice lifestyle, but I was really fed up with living on £25 a week, it was a killer. I'm not unique, I'm not cold or bitter or anything like that, it's a fact of life.

There's good and bad things about this job. One of the bad things is being an illegal worker. I can't tell my friends about it. I can't use it in a job description – 'Oh yes, I've been a hooker for four years' – but you know, it's quite a qualification. Think about the experience I've had working with people. For friends of mine there's a chance they could have their kids taken into custody, or get cut off the social security, or their boyfriends could be done for pimping. There's really a hell of a lot that you can be done for – share a flat with another girl and you get done for running a brothel. I've been cautioned but I haven't actually been arrested, but once you have a record for being a prostitute (they label it 'common prostitute'), it's hell when you want to get off the game.

There is the glamour side, and being with money, you know what I mean, it feels good. Not having to work too much. I can work maybe one night a week, two nights a week, and I would be taking home in one night what would be a week's wage for someone who's doing a nine-to-five. So it gives me a lot of time to do other things that I want, like swimming and aerobics or going out for a nice meal and thinking, 'Yeah, I'm paying for this.' And also, I can afford more things, like nice clothes, it really does give me that financial independence, and if I have money in my pocket that's mine, it means I can choose who I want to have a relationship with.

It isn't embarrassing saying, 'I'm a prostitute.' I wish I could say it more. I wish I could but I can't, purely practical, I can't. I'm not ashamed of what I do.

The actual sex is not a great amount of the work. Generally, the English guys are the kinkiest. They like you to dress up and that kind of thing, but I don't usually do that, although I do have a few outfits. They also want you to talk dirty to them, they love you to be really crude. Generally the Japanese are very businesslike. They're great to work with because it's really laid on the line and you know you're going to get your money and you're not going to get ripped off, so you can relax more. But generally it's quite straightforward what people want, you know, bang and bash, putting it crudely.

If they're considerate, generally it's gone through the evening, it's not just in bed, it's also part and parcel of the evening. Little things like, 'Do you want a drink?' and if you don't, not forcing you.

After we've had sex I go home. I'm not going to stay till morning, unless we make an arrangement. Even if I'm tired I always have my wits around me. Generally if you stay all night then there's another screw in the morning, which you get paid for, of course.

I've had jobs when I haven't had to have sex, which is great because it's a whole bit of work I don't have to do. It's kind of like taking time back. It's like getting paid for some work you haven't done.

I'm never sexually aroused. One thing that does strike me is that blokes have a lot to learn about physically and mentally pleasing a woman sexually. Instead of going in there from the beginning and thinking once they've blown their lot that's the end of the sex act, they should take into account what a woman wants to please her, looking at all the signs that it is pleasing her. I find there are very, very few blokes who actually care about a woman, if she's happy, if she's satisfied. I'm a lesbian woman, so I do know about that.

Restaurateur
Peter Godwin

The majority of the people I've worked with seem to be happy with their lot, which I think is a bit sad in many ways. Perhaps good for other people who want to achieve more, because if we were all at it, it would be a terrible scramble and rat race, wouldn't it?

But having my own restaurant and being my own boss is the ambition I've always had. It's not being held back by other people and other situations. Freedom, I think, is the word. The beauty of being your own boss is that you don't have to admit your mistakes too readily. It's much better to be number one than number two. Number two gets his arse kicked around, and number one can make a few mistakes and nobody really notices.

Most restaurant owners work very hard. It's not as glamorous as it might appear from the outside. Ninety per cent of my time is administration. Paying bills, checking invoices, staff problems. We have twenty-eight staff, each one is a lovely person, but each one is a problem of one kind or another. Sometimes it's the job. Perhaps they've been too long in one place and they really ought to be doing something else but need a push. You find out what the problem is. Often it's family; perhaps it's their children, wife or something. You don't want to get into their personal lives too much, but you must talk to them and communicate.

There's nothing better than to go to the markets at five or six in the morning when the day is starting, the sun's rising, and you get the feeling of actually buying produce which is going to fuel the people of the metropolis to get them through the day. It sounds a bit sort of glossy, but you get this kind of feeling, it's not far from religious. Very early in the morning when nobody else is up, and as you're coming back with a vanload of food and goodies, everybody else is bleary-eyed, going to work in the office. You feel as if you've seen more than they have. It's hard to explain.

Then you have to pick the merchandise. Rather than phoning somebody up and saying, 'Send me a pound of potatoes,' you go there and say, 'Those are better, so I'll buy those.' That's a real pleasure.

The days are gone where you could look to your accountant and ask, 'How did we do last year?' You can't do that. You need to be aware here and now, what happened, what was the make-or-break situation. You need to be living the business.

We make more money on food than drink. I think we're entitled to, because that's the produce area. We buy the raw product, prepare and cook it, whereas with alcohol, you buy a bottle of wine and you don't do very much to it, apart from look after it and take the cork out. But then on a menu you can't set out with a straightforward profit percentage on each item, you obviously have to subsidize things like best Scotch meat, and make up for it perhaps on a bowl of soup.

Take, for example, one person coming in on his own for a cup of coffee. The waiter has got to go make the coffee, bring you the cup, and perhaps miss out on other clients; but with a full meal, the man can come back and serve four people at the same time. One person takes up a chair, a table, a cup and saucer, and a cup of coffee, and although the actual sale point of the article involved is not high, in effect you're subsidizing it.

Unless you're up to date on your purchasing, and your menu prices, then you can come very unstuck. It's a matter of life and death. We try to monitor it and get it right all the time. We reprint the menus every six months, so I don't rush out and change the price of something, but you have to look forward and project and anticipate increases in the future so you can cover them. Something terrible may happen in the Budget and you need to reprint your menu to cover tax, duty changes, that kind of thing. You have to be constantly aware of the market outside, and have a feel for it. Just because the price of beef goes up on a Friday, you don't run out and put the price up on the Monday. It is much harder to make money than it was, say, ten years ago.

I find it exciting. We open our doors and the public comes in. You're not going round knocking on other people's doors. They come to you. So what brings them here? I wonder what they're talking about, I wonder whether they're happy. Every day, so many people.

The majority of people are very pleasant to handle, but with a turnover here of about three thousand people a week, one in every hundred can be a bit of a pain, but by and large they're very easy to get on with.

Once there was a middle-aged couple who came in with a child, and perhaps the man was a bit high, and next thing I knew, the guy picked up his two-year-old child, or a year-old child, and put her in the middle of the main road outside. And then he ran away. The traffic was going round this baby sitting in the middle of the road. It shocked me so much, I just looked on, without doing anything. I regret not having rushed out, but I just couldn't believe it, I was paralysed. And then his wife ran out and picked the kid up.

I either like to work very hard or do nothing. One or the other. But I can't do nothing for very long, so work is important to me. Through the restaurant I meet people and that broadens my mind. The whole thing is '*la ronde*'. It fulfils everything that I love and need and I can use it for my own purposes as well. For example, if I speak to customers who are involved with the wine business, or the stock market, or talking to the journalists and photographers who come here, by getting to know these people I can perhaps further my knowledge and interests through a friendly relationship.

I don't think anybody should be tied one hundred per cent to their job because that gives you tunnel vision and doesn't let you get out and see what else is going on. Have a couple of weeks off and come back and see things differently. I've accepted that for years.

In many ways I feel that a woman who doesn't have a career loses out, because she has only one life. She has a home life, whereas a guy has two lives. He has his career and his home life, so it's very rare that both are going badly. One will compensate for the other. At the end, when he retires, then he has a problem. He has to give up one of his lives and go back to the other, so at the end of the day he has to pay for it, but basically I think that working men have it better than non-working women.

I find it very sad that so many people accept their lot. They are born, they are educated and they are given a job. Then they get married, they have children, they accept it. They don't look very much further. They're happy with their annual holiday and Christmas with Aunty Lill, and that's it, and there's so much more to see and do in life.

It's their attitude. Nobody says you've got to go to work every day, five days a week, and bring home so much money to pay the bills.

There's nobody says that. We just accept it. That is the norm. That's what everybody else does, and so they do it. Life to me is to be enjoyed and I enjoy being here and being involved. I'm not just here to think, 'Oh Christ, another week, another Monday to Friday.' I'm living my life the way I choose to live it, and not being told, 'This is your life, Peter Godwin, off you go, here's your ticket, you'll retire at sixty-five, you'll be able to afford a small single-bar electric fire, and a newspaper on Sunday.' That's crazy, but so many of us do say, 'That's my lot,' and that to me is sad. Someone said to me, an Austrian guy, 'Peter, you know what success is? Sunny day like today, I say, "I'm not going to work; I don't have to go to work – that's success."' That's what he said to me, I'm not sure whether he's right or not, but it's a nice thought.

Sales Representative
David Fuller

I've never sold anything other than books, but I would imagine that selling some other product such as canned beans is just a case of selling one particular product against another, Heinz beans versus Crosse and Blackwell, or whatever. But when you're selling books, you're selling individual items for different markets. On our current list, our lead title is Anita Brookner and our second lead is Gore Vidal's book on Lincoln which really is more of an up-market-type book. The Stephensons' bookshop in Norwich, where I met you, is an excellent case in point, it's for a very literary audience and you'll expect them to take a lot of those particular books. On the same list we've got Gyles Brandreth's *Great Sexual Disasters* which is a very funny book, a very good book of its type, but you'd expect to sell that in your W.H. Smith, and the lower type of range. So books are very individual products, not only from publisher to publisher, but from one book on your list to the other.

I went into books when I left school. I left school after doing A-levels at eighteen, I had no idea what I was going to do when I left, and I thought, 'Well, what do I enjoy?' And I enjoy reading, so I wrote a letter to the managing director of Jarrold and Sons in Norwich asking if he had any vacancies in their book department. He had a vacancy in their educational department and I started there, serving on the floor, and I was on the bookselling side of the business for the next twenty-odd years. I then went abroad to Zambia and did bookselling there, and then managed a university bookshop in Papua, New Guinea. When I arrived back in England six years ago, again not really knowing what I was going to do, all I knew was I wanted to stay with books. I thought the obvious thing is to do representational work, and I applied for jobs and I was lucky enough to get this one, so really I've been in books all my life.

My area covers Norfolk, Suffolk, Cambridgeshire and part of Essex, as far as Colchester in the east of Essex, and Harlow in the west, and I also cover parts of Hertfordshire and Lincolnshire.

I have a three-weekly journey plan; in other words, I get to see each of my accounts hopefully once every three weeks, and I work out what part of my area I'm going to visit on a particular day. For example, today I am going to Letchworth, Hitchin and Stevenage, and then on the way back from there to Norwich, I'll take a detour into Saffron Walden.

I make appointments to see the particular accounts, I don't just drop by. By and large booksellers treat reps fairly well, but there's a few frustrating little things. For instance yesterday, I was trying to get a lot done in the morning – and it is always very difficult when you are travelling on the road from one place to another, you're always five minutes early or ten minutes late, but I was pretty well on time, and they kept me waiting for half an hour, and I'm looking at my watch and thinking, 'My God, this is making me late,' and that's a frustrating aspect of the job, but really that's the worst that accounts do to me.

I average between 800 and 1000 miles a week. I don't mind it. One of the questions I was first asked at the interview when I went for the job was, would the travelling upset me? But I've always enjoyed driving, I don't find driving a hardship, so it doesn't worry me. There are times, particularly in the winter when I'm going to Lincoln, and I get up at six to leave at seven, and I think, 'God, that bloody awful journey again!' I never have the time to admire the scenery because I'm blazing up the road for the next appointment. I find the wireless a great comfort in the car, I have it on from the time I jump in the car until the time I jump out of it, every single journey. Sometimes, if I'm feeling in a fairly intellectual sort of mood, I put on Radio 4 and listen to the discussions, very often I listen to Radio 2 or Radio 1 and sing along with the music.

It is a pressurized job. One's given annual targets and one feels a sense of achievement if you reach that target at the end of the year. You've got to sell X amount of books in a year, and one always wants to beat that budget, but you must also accept that however well you do this year, you are going to get a slightly larger target next year, and so we are always chasing our tails, because however well we perform, we're expected to do that much better the following year. Say I've got 8000 Anita Brookner to sell; there are times when however good a book is, however well you present it, it's not met by the same approval in the trade and you don't sell as many of those books as you would like to do. And then you get the occasional memo saying, 'Good God, what are you doing? You can do better than this, ring us next week and tell us how many more you have sold.' You get that sort of pressure quite a lot of the time.

Whichever book I'm selling, I try to find something that is going on that is topical, and bring that into the conversation fairly early, just to sort of personalize the chat. I tend to agree with people rather more than I actually do agree with them in my own mind, and I suppose that I compromise some of my own ideas and opinions to go along with the people that I'm talking to. For instance, I serve a number of left-wing bookshops, and although I don't particularly go along with some of their political views, it might sound as if I'm a rampant left winger when I'm in that particular shop.

I try to read most of our lead titles before I go and start to sell them. Obviously there are books that I'm not going to like, but I can't tell you if I'm trying to sell you a book that it's bloody awful because it's not exactly going to help me sell the book to you, and it's only my opinion anyway. We don't con anybody, I've got to be insistent upon that, but what you have to try and do, however much you may have disliked the book, you've got to try and make yourself completely objective, and you've got to say to yourself, 'Okay, *I* didn't like it, but what are the good points about it, what are other people going to like about this book?' and you highlight those.

Sometimes you can be selling a fairly specialized book. We do a lot of books on the occult which is not a particular interest of mine, and I get awkward questions about the content, facts about the author which I may not know a hell of a lot about, but I have read the blurb and I can make up an answer which is a fairly genuine honest answer which satisfies the customer. But I've got to think fast on my feet.

I think they respect my views. There are some reps on the road that are perhaps treated with suspicion, there are some people who push too hard, and booksellers have got to be a bit careful not to be led by the nose and order too many of a book that they are not going to sell. I think trust is a big word in the book industry, and I like to think that they can trust me. Despite what I said about the pressure of reaching targets, it's a policy of our company that it's as much a crime to oversell a book as it is to undersell a book, because in the peculiar world of paperbacks, anything that's not sold we accept back for returns anyway, and they have got to feel that they can trust you to say, when they order fifty of something, 'Look, you're not going to sell fifty of that, let's try thirty and if it does go, great.' I think trust is a very important thing.

With most of my customers it's a friendly relationship within the job, but I see very few of them after work. I get the impression that people who work in an office or factory or a shop, or whatever, have the opportunity at least to make friends within that working environment and go down the pub in the evening and meet three or four of their mates and have a few drinks. I don't have that potential to make friendships in my job, so I don't have a great deal of social drinking buddies that people in jobs such as those would have, and I miss that. I think I'm a fairly friendly sort of bloke, I like to have a few beers with the lads, but I only do it twice a year when we have conferences, rather than, say, once a month as perhaps most people would do.

I suppose in a way I'm a bit of a loner. I don't like people looking over my shoulder all the time, I like to be able to get on with the job, and then I'll either stand or fall on what I've done, so in that respect the fact that it is a lonely type of job suits me.

I work very hard. It's irregular, long hours, I mean it's not really a nine-to-five job. Fifty per cent of the time I'm leaving home before seven-thirty in the morning and I can very often not get home until six, seven o'clock. But I can't forget about it because I've then got to write up the orders I've had for that day and get them into the post. There is a lot of reading to be done. Many reps, in a bravado type of way, will brag that they have hardly ever read a book in their lives, but there is a lot of reading to be done, quite apart from the books, there are blurbs about the various books, instructional memos, reports to be written, so you're working quite a lot at home.

I don't think that I'm particularly well paid, I look at advertisements in the newspapers and see other representational jobs where they are talking about a salary at least 50 per cent more than I'm earning. But personally I can't see changing. I don't know whether that's a flaw in my character, but I have been in books all my life, I enjoy books, and books is all I know. I am so enthusiastic about reading that I can ramble on and on for hours to people about the value of a book as I see it, and this may sound very pretentious when you put it this way, but I like to think that I'm getting the books out to the public at large and getting more and more people to read, and enjoy themselves by reading.

What can I say about reps? I think they are a hardworking bunch, I think it's in the nature of the job that they have got to talk fast and so they sometimes give people the impression of being rather more glib than they are. Most of the reps I work with are dedicated, loyal to the company they work for, and also dedicated and loyal to a lot of their accounts as well. They are pretty friendly with most of the people they deal with on the superficial, chatting basis – you know, 'How are your kids?' – you may never have met their kids, but I think we are fairly genuine sort of people.

The problem of dealing with booksellers is that by and large they are just too nice, so that if you feel they are not doing as good a job for you as you would like them to do, it's very difficult to get narky or unpleasant. That can be a bit of a drawback at times.

There are some mornings when you may not feel particularly like going to work, or there might be some mornings where perhaps you haven't done as well with a couple of books that the head office thought you should, and you've received a couple of pretty snappy memos in the mail, so you are a bit depressed. Or you're a bit worried about your figures. I'm worried, I'm depressed, but as soon as I go into my shop, I've got to have a smile on my face, and I've got to be happy and enthusiastic, it's part of the job.

I suppose the fact that I know something about the business, I'm able to show that I'm not selling completely blind and I know to a certain extent what I'm talking about. You don't like to be thought of as a know-all, but I'm the sort of bloke that sits in front of TV quiz programmes on the television and sees if I know the answers when they trot them out. Yes, I suppose it is a little bit ego-boosting, isn't it?

Schoolteacher
Lucy Adams

The school's called Norwood Girls. It's just south of Brixton on the South Circular Road, and it's a girls' comprehensive school. We've got about 850 girls. It's called a 'social priorities' school – some schools are designated in that way, you score up points on various scales, like what proportion of the children have free dinners, what proportion of the children come from one-parent families, what proportion of the children don't have English as their first language. If you score enough points on all of those things, then you get extra money and smaller classes, which is what a social priorities school is. So it's one of those, but so are lots of schools in London, it doesn't mean that it's a particularly difficult school or anything.

At the moment I teach everything. I'm nearing the end of my second year at this school, and my title is Teacher in Charge of the Support Centre.

I wanted to do this particular job. The Support Centre is a hut in the playground, one of those big temporary classroom structures withdrawn from the main stream, for girls who aren't coping. It's an idea which quite a lot of ILEA schools have which is to cater for a different sort of 'special need', which aren't strictly academic special needs. The girls I have are extremely disruptive in the lessons, so they will fall out with a teacher, refuse to work, shout and swear, and all that kind of thing. Children with very different kinds of problems come to the centre, and it's difficult to make generalizations, but typically there is a disruptive who systematically is ruining some teacher's lessons by rude, aggressive behaviour. I've seen some of my girls doing it. I sometimes go into the lessons to watch them in action, and what they do is they arrive late so that when the teacher has just about got the lesson quiet and is doing the kind of exposition at the beginning of the lesson, at that moment one of my girls might come in. Typically, they'll sing loudly, they will not apologize for being late, will cause an argument simply for the sake of it, and then they will get sent out.

Sometimes there are terrible fights between the girls, and one party of a fight might be put in my hut in order to remove her from the other party. Another group of girls I have are truants, children who for one reason or another have been out of school for a long time, or aren't coming to school, or have massive difficulties in getting to school.

Some of them are actually school-phobics, school makes them feel sick. A girl this afternoon, who I'm in the process of reintegrating into the other school building, when it came time for her to go to her maths lesson, she set off up the road (usually I drive her, but today was the day she was going to walk herself), and she came back after a few minutes shaking like a leaf, bright green, and said she had been sick – and she had, I checked. She actually had thrown up because of anxiety. So there are those kind of children, then there are those who aren't coming to school as an act of aggression. Sometimes we have short-term traumatic cases. For example, two sisters arrived from India, speaking not one word of English, and they were put into my hut for a couple of days, just for them to have a secure base so that they'd know where they were. Another time, a girl with a broken leg came and worked in my hut for a couple of weeks, because she couldn't really trail around the school. It's a very, very mixed bag, and mixed ages, I have from eleven to sixteen in the same room at the same time.

The reason why I took this particular job was because I had learned over the five years I'd been teaching that there are a whole lot of children with special needs which hadn't been even vaguely met by the school where I was working before. At that school, where I used to work, when the children were naughty they were sent home, or they were made to sit outside the staffroom, sometimes for days at a time, and meanwhile, the truants just stayed at home, and that was that. So I wanted to see what could be done for all these kinds of children.

But now I think the whole philosophy behind the thing is unbelievably confused. I mean it's not really my job to make a philosophy for the place, because I'm not in control of the referrals, I'm just a service to the school. I have no control at all over who's sent to me, anyone might turn up. For example, yesterday, a girl whom I'd never set eyes on before suddenly turned up in the middle of the afternoon. She'd been sent by a magistrate. She'd been up for truancy, and the magistrate had said that she had to do a two-week test attendance in my hut or she would be fined.

For some girls it is a punishment in a way, but it's giving them some horrifically mixed messages, because when they get there it's very nice. Compared with an ordinary classroom the room is quite fun. Lots of my own things are there, my own books, for example, there's a carpet, a little animal (a gerbil), there's a basin, there's tea and coffee, as much as you want, it's all very cosy, and the children enjoy the work because they don't have to wait for help.

But it doesn't really make sense, and the motives of the people who refer them aren't at all clear. It's really interesting, because although I see myself as quite a friendly person, I have had a lot of trouble making friends with the teachers in the school. I think one of the reasons for it is because when a child is very naughty in a lesson, and this behaviour ends up with a referral to me, the teacher feels very angry with the child, but also feels a sense of failure, because they've failed to get what they want out of the child, and I'm supposed to be the big expert on the naughty children. And then when the child meets her friends again, she'll say, 'Oh, it was great in that unit, it was fantastic, you don't have to do any work at all. You can chew gum, you can put your feet on the table, you can drink tea and coffee all the time, that Miss Adams is a total pushover, it's wonderful there.' But, of course, they really say it to stop themselves being so ashamed; but then surprise, surprise, the teachers won't speak to me in the staffroom.

I'm increasingly worried by the whole thing now because I think it's rather woolly thinking. There's no doubt that for some children, I make their lives a lot happier than they otherwise would be. But the primary purpose of the whole thing is to make sure they get some education. I see my job there very much as a teacher, and not as any kind of counsellor or social worker or anything like that.

The only ground rule is that they are not allowed to spend years and years there full time. I might have some kids part time through their whole school career; for example, there is a case where a particular girl has to spend the first hour of every day with me because she needs to be greeted as a person every morning. She needs someone to say, 'Have you got everything you need, do you know where you're going, are you all right?' – all because she needs kind of getting ready for the school day in a calm, very controlled sort of atmosphere. And then she'll be okay for the rest of the day. Something like that might go on all the way through a girl's career. Mostly the full-time kids I have are waiting for places at other schools; for example, at maladjusted schools.

I'm pretty dedicated to the job, I should think highly dedicated really from the fact that I see myself doing it for the rest of my life really. I find it endlessly interesting. I enjoy talking about it and thinking about it. The only other thing I've done in my life I suppose is academic work, and compared with that, say, I love the instant feedback, I love the way you know straight away whether you're doing it right.

Sometimes you've planned everything out really well and you've been to bed early the night before, and you're in a good, good mood, and the sun's shining and you've really got your head together, and you know what you're doing. You can see straight away that things are going fine and the children enjoy the lessons and they say really interesting things, and you know you're doing it right.

If, on the other hand, you're doing it wrong, you know instantly as well. If the children are horrible with me I tend to think that that's usually my fault. I mean something horrible might have happened, they might have just had a huge row with their mother, in which case they're in a filthy mood and they transfer their anger with their mother on to me. But, on the whole, I would say that on a good day I am capable of overcoming such things. I think probably the reason why they're bad in lessons is because the lessons and the whole structure and ethos of the school aren't good enough sometimes, you know.

I think my whole identity is defined in terms of my being a teacher. When I started teaching I loved it, I fell in love with it straight away, and now, in a way, the love affair is over, but it's a good relationship still, seven years later. In America there's been a lot of research on urban burn-out, and I can certainly feel strong twinges of it in me now. That's what I mean by the love affair's over. For the first few years I didn't have any twinges, but now I certainly do have quite strong twinges, and some of the things that I'm saying about my disillusionment with my particular job are certainly to do with that. Sometimes, I feel as if I'm perpetually putting my fingers in dykes. The realities of the children's lives are poverty and racism, and the way the whole thing moves on from generation to generation is so predictable.

Sometimes the awfulness of so many of their lives just makes it seem that there's absolutely nothing that you could do, and you feel yourself getting tired. Plus a little cynicism and feelings of – 'Oh well, what's the point, what can I do?'

But I'm not less interested in the children and in what they say than I was. That's the nice thing about them, they're continually changing, you get new kids all the time. I like their cleverness, I like their passion, they're adolescents and therefore very passionate. The things about which I get cynical and make me feel tired and worn down are things like when yet another of them tells me some appalling story of being assaulted or something like that. Or when some mother rings me up and tells me the next kind of appalling thing that's happened to them. The level of street violence seems to be higher in this area of London.

Well, they mostly love me in this present incarnation, and the reason is because I get the luxury of dealing with them in a small group, you see. So, I have got space to give them a lot more time than most other teachers have. Some of them get hideously dependent on me, and then get very upset when they think that I'm leaving them in some way, which, of course, I always do. I have a lot of trouble trying to get rid of children out of my unit. That's another thing that I think isn't so good about it, because the whole system encourages them to get very dependent on me, it has been such a relief for them to only have one teacher instead of about five teachers a day.

I don't find it sad when the children leave because they are looking forward to something else. They're excited, the poor little brutes, about leaving school, so they don't feel sad. So, you don't feel sad for them. Anyway, I often think, 'Lucky them, leaving school.' Although I emotionally like schools a lot because they're exciting places, intellectually I don't like schools. I mean a big institution is a big institution.

I think I'm different all round since I've been a teacher. For example, my family tell me that I'm very teacher-like at home. Well, I think I was always quite bossy to start with, and I certainly haven't got less bossy since being a teacher; if anything, more. It all fits in – eldest of four kids in my family. As a child I obviously had a supervisory responsibility. I was very conformist when I was at school myself, I was a real goodie-goodie.

It felt natural, somehow, this whole thing, although it was a late idea. When I went to the appointments board of Oxford University to find out what I was going to be when I grew up, the woman there interviewed me and she said, 'Well, I've made a resolution because of the present situation in employment, I'm not going to tell anybody to be a teacher this year except people who are clearly dedicated to the idea, which you clearly are not' (because I wasn't at that time), 'but, I must tell you,' she said, 'that I really do think that you are teacher material.' I was really upset and disappointed and I went home to where I was living with all my friends in a student house, and half of me was ashamed to tell them what that woman in the careers office had said. 'How could she judge me in twenty minutes? She's just a horrible old thing.' And my feelings were really hurt because up till then I was extremely prejudiced against teachers. In my group at St Paul's, all the thick ones wanted to be teachers or nurses, and all the clever ones went to university. But then, as it turned out, that's how I ended up.

I do think of it as work, and I'll tell you why, because in a rather babyish way I'm quite proud of working. I like having a working identity. I like being a professional as opposed to an amateur. I don't mean a professional in terms of 'the professions'. I think the idea of work implies a seriousness which I like. I would like to see myself as serious rather than amateur or dilettante or anything like that. I like the idea of being a working person.

Submariner
David White

Well I must have been influenced from the fact that I come from a very military family. None of them were in the Navy, but my uncles, my father, my grandfather and great grandfather were all in the Army. I joined the Navy because I love the sea, and in fact there was a certain amount of boyish fulfilment about joining the submarine service which has got a certain mystique to it. My father loved the sea as well; he worked in Lloyd's, which is to do with the sea, and so he was by no means disappointed that I joined the Navy rather than the Army.

However, I didn't join the Navy immediately. Having left school, I worked for over two years on lots of different jobs. The Navy was my sixteenth job. I worked in France on a vineyard, I worked in the wine trade in London, I went out to Singapore, and then to Australia, worked on building sites, washing up saucepans in restaurants, became a carpenter …

When I came back from Australia, aged eighteen, I joined the Navy. My vision of the Navy was sailing through sunsets and firing guns on exercises, and cocktail parties, and all being really a very pleasant way of earning money. What I actually discovered was that it wasn't like that at all. The fun side was very few and far between, there was a tremendous amount of administration involved in everything you do, and of course life never is as easy as you think it's going to be.

For instance, I went to sea when I left Dartmouth eleven years ago, and since that date, the longest I have been ashore is about two months, and that was on a course. And the longest leave I have ever had is three weeks. I live in Hampshire, and for nine years I was based in Faslane in Scotland. In fact, I actually keep a record of the number of days that I spend at sea in a submarine, and I have spent four of my eleven years underwater.

I'm not married, and one of the reasons is because I don't actually have much of a social life. I find it particularly difficult, having come in from a three-month patrol, or something like that; we go to a cocktail party and there's not very much you can talk about, because your life has been devoted to submarining since you were last on leave, you haven't read the papers, and you're actually a pretty boring person to talk to. I can't talk about my job because it's too classified, and when the topic of conversation might be something that's been in the news, you haven't a clue what anyone's talking about.

It is screwing up my personal life, indeed. I don't have anything else at all, really, other than my work. I'm frightfully romantic but I'm quite content to have a quick relationship. I find that, you know, a damn sight easier and less complicated than trying to prolong one when you're away at sea. There are a number of people in my life who've said, for obvious reasons, 'Sorry, chum, I'm not going to put up with it.'

So one might think, 'Well, why one earth stay?' But in fact, my reasons for staying are very different from my reasons for joining. When I went into the submarine service, I found that we are much closer to the coalface than any other element of the services, and the work that we do in submarines now and again is extremely fascinating, although I can't talk much about that for security reasons.

Okay, there are many times when you think, 'What the hell are you doing in this job?' But on the other hand, I have my own command at the moment – I mean, command of one of Her Majesty's ships, and it's not just any old boat, any old minesweeper or something, it's a major warship, a most powerful one. I'm responsible for seventy lives – and that is quite good for one's ego. It's a very exciting prospect from that point of view, and I enjoy taking my submarine to sea and commanding it. That is the carrot – that is what I've been working towards, you see, and now it's happened and this job is the most marvellous thing you can possibly do.

You get a tremendous amount of responsibility; as a watch leader of a submarine, you're in charge of £300 million worth of equipment. Tremendous stimulation. Submarining is not without an element of danger so there's a certain amount of adrenalin pumping through you. I mean if you didn't find it exciting, or if you found the responsibility frightening, then you might as well go and be a manager of Tesco's, quite frankly. Probably earn as much!

The exhilaration comes from being at sea and commanding men. It's hard to explain, but sailors are the salt of the earth, and it's a great pleasure and a great privilege to be in charge of them. The relationship between officer and rating is very close on a submarine because we know them so well, we live within feet of them for weeks on end, and you can't be too stuffy. They're still required to call officers 'Sir', and I'm always called 'Captain', but a rating will express his opinion to an officer rather more freely than perhaps in general service, where the officers are much more remote. In a frigate the captain wouldn't go anywhere near the wardroom: he has his own cabin, he eats by himself and he's on a much higher plane. I eat in the wardroom and I spend a lot of time there.

I work my cotton socks off in terms of being up and about and commanding that submarine. Most civilians would be pretty astonished. It's very much a one-man band. As a submarine CO, I'm responsible for everything. On the surface I'm called for every ship that comes within four thousand yards and so one is constantly alert. I never get undressed at sea. One always sleeps fully clothed, including shoes, and I have the loud speaker on so everything that's going on in the control is being broadcast into my cabin. So if something is going on up there, I'm awake immediately, because one is only actually half asleep. I try and sleep for about two hours in the afternoon and then I don't normally even think about sleeping until about three in the morning because that's when I do my paperwork.

It is bloody uncomfortable. We live in absolute squalor. I mean, we all live on top of each other. I have my own cabin, I'm lucky, but it's about as big as a medium-sized sofa, and the wardroom is absolutely minute. But because of that lack of space, there's a certain comradeship that goes with it because it's so bloody uncomfortable. The boat rolls a lot, you get covered in oil, it's cold, a howling gale comes down the tower, you get covered in salt water, and when you dive it's hot and close, and with the engines running a few feet away, everything smells of diesel. You can't see anything when you're submerged, it's like being in a tube train with the windows blacked out, about that sort of size in fact.

Obviously you have a limitation on fresh food as we can be under the water for weeks on end. Your potatoes will probably last the trip. Potatoes are the last to go and the lads like chips. Your salad will probably last a week, fresh vegetables a week and a half. After a fortnight it then begins to pall a bit because everything is tinned or frozen, and if you're away for a very long time, things start running short. And then the food gets a little boring and one is rather fed up with having the same thing twice in a week or whatever. I was on a nuclear submarine which ran out of every single thing with the exception of tinned spaghetti and tinned tomatoes, both of which I loathe, and that was all we had for a month, but that was probably a cock-up on the supply front.

We are not particularly well paid compared with somebody who puts in the equivalent hours or has the equivalent responsibility in civilian life. If you go away to sea for a long time you get paid more than somebody in general service. Well, I do as a lieutenant commander. My submarine pay, for instance, is nearly £6 a day extra, which is worth having, but it's not much when you consider the lifestyle. I consciously say to myself – that is the extra pay I get for being buggered up and I will use that money to enjoy myself when I'm on leave. For instance, I'm going to go to Kenya next week to stay with a friend, and I do it without any compunction whatsoever, and I'm bloody well going to spoil myself for a week on that money. Mind you, because you don't see much sunlight in my job, I'm allergic to the sun, I get prickly heat and burn.

You've got to be pretty dedicated. I feel that I've sacrificed quite a lot, doing a job like mine. I wouldn't do it for all the money in the world if I didn't find the job fascinating, because it does ruin your personal life. There are a lot of broken marriages in the submarine service for that very reason, and actually I'm relieved that I'm not married, because I would hardly have seen my wife at all over the last ten years. And should I be lucky enough to have the social life in which to meet somebody, I would be quite content getting married at about forty when my chances of seeing something of my family were higher.

The Queen is our Lord High Admiral, we are responsible to her as well as to the Government. We toast her when we have our dinners, we pray for her when we have church every Sunday – I have to do the church services. I'm a fervent royalist. The whole navy is a very traditional service, and a very royal service, very much involved in the Royal Family, with the royal yacht and all that sort of thing.

I'm fanatically patriotic. Fanatically. It's a very significant motivation for doing the job, actually. We are not political, but we are patriotic. Our job is to serve the Government, and we will do whatever the Government tells us to. If the Government turned around and told me to attack the French or something, I'd do it. I served in the Falklands and I think we came back feeling pretty proud of what we'd done.

Taxidermist
Philip Milne

It all stems from an interest in bird-watching when I was a child, and an interest in natural history. I used to do quite a lot of bird-watching on the Broads here, and as you go about you tend to pick up dead birds and that sort of thing. In a lot of cases they were quite pretty and it seemed such a shame to throw them away, and it was quite coincidental really that I happened to find some books in the attic with instructions on taxidermy. They were Victorian handyman hobby books which were quite well written, and I started from then on. And luckily, I suppose, the first one I did came out rather well, it was a teal, a small duck. I've still got it out there in the shop, actually. It gave me the encouragement to carry on. I've done a lot worse things since.

I don't sell very much actually in the way of taxidermy, my main work is nearly all commissioned work. The stuff that's here in the shop, none of it actually belongs to me, it's just things that people have brought in to be set up, mainly things that people have found. The lizard there was a pet, in fact, but the rest are road casualties mainly. I don't like to do pets actually because people tend to be too close to them, and unless you've got lots of photographs to work from, or you knew the animal, it doesn't look anything like the original, or as the people remember it, so they tend to be disappointed.

I suppose grey squirrels are a popular item, foxes, and lots of birds, particularly owls. Everybody wants owls. I skin them and make a false body, fit the skin to the false body and allow them to dry.

It's a completely different process with insects because the mammal being a vertebrate, the skeleton is on the inside, covered in flesh, but an insect, like a spider or a butterfly, has an ecto-skeleton, the skeleton's on the outside. So we simply pin them out, allow them to dry, and in the case of these big spiders, like this Brazilian bird-eating spider, the body is squashed and the inside comes out and you simply blow them back up again; you see it's hollow inside.

Skeletons are quite a specialized thing, I don't do as many skeletons as I'd like to be able to do. Skeletons and skulls are quite easy to come by from the abattoirs and that, but then they have to be cleaned and pieced back together again. Also they tend to be quite expensive. Nevertheless it's amazing the amount of people who want skeletons. I had quite a collection of skulls just before Christmas, and they sold well as presents, which quite surprised me. I've got quite a few fox skulls, badgers, birds, any animal that is decayed beyond actual saving, rather than throw the thing away, I'll keep them in the shop for their skeletons. There's quite a lot of money in the rarer skulls – lions, tigers, monkeys and that sort of thing. It's quite interesting actually that a lot of birds and animals that you wouldn't readily recognise as coming from the same genus are related and you can see the resemblance in the skull, perhaps more readily than from looking at the actual animal itself.

I've had some quite nasty things, really messy. Sometimes maybe a fox or badger that's been run over and the skin's split and the entrails have all come out, the skin is covered in blood. But in the main, it's a lot less messy than people would imagine. I have been bilious plucking and drawing well-hung pheasants, but in taxidermy you can use lots of cotton wool and sodium borate which absorbs the smell. If the body has died from natural causes or even been hit by a car, rather than actually run over, you take the skin off, and the body is complete inside. You get very little leakage of blood or any of the body fluids, and the messy part, the entrails and the heart and lungs, are still inside the body, and you don't need to come into contact with them at all.

In the evening before I go to bed, I will take something out of the freezer and then that's the job for the next day. It usually takes me all day to do one thing unless it's a big animal, which could take three days or more. The taxidermy part of it, the actual setting the bird up, is the part I enjoy, I don't particularly enjoy making cases or doing ground work* or things like that.

What I enjoy is something different, something that I haven't done frequently before, like monkeys and that type of exotic animal. I did that flamingo a few years ago. It's not that I find the other things

* Ground work is a small part of the bird or animal's habitat which is reproduced inside the case to give some idea of how the creature would look in the wild.

uninteresting. Every one of those little owls is interesting and every one is different, and you can work towards making each one better than the last one.

I've got one or two exotic birds from the local aviary, like that gallinule over there, a relative of the coot and moorhen. It's quite an unusual one, a grey-headed, purple gallinule.

I get corpses from wildlife parks and aviaries, and they're my particular sources, other than what people bring in. Although I know the animal rescue people, they tend not to bring things to me, and I don't like to press them, I don't actually like to ask for things because you never really know how they are going to react. I'm not sure what they think of me when I go and see them. They're usually quite friendly, but they tend to say things like, 'Well, they're all healthy this week,' and I say, 'Good, I like to see them alive.' Mind you, perhaps it's just me being oversensitive rather than them being nasty.

There's quite a lot of competition actually for birds and animals that do die in captivity, particularly the more valuable ones. Things like eagle owls and snow owls are worth more dead than alive. A breeding pair of eagle owls might fetch £100 to £200 alive and might fetch, dead, £500 each, which seems ridiculous really, doesn't it? Zoos have a great deal of trouble getting rid of lions, so much so that they even introduced contraceptives, and yet dead they're worth quite a bit of money for making into rugs and things, when you can get them.

I did have a European bison which died at the local zoo, and that was quite a big thing. I didn't do a full mount on it, I just did the head and shoulders. That was a real challenge, I enjoyed that, it was something special. My dream animal would probably be something like a gorilla, although I don't actually dream about dead animals, I do prefer to see them alive. When they die, all well and good, you can preserve some idea of what they were like, but you can never make them alive again, however good a taxidermist you are.

I'm not ambitious to make more money, but I have ambitions in that I'd like to do better work all the time, and I think that any sort of recognition or money would come from that, from being able to do better work. I'm very comfortable here, actually, there's interesting people coming in all the time and telling me all sorts of stories and I talk to them, it's really nice.

However much artistic talent you've got, you've got to have a knowledge of natural history. The thing that I think has helped me a lot to improve is watching the birds alive, seeing how they stand, their different positions and that sort of thing. Like that gallinule over there, I could have done it just legs straight down and probably in the beginning I would have done that. But through observation, you see that they don't stand like that, you know the legs are very mobile, and moving all the time. And they do hold their head very parallel to the ground. I'm quite pleased with that, actually.

I work all the time, I very rarely take any time off, because what I'm actually doing is what interests me. So when I'm not at home, I'm looking for examples of Victorian taxidermy or I'm collecting moss or twigs and branches, I'm looking for new ideas all the time. I think that's what really interests me, looking at new ideas, different ways of doing things, better ways. My latest idea is casting insects in resin.

Taxi Driver
Denis Jacobs

I get very frustrated and wonder what the hell I'm doing, sitting on that seat doing the job, so I don't get annoyed with other drivers on the road as much as I do with myself. I feel frustration because I feel I shouldn't be doing the job, I should be doing something else – writing a book or whatever – because I feel I could handle something a lot better than driving round, as much as I love driving, and if you asked me to take you on a job for £5000 for the next two months driving across America, if it wasn't for the family I would do it for nothing, 'cause I love driving, but driving around in circles from Knightsbridge to wherever, you don't need much of a brain for that. Once you've learnt your original stuff you don't need a brain at all, so it tends to vegetate.

I was twenty-one, unmarried, looking for something else, but then I heard that you could drive a cab and earn a nice living, and I thought, well, although I didn't want to do it, I'd do it anyway, what the hell, I was still young, I had my whole lifetime ahead of me. I had a plan of travelling around, getting a TR4, which it was then, go across Spain on my own and tour. Well, between the original thought and the TR4, I met my fiancée, now wife, so they never materialized, and really I suppose frustration had set in by then, you know. I mean I didn't fulfil even that bit. And since then I have been trying to get out of it. I've been out of it once, sold cars for someone in the family. That didn't work out so I came back still frustrated, tried to get out of it again, opened up a retail jeweller's and then the recession came along, a bit of bad timing there, unfortunately. We kept it going as long as we could and eventually we had to close. We could have stuck it out and maybe in three years we would have been doing fabulous, but at the age of thirty-eight, as I was then, I wasn't prepared to pull my horns in.

See, everyone says, 'Oh, you're so lucky you've got a badge.' This is the thing, this is the centre of the whole thing. Everyone says you are lucky to have that badge 'cause you can always fall back on it. Well, I would have been a success, I guarantee, years ago if I hadn't of had that damn badge to fall back on. You know, I think the guy who has the safety net falls down a lot more than the guy who doesn't have one at all, because he knows if he does, he's dead, and so he's a damn sight more careful than the guy with the safety net. And that badge is my safety net and I don't like it. You know, I have been so frustrated some days, I might just walk into the first police station and hand the damn thing in – and then I would have to do something else.

I hate the job, every minute of the day. You've got nothing else to do except think, you know. I take you from here to there, okay, we might speak, but nine times out of ten, you have a quick jaw, and that's the end of it, so you're thinking the whole time, you know.

You can't take me as your average cab driver really, because probably they are not as frustrated as me, they're very content, they feel free, they can come and go as they like, they can get up at eight o'clock, nine o'clock, whatever, and do as they like, and generally speaking a lot of guys are quite happy with the job, but I don't feel that way.

Without realizing it, even if I'm not at that moment actually saying, 'God, this is Dee's fault,' I know subconsciously I am blaming her anyway. We've gone through some heavy times. If Dee was here she would say the same thing. We have got a son who is now fifteen, so the usual thing, you stay together, but I'm not knocking the marriage, the marriage is basically very good, you know. But there are frustrations involved and I don't completely blame her as far as the work is concerned, not entirely, sometimes it comes out that way. It's just a matter of circumstances. I blame the badge pure and simple, really.

My father was a textile buyer and mother was just a housewife. She died this year, a great loss to me, that was. We lived in north London, Stamford Hill. It was a real loving background. I mean if I had been looking down and been able to choose two parents out of the whole world, I would have still picked my mum and my father, so I was very lucky there.

My father, even to this day, I can't make him understand, you know. He sees money coming in, he sees me living very well, and I do live well. I wish I could actually stick him behind that wheel in that cab for a week, although he wouldn't last it, he wouldn't last a day, but he expects me to do what he couldn't do for five minutes. He thinks I should knuckle down, and as long as I'm working he feels that's enough. Of course my mother, being a mother, I used to worry her sick, I mean she knew I was unhappy and I must have given her a lot of heartache. Everything she had she would have given to me, I know that.

My wife understands too, and she is trying hard and we are constantly thinking of new ideas. She's even getting a new knitting machine, picking it up today, in fact. And we are going to do that. I don't care, I've got no macho hangups, if this turns out well I'll sit there and knit, and if I can earn £20 a pullover I'll do it, if I can make it better than driving a cab.

Well, you work according to what you need, and that is the downfall with a cab badge, because you can do as you like and the chance to earn money is as much as you want to work without falling asleep at the wheel. So you work and you earn so much, and then you think, well, we want this or that, anything, a video, a television, I mean you see anything advertised you think you want, you can work for it. Particularly when you are young, you've got the energy, you need everything, or you've just got married, and you work as much as possible and you've got the initiative and incentive and the opportunity. If you are willing to graft, the money is there, you know. Some guys live in the East End still because they have never worked hard; you know, if you want to work hard, you have got a very nice living, if you want to be a bum, you'll have nothing.

It's really really bad, this job. It's frustrating because you are sitting in traffic and even though you are ticking up that much more, at that moment I would earn less just to get away from the traffic. The traffic is just unbearable, the traffic is non-stop. In the summer, because the British go away on holiday it eases off a bit, but basically the traffic is constantly bumper to bumper except for the odd moment, and it really grinds you down. I think this is what gets to you more than anything; it certainly gets to me more than anything. It's unbelievable. And the noise is horrendous, it drives me mad. The fumes you breathe in are getting worse and worse. I don't smoke during the day but I must breathe in God knows what, worse than if I was smoking twenty cigarettes. I'll be very glad when they improve the exhaust systems.

Drivers on the road, well, what can you say? Basically they are okay. Like all things in life, you only notice the bad ones, you know when someone is really horrible to you and you think that's when you want to kill. It is frustrating when after letting people in traffic all day and being polite, and you're trying to get out of a small street into a big main high road, and they won't let you out. And you have been doing it all day for them, so why won't they let you out? They won't let you out just because you are a cab, sometimes.

Maybe that's the difference between me, not meaning to sound big-headed, and the next guy who really doesn't mind if he sits there. It's not my character and personality just to sit there. Although I'm a Leo, and give me a million pounds I could be the laziest guy in the world, until I've got the million I will be frustrated.

There's something about lady drivers behind the wheel of a car, I just don't think they have the know-how, I don't know what it is. Just like the guy in the kitchen can't cook, if I go out with my wife, I drive, when I go home for a meal, she cooks. So over the generations we both get experience in one particular thing. But I really can't stand women drivers. I wish I didn't have to say that because now I sound very chauvinistic, and otherwise I'm completely behind women in everything else.

Because of my attitude, when I'm in company with other people, to say I'm a London cabbie is like dragging out teeth, whereas if I had my own company I would be proud of it. I know it's wrong because there are a lot of guys who would cut their right arm off to have a badge, but I can't help the way I feel.

It's been eighteen years, and I've got no more to sell now than I did then, because this is not a business you build up, you go to work, you get your money, you park your vehicle, and that's it. You're not building up a hairdressing clientele or an export business where at the end of it you can sell out for forty thousand, a hundred thousand, quarter of a million ... you've got nothing.

I haven't bought my cab purely because I'm constantly trying to get out. The only time I would do that is when I decide that I'm knocking my head against a brick wall and I can't get out of it – but I would be banging the last nail in if I buy the car.

I'd say eight out of ten conversations start up because of the traffic. 'My God, how can you bear this?' And I say, 'I can't bear it,' and so on and so on ... and then you talk for five minutes about that, and then the conversation might go on to something else.

I'll often wait to make conversation. Sometimes with a pretty girl you feel that they are so big-headed you don't want to even strike a conversation to give them the satisfaction of being chatted up. So I wait until they say something to me … whether I'm disappointed or not, well, that's another thing. Some guys are interesting to talk to, getting another view. Sometimes I hear a view I disagree with. I don't always argue back because you usually haven't got the time because they are going to get out in five minutes, and so I just store it in my mind, it's another sort of person, you know.

I'll tell you what cabbies talk about, they talk about cabs, their jobs, what's happening within the cab trade, things of that nature, which is why I don't get involved with them. I'm very snobbish when it comes to that. The ones who talk like that are your typical cab drivers. I'm not knocking them for it. I envy them in a way because they are content. They're happy driving the cab, and good luck to them.

If I wasn't a cab driver, talking to another cabbie I would respect him for what he does; as a cab driver I feel a bit snobbish about it. But if someone is funny about my being a cabbie, my back goes up and I think, 'Well, it's not good enough for you?' It's not, as it so happens, it's not good enough for me, but it's okay for me to say it because I suffer the ten hours a day in traffic, and he doesn't know what the hell it's all about. He's only seen a cabbie as a stereotype and that's unfair because he doesn't know anything about it, and he's just a snob without reason.

Absolutely over my dead body would my son be driving a cab. I don't want him to be top in the lists of professions most liable for heart attacks, for divorce, and there are several other lists which we seem to be in the top four or five, none of which are good for you. Driving around London, breathing in the fumes, I don't want him to do that, I don't care if he becomes something more menial, if he likes it enough, great. So long as he's happy with it and enjoys it, and he can keep healthy and find the right woman, that's good enough for me. He sees the way I come in at night, and so he knows, he knows not to do it.

I feel now that I don't want to work more than eight hours a day. I feel that I shouldn't have to. Whatever I owe, I'm just not going to do it, I've had enough. I think it's a combination of age and attitude, I'm not going to let it run me. I feel really that I can't take more than eight hours of that torment anyway. I don't work as hard now as I used to, I can't honestly. I turned forty this year. It's a big landmark. I've never felt old, I've never been conscious about my age until this approaching forty. And this has been a hell of a year for me, what with my mum, and turning forty.

The perk of the job for putting up with all this nonsense is it's a cash business, and you really don't have to declare anything you take, and that is the biggest perk of all. I don't want to say too much financially because of the old tax man, and if you pay a reasonable amount I'm sure he's satisfied as long as you don't take him as an idiot.

I've got something I'm trying to get off the ground as a business proposition which I hope will work, it's an import business involving Spain. If it comes off, fantastic, great. I would build the business up, give myself a nice living and then hopefully retire with a bit of money. If it doesn't I would have to resign myself to driving the cab. Then hopefully I will semi-retire when I'm fifty. Not necessarily with any more money then than I have now, but I don't care if I'm skint when I'm fifty, I will arrange my life so we can travel around the world for six months. I'm not going to drive that cab for twelve months of the year. I'll wash dishes, sweep the streets, I don't care, it's got to mean I'm travelling, I'm seeing the world, and that is everything. And I won't be driving. I don't know which is more important. The most important thing is for me to travel, but at the same time it gets me off the cab. This business, say it comes off and becomes a big business, I've still got to work, but I will be able to get away and do what I want in my life. I don't want to become a businessman up till the age of seventy making money I can't spend and unable to travel. If it becomes big enough, then I will just sell out, hopefully that will be the way, but one way or the other, I've got to travel, that to me is the best way to spend your life, coming and going and seeing the world.

I do at moments feel like driving into a wall, I mean I've got really that bad. Suicide is a good way out, I've been that way a couple of times so I'm not sort of speaking light-heartedly about it, I could see the men in white coats coming over the hill, I really felt that bad.

That jewellery business I was telling you about, it wasn't all my fault, although there were things that were my fault. But the state of the country was not my fault and I picked a trade, jewellery, which when there is a recession, that's one of the first things to go. That was hit very, very badly, obviously.

It was a relief to start earning money again in a sense, to get back in the cab, but it was like fool's gold, you know. For a few weeks you think,

'Oh, this is not so bad,' bombing around enjoying yourself and free, no tax man and VAT man to worry about. But then the rot started setting in. It's funny, when I was in the shop, after a very short while I could hardly remember driving a cab, and yet back in the cab again after the shop, the shop seemed to disappear, you know, like you have a lovely holiday, and then two days after you can hardly remember being there.

At the same time as hating it, I do feel ashamed, because basically, apart from the personal things that have happened to me, I must be lucky, I'm not living in Ethiopia, you know, I remind my wife and son about these things, and I have to remind myself as well.

I should have gone to a psychiatrist, really. I was going to and it came down to money, I couldn't afford it. This is what a lot of things come down to, you know. Shrinks cost about thirty guineas. I can't afford that, so you don't bother. And when they say, 'Go and get one off the council,' well, what sort of shrink is that? I mean you just don't do it, well, I wouldn't anyway.

The way I'm talking is ridiculous because I'm saying no more than what everybody wants, not to worry about money. But what annoys me is that I feel if I put my life on the right path I would never be in this position and I would be in good shape. It's so hard to put it into words, but I feel because of that little oval-shaped thing I've got stuck down there, that badge, I would have taken many different paths and I would be loaded, loaded. I know I would because, you know, I'm not an idiot. If I was an idiot, well, what could you do? Settle down, drive a cab and be thankful. But I know I could have done many different things. Possibly due to myself, maybe a bit of laziness, maybe the right person at the right time would have helped, I don't know. But what frustrates me about money is that I constantly have to think of it, and really I know I shouldn't at my age, I shouldn't have to think about it at all, you know, I should be able to do what I want, but then I suppose that's what everyone wants, so that's it ...

Tax Inspector
Marjorie Wilson

The general perception of a tax inspector is of a middle-aged chap about five foot five in a bowler hat, pin-striped trousers and pebbled glasses. And of course they aren't expecting a female, so they tend to be very surprised when they meet me.

I certainly didn't grow up with a burning ambition to be a tax inspector, but then very few people that I know in the job actually did. I got into it sort of by accident. I was living in Dulwich, bored out of my mind with a small infant, and I thought, 'I've got to get a job, doing something.' And I saw an advert in one of the Sunday papers. They wanted people with legal experience for what was then the Estate Duty Office, now the Capital Taxes Office. Well, I've got a law degree, and so I applied for that. You have to go through the whole rigmarole of the selection procedure for civil service jobs, which takes ages, and by the time I had got through all that, they didn't actually have any jobs in the Estate Duty Office. So they said to me, 'Would you like to go into the Inspectorate instead?' And by that time I was really so bored with doing nothing that I would have taken anything. So there we are, I ended up in HM Inspector of Taxes, Walworth District.

Actually most tax inspectors are really very nice. It's not like Big Brother at all, really. We don't go round snooping on people. The powers of tax inspectors in this country are very circumscribed. There's not a Big Brother system, we don't have nearly as many powers as they do in the States, for example. I don't think the British on the whole would tolerate a system where tax inspectors were able to go around and bash on people's doors, get them out of bed, and cart them off to the Tower of London. I think the system as we have it is fairly gentlemanly and reflects the British character.

Well, yes, we do check on returns, but not every one by any means. I suppose I probably look at something between two and three thousand sets of accounts over the course of a year. Most people we take absolutely on trust. When somebody sends in their tax return, one normally accepts what they have sent in. But sometimes you get a set of accounts or a tax return which you don't think is right, maybe for entirely innocent reasons. Often it's just a difference of opinion as to what is or is not an allowable deduction in calculating a taxable profit. I mean the Taxes Acts are fairly complicated things. So there is room for genuine disagreements which have to be thrashed out.

I see quite a lot of people. Obviously not under the happiest of circumstances. They are often very tense, but in fact that in itself is a challenge, trying to get people to relax and realize that in fact HM Inspector of Taxes is not an ogre. It's quite nice when you get somebody who comes into your office who is really tensed up and ends up actually being on friendly terms, going out feeling, well, as happy as you can feel when you've got to actually fork out some tax.

I think you have to have a certain amount of sympathy. You have to be able to put yourself in the place of the taxpayer that you're interviewing. Sometimes one can lose sight of the fact that it is fairly traumatic for the person coming to see you. At the same time you've got to be a realist. You've got to have a certain tough streak in you because you are going to have to argue your case, probably against a pretty bright accountant, and also, you do get told quite a lot of tall tales. You have to be able to say, 'Come off it,' or 'Pull the other one.' *You* might put in a claim for £500 worth of thermal underwear for your trip to Norfolk to interview the gamekeeper, and think that's a perfectly reasonable deduction in arriving at your profit, whereas the tax inspector might say, 'No.'

There's no mystique about it. When you're talking to somebody, you form some sort of opinion as to whether you think they're telling the truth or not. There's none of this Captain Kweeg business, fiddling with marbles. If we've disagreed, I have the power to make an assessment under the Taxes Acts to assess a person on the profit that I think is reasonable.

I think that a lot of people mistrust tax inspectors unnecessarily. We are not out to grind people into the ground, and I don't really see that people have anything to fear from a tax inspector. I suppose I could be unpleasant. There's scope up to a certain level, but at the end of the day, the tax inspector is only a public servant. If he's really too nasty to you, you can always go and complain to the Ombudsman or to your MP and get the thing looked into. But I can't see that any tax inspector has got a vested interest in being sadistic or nasty. Basically they're professional people doing a job of work. And on the whole one gets the job done much more easily if you're pleasant and cooperate with people. I don't think it's a job where a sadist says: 'I really want to inflict pain. I'd better become a tax inspector.'

People get very hyped up about coming to see me sometimes. I remember one woman came in and she was shaking like mad. We had a good chat and a laugh and I said to her, 'It wasn't as bad as going to the dentist, was it?' and she said, 'Oh no, it was ten times worse.' That sort of puts it in perspective, because I know what I feel when I go into the dentist, and if she sees it that way ... it actually brings it home to you. I think it is a sort of fear of the unknown.

On a personal level I find the job causes me problems. When I go to parties and things, I usually don't say what I do, but you often find it's gone before you. You might be introduced: 'This is Marjorie, by the way, do you know what she does for a living?' Nudge, nudge, wink, wink. And it all gets dragged out. You either get somebody who'll try and take you into a corner and give you the long saga about the problems they are having with their tax returns, probably a bit like doctors get, or you get people who immediately say, 'Oh God, what have I said? What have I told you?' It's tiresome, really, but it's something you've got to live with.

I suppose I am a bit defensive about my job. I think almost inevitably, if you're in a job where you're regarded as Public Enemy Number One you do get defensive about it, and so I suppose in my private life I am particularly sensitive and react a bit. I get irritated with people who make stupid comments about what I do. In a social context I'm not HM Inspector of Taxes. Outside the office I'm just Marjorie Wilson, and so I do get uptight if I think people are imagining that I'm taking things down or remembering them in my head to rush back to the office and feed them into a computer or something, like some sort of undercover Revenue spy.

I think it's because the British have a general antipathy to disclosing personal details that we are regarded as not very nice people, and it grows from there. In fact most people have never come into contact with their tax inspector, and they just see what they read in the press, and that's usually pretty unfavourable.

We live in a society where earning capacity is a great status thing, and men in particular are not keen on telling other people exactly how much they earn, although they are quite happy to have the 'I have arrived' symbols around them, like the Jag outside the door and so forth.

Most tax inspectors feel that they are doing an important job that is of service to the community – even if the public don't see it that way. I mean what would happen if we didn't actually bring in any revenue? Where would society be if the government didn't have any funds to pay the police, for instance?

But this is the whole trouble, people just aren't convinced. I've got one friend who says to me, every so often, 'God, I don't know how you can do that job.' You know, the Public Enemy Number One bit. And maybe a lot of people see it that way. But I think society is very hypocritical. Everyone wants society to continue in the way it does so that they can have their nice house, and be safe from the Russians or whatever. But they can't have all that unless there's the money there to do these things.

It's not a glamorous job. You go into an Inland Revenue office and it's usually sort of ghastly tubular steel chairs with psychedelic nylon covers on them, and grotty views out of the window. It's not a job you go into if you want to get rich, it's not a particularly well-paid job. And so I don't think it attracts grasping, greedy people. Most of the tax inspectors I know are very caring people. You know, they're *Guardian* readers.

I've been doing the job for nearly twenty years, so I don't know whether it's the job or just age, but I feel that I have changed in the time I've been doing this job. Politically, I have moved further left. I suppose I'm more aware of how unequal society is really, and it's actually given me quite an appreciation of the haves and the have nots. I do come across quite a lot of poor people, and I'm less tolerant of those who earn a great deal of money and still moan about how much tax they have to pay, and things like that. I think that people who are lucky enough to have a job and lucky enough to be earning a lot should jolly well pay their whack.

Television Producer
Richard Denton

I decided I wanted to be in television by the time I was eight. I imagined that much more than I imagined being married or having children or living in a house. I never saw myself in any other context, and if I hadn't done it, I'd probably have been even more bloody neurotic than I am now.

My job is such a cliché that I'm often embarrassed to have to say, 'I'm a television producer.' I don't know what the psychology behind that embarrassment is, but equally if nobody asks me, I feel rather cross, I haven't been able to show off. Although it is a cliché, I'm sort of proud of it as well, it's what I've always wanted to do.

It is a wonderful job making documentaries. I fell very madly in love with it. I think one of the reasons it appealed to me is that in a sense it's almost one of the last *auteur* styles of film making. When you make a documentary it really is entirely yours, you're not working with somebody else's script, you're not working with actors. Also I am a terrible nosy parker, I suppose I'm a voyeur and I have no sense of anyone else's privacy. And here you are going into other people's homes, asking them very personal questions, invading their lives. You are actually living their lives with them, having their successes, watching their failures, being involved in all their moments of vulnerability, and in the kind of work I do, which is observational documentary work, it is those moments *par excellence* which make your film, seeing people with their guard down in moments of crisis. I find that I have very close relationships with these people for rather short periods of time. It's the way of my work, I suppose, great bouts of intensity followed by retreat.

Television itself is the most ephemeral of all art forms. I used to get postnatal depression. You spend two years working on something, and then that's it, never seen again, but I suppose that's more of the same thing, intensity for short moments. That's what television is about – an intense experience and then it's gone.

I find my work very easy. Other people look at what I do and think, 'Jesus, how do you do that, going somewhere with five hundred rolls of film and no fixed idea of what exactly you're going to get?' A lot of people would find that very nerve-racking, but I find it easy. If I didn't find it easy, I wouldn't do it.

When I am not working, or not at work, I mean there is a difference: I spend a lot of time at work, it doesn't necessarily mean I'm working hard, because I don't feel I work very hard, but as often than not, when I come home I just go to bed. I read a book and watch the news, make myself something to eat and then go to sleep. Since splitting up with my wife and living on my own, I've become almost reclusive. I think it's part of not exactly knowing now what your function is outside of work. I do need people, but on my terms. I need people to need me – and then only for as long as it is convenient. I'm not very good at fulfilling the obligations that that need dictates.

I know what I'm supposed to be doing when I'm at work, I seem to know less and less what I'm supposed to be doing outside of work. I seem to become less and less capable of being a friend or a father or a husband or a whatever, and so I get more and more scared of trying, I just go back to the office where I know what I'm supposed to do ... at least I know what I'm bloody supposed to do there, and I can more or less do it.

I envy the fact that other people are happy doing things which, it seems to me, give them an easier lifestyle than I've got ... but as I don't feel happy doing those things I couldn't do what they do. It's like envying somebody who never feels hungry on the grounds that then you would never have to eat, which is a kind of intellectual envy. You know, I'm quite sure that other people to whom work is less important are more adequate human beings, but there is nothing I can do about it. I mean the old psychological thing about knowing what's wrong with you doesn't actually make you any better. It's like being terminally ill.

Because I enjoy the job so much and I find it easy, I think actually I'm paid very handsomely for what I do. If they said tomorrow, 'We will have to halve your salary,' I'd say, 'Fine, okay, it doesn't worry me.' On the other hand, if all of my problems are in fact the result of my work, then maybe I need a bit more financial compensation. But I don't honestly think that this job can be done any other way. I mean I'm that sort of person anyway, so that's presumably why the job suits me.

I can't see a point where I will step outside the role of television producer to search for myself. Not till I get on the first step to becoming sane, and I can see no sign of that. I can remember, I used to drive past BBC Television Centre when I had just left university, and think, 'If I could just get in there I'll be all right, I'll be happy then.' I got in there, and of course that wasn't enough, and every step of the way you think, 'If I could just get to there, everything will be all right ...' but it never is. I think in a sense the whole thing is a kind of vain exercise. I don't mean vain, vanity, I mean vain, useless, in the sense that people who use their work to work out all their insecurities and to redefine themselves as worthwhile human beings never will succeed in doing so, because that's not how you do it. You actually do that from inside.

Work is a formalized environment in which there are things you are supposed to do, which you can either do right or wrong. It's comprehensible, it's relatively simple to understand, and in comparison with life, it's got a lot going for it, because life is so terribly confusing. The goals aren't clear, and there's no kind of consensus about how to do life right. I think that for some people work becomes a kind of alternative to life. And it's a way in which they can be successful for themselves which is actually much simpler than life, and that's why a lot of people retreat into it, I think, including myself. I have a theory that an awful lot of people who push themselves very hard at work actually have low self-esteem. They use their work to kind of redefine themselves upwards. But it's a losing battle, because if you can do it, because you have low self-esteem, you reckon anyone can do it. You set yourself another goal but you are never impressed with what you have done.

Looking back at your life you can give a kind of shape to the things you did in your youth that makes it look as if you have been very single-minded and ambitious about it. In fact it never occurred to me that I wouldn't do this job. I just assumed this is what I would do, I never planned it or anything. Because of the personal problems, splitting up with my family, all the rest of it, I have spent quite a lot of time thinking about the price of what I do and if it's worth it, and I think in the end, the price is high. I'm not sure it's worth it, but I don't feel that I had, have, or ever will have much choice in the matter.

Tour Guide
Ian Fancy

I've done an office job. I used to be in shipping offices up in the City of London, and also I worked for Associated Newspapers as a clerk, but working in four walls just didn't interest me. I used to be fed up when Monday morning came round, I was dead depressed and thinking to myself, 'Oh, I've got five more days at the so-and-so office.' My wife didn't want me to do any job other than a normal nine-to-five type of job, but when we split up, I did what I've always wanted to do. I wanted to join London Transport and I started off as a conductor on the buses. *There* was an interesting job, and you met people, the same as I do now. Then I went driving, then I became a bus inspector and then I had the opportunity of putting in for the Tourist Board.

I don't know whether you know the ins and outs as regards the London Tourist Board? But to be a qualified guide lecturer you have to pass written and verbal exams before you can get the blue badge, and they are very strict over it, but then they have to be.

You must study for months to pass those exams. Where is the oldest church in the country? St Martin's, Canterbury. Who was the only Prime Minister to be assassinated? Spencer Perceval in the Houses of Parliament in 1812. Whose series of mosaics can be found at the National Gallery and the Tate? Boris Anrep, who quite frankly I hadn't heard of until I did the course. And then there's the Americana, as a quarter of all the visitors to London are Americans. With what London places do you associate John Smith? He was the founder of Virginia, the one who was rescued by Pocahontas. Well, he's buried at St Sepulchre, Newgate, and there's a statue of him in the courtyard beside St Mary-le-Bow, Cheapside, where it's said you're only a true Londoner or a Cockney if you're born within the sound of those bells. Where were Mary Tudor and Philip II of Spain married? Winchester Cathedral. There were over three hundred questions: addresses of hotels and embassies, where the street markets are, oh dear, it covers the whole spectrum, times of services at Westminster Abbey, burial place of Henry VIII's wives, all six of them, of course.

I was brought up in Worthing in Sussex. My mother has always referred to the times as a child when she used to take me for outings; she would ask where I wanted to go and I used to say, 'London,' and my Mum still says that she remembers me saying, 'Oh, look, there's St Paul's Cathedral, built by Wren, 365 feet high,' and this must have been when I was not even eleven or twelve.

I didn't like school and I was a shy character, but this job, I'm so enthusiastic about it, I don't even think about shyness. I'm doing a job I like. My old headmaster used to say, 'If Ian liked a subject, he was good at it.' I came top of the school in art and I did very well in history, but subjects such as – and I must be honest – religious instruction, I probably came bottom, but at the same time that was because I wasn't interested. So doing a job you like is all-important.

Take some of the guides, I won't say our own guides, but some of the freelances, they smoke nineteen to the dozen ... they might have problems or it's nerves but I've never felt that. I think if you are doing a job which you enjoy you can't be shy, I mean I'm not a handsome person by any means, but I don't care what anyone thinks about that. I give them what I know, and some people have said in the past, 'That's the best tour I've ever been on,' and I've never had any detrimental comments as far as I can remember in all the years.

Well, everybody has got their own favourite subjects, naturally. Things that interest me are questions on Parliament and its procedures, so if anyone asks a question regarding Parliament I'm well away. We get people asking questions on history, and I'm very keen on the Tudor period of our history. I think a mistake I probably made when I was younger, I used to mention Henry VIII more than anybody else. I mean he was a larger-than-life character, but at the same time you have to realize that there were so many others.

Windsor Castle is fascinating. As you probably know, it was built for William the Conqueror's protection, and I find it most interesting because it's built over so many periods of history, and of course the original tower, where the Round Tower stands today, is artificial, built up by the Normans of chalk.

You have to like researching and studying. Even after getting the London Tourist Board blue badge, you can still improve your knowledge. I like pottering around libraries and bookshops, I love going to second-hand bookshops.

Some groups are very responsive. I always test them out with a silly joke about Harrods. 'Londoners can buy anything from there from a gold pin to an elephant, and I've never yet seen an elephant walk out the shop,' and we just see how that one goes off, and if they laugh at it then you can add a few more, and you apologize: 'It's going to get worse during the day, the jokes, that is.' Jokes that might be silly but it's how you put them over. For example, when you go through the Royal Farm area you say, 'Always look out for the Royal Sheep, they are not the common sheep you see in other fields, the Royal Sheep are brought up by the Royal bleat master to say "Your Maaajesty".'

You often do get a child that seems to be under your feet every five seconds and either you trip up or the kiddie trips up, so I always tell the people to make sure they look after their children because I don't want to hurt them. You have got to be tactful, that's another very important fact as regards guiding, being tactful. On occasions we get the child who I feel is much too young to go on a tour, and it sometimes might start crying, and that obviously doesn't just put me off, but it puts all the other passengers off, who have paid a jolly good price to go on the tours.

I love Hampton Court. The atmosphere at Hampton Court, I feel, is very cosy, even on a cold winter's day. Do you know it was one of the first buildings to be built of brick in the country? It wasn't built originally for Henry but for Cardinal Wolsey ... but I won't go into a history lesson now. One of my very favourite places are the Tudor kitchens in Hampton Court which are only open in the summer season. I've been looking at various books regarding Tudor kitchens, and the type of food they cooked; they would roast whole oxen with the trowel underneath where it used to catch the dripping fat from the animal, hence the expression 'dripping'.

The grounds at Hampton Court are interesting too. Hunting went on in Bushy Park across the road and you can still see deer there, and always corny jokes – 'That's where Henry used to hunt his little dears, oh pardon me, slip of the tongue, his deer' and this sort of thing, it's just that if you like to do a job like I do. ... People will often remark that I sound enthusiastic, and I feel that's very, very important. I am very enthusiastic.

I don't think of it as a job. I suppose it has to be a job because you are paid for it, but I look upon it as a day out. I think the job is more important in one respect than the money, although money has to pay bills and rates. With British Rail fares, you've got to be paid something, but I'm not in an unfortunate financial position, put it that way, what with Rosemary earning as well, it's not too important. We are not well off by any means, but we are comfortable, so I don't really think of the money.

Well, I must say, a bit of praise for Rosemary, my wife. She knows that my sort of job is not a nine-to-five, Monday-to-Friday type of job. I work many weekends, and, for example, on Friday night, I went on a tour which included a pub meal and a drink in the evening, and I didn't get home until about half past ten. But she knows I've got a job to do, and she accepts that I don't work normal hours, in fact you could call them unsocial hours.

When I first remarried she was very enthusiastic, coming around with me on certain tours, but nowadays I don't think she bothers. If we have a day or two off together, we nip down away from all of it, down to a place we're very fond of, Bexhill-on-Sea. You might say, 'Well, why that place?' But Rosemary, she works at Midland Bank, and she gets a bit aerated. I think the job gets on top of her from time to time, especially now they seem to be cutting down on staff, which means they've got more work to do, so to get away from it, we like going down to a place like Bexhill which is very sedate and very quiet and you can sort of unwind.

One thing a tour guide doesn't say to the passengers is, 'My favourite tour is this or that place.' Naturally you keep that to yourself, but they can always tell, I believe, by your enthusiasm. I like looking at the vine at Hampton Court, particularly in the period from July until the time the grapes are picked, because you can see the hundreds of grapes, thousands, down on their bunches. I have heard stories that the roots of the vine are so long that some go underneath the bed of the River Thames, and when you say it was planted from just a small shoot, people are just amazed by it.

By walking along the canal, looking back straight down the path, with a little round pond and the fountain, and with the water lilies in the summer you can see that lovely view of the east front of Hampton Court, based loosely, of course, on Versailles. And that often causes comments, and this is what I like. Some people have been to Versailles in Paris and they say, 'I preferred Versailles,' and you get other people who say, 'Oh, I much prefer this.' But with the tulips out in May, and then before that you've got the daffodils, where you can see a whole carpet of yellow daffodils leading up to the Lion Gate, there is always something to see, whatever the time of the year. This time of year you can hardly see any flowers but you can see the layouts of the gardens. The only thing I do hope perhaps is that the gravel path outside the east front might one day be concreted over because it makes a bit of a muddy mess on the coach floor when you go back on the coach, but apart from that, the gardens are beautiful.

So in my job you can see Hampton Court gardens throughout the seasons, the winter without the flowers, the early spring with the daffodils, and then the tulips, and then going into the early summer flowers, the begonias, and the different types of trees. I'm not an expert on trees and I don't pretend to be, but people always seem to be fascinated with the yew trees and the two holly trees near the tennis courts. And that's another thing which interests people, they are said to be the oldest tennis courts in the country, where Henry used to play the game of royal real tennis, which of course they still play there.

When I sit on the coach, especially after leaving Hampton Court, and we go back to London, sometimes I think to myself, 'I've done this job so many years now' . . . and I remember the days when we used to be on forty-nine-seat coaches, perhaps even smaller, and the drivers are different today. I can't remember any driver who started with me, and I think to myself, 'All the years I've done this, am I mad?' And then I think, 'No, I enjoy it.' I do start feeling a little bit long in the tooth now as regards the number of years I've done it, but that's only if I feel in that type of mood.

Vinekeeper
Jill Strudwick

I'd been working at Hampton Court for nearly six years and I thought I'd like to have a go in the vines. I didn't know I would take it over, I just thought it would be interesting to learn about more specialist than general gardening.

I didn't know that I would like working in the vine when I first started there because it's like working in a goldfish bowl, you've got people looking through the glass at you all the time, and there's a lot of gardeners wouldn't do it just for that reason. And also, if one job takes two months, that can be a bit tedious to some people. When I thin the grapes, for instance, that takes me a good six weeks. Well, it's not everybody who wants to spend every day of six weeks, snip, snip, snip with the scissors thinning grapes. It doesn't suit everybody, but I like it very much indeed.

It's not so much structuring my day, as my year, because there are different jobs in the vine at different times of the year.

I start with pruning in the late autumn, and after that I scrape off all the bark, let down the branches and paint them with insecticide, then I tie all the branches up and that takes about a couple of months. I need a good three weeks to prune it and then a couple of months to paint, scrape and tie it back up. And when it starts to grow, end of February, beginning of March, then I have to tie in all the new shoots which takes from April into May, when it begins to flower.

The vine is in control, really. When it flowers then you go on to the next stage, which is when the grapes form, and as it develops you have to go from one job on to the next. It's always quite obvious, provided you know what you're doing with vines.

I love the job. It's not everybody's cup of tea, but I like working on my own, and I like to do something which might only be a little bit, but it's my little bit, and nobody interferes with my doing it. And if it's wrong, then I did it wrong, and if it's right, it was because I was doing it right.

When I first started, I didn't dream of ever doing any job that would last a whole lifetime, but now I can see myself going on for years and years just doing the vine, because it is that sort of job.

The lady I took over from, she was very sad to go, it was her life. She was so very fond of the vine, but she was over retiring age, her husband was retiring, and perhaps she knew it was time that she go. I worked with her for eighteen months and I gradually picked it up as we went along.

I found her attitude difficult to understand at first, but now I'm beginning to see how you become very attached to living in this place and working in it. I like the feeling of being a small cog in a big wheel, where lots of people have been before and lots of people will be afterwards, hopefully. I like working at Hampton Court for the reason that it's old and you're just a tiny part of one long stream of history.

People are usually very interested in my job, and that's where gardening can take over your life, because if you're not careful you spend your whole time talking about vines instead of conversing with people about themselves or about things in general, and that's one of the ways in which you can find yourself forever talking or doing gardening.

Gardening is not a very well paid job and I don't know whether it should be or not really, I never know whether it's quite on the same scale as, say, doctors or lawyers. I don't think it is, not quite the same, although I think gardening is very valuable socially because gardens mean a lot to people who come round and look at them. You can't put a price on what that might mean in their lives, or the pleasure that it gives to people who are unemployed or sick or old, but that to me makes the job worthwhile doing.

I'd feel guilty if I didn't have a job that I couldn't in some way think of as being socially useful. That's partly why I gave up the job I had before I took up gardening. I was a window dresser for menswear at John Collier's. I used to travel all round the country, which I loved doing, but one of the reasons why I changed was that it didn't really seem of much use, somehow, not very real, not very important in life.

You see, my mother was a nurse and my father was a surgeon, and I don't know whether we are going to have to account for ourselves at the end of our days, but I kind of feel that you have to do something that is of value somehow or other in life. I wouldn't go around discussing it with everybody, but I do feel that's terribly important, and I sometimes wonder whether gardening is going to be good enough. If it is, it's in the way it gives pleasure to others, that's what I tell myself, and I hope it's important enough to be of some use.

Sometimes people knock on the glass, or they catch me outside, and I have a little chat with one or another, which is very pleasant. I quite like doing that when people are interested, but because of the glass, I can always pretend I can't hear if I'm feeling particularly fed up one day, but that's not really very often.

You'd be surprised at the number of people who think that we tie the grapes on to the vine, that they're plastic ones, and I've gone to all the trouble of tying them on with raffia, which seems to me to be almost as much trouble as growing them. I don't know whether I'd claim that they taste any better than grapes you can buy at the greengrocer's, they're just ordinary black dessert grapes.

The vine just ticks over and we look after it in a very traditional way. I've got some old Victorian books on vinekeeping and we look after it more or less the same as then. I collect books like that, because there aren't many modern books on vinekeeping, not under glass at any rate. But there are plenty of old books, because it was in its heyday in Victorian times when every big house would have a vinery.

The only time that I can go away is after the grapes are sold, which is the end of September, because it doesn't matter too much who looks after it then. There isn't anybody to look after it when I'm not here that really knows what they're doing – there's loads of people who think they know what they're doing, which is an entirely different matter, so it has to take pot luck with somebody else looking after it for a week. That time of year the vine can look after itself for a couple of weeks at any rate.

But there are times of the year when it's vital what I'm there; the ventilation is very important, it must be correct, and so I can't really go away then, or be sick either, I don't think.

It's a full-time job for just one person really, but at certain times somebody gives me a hand for a couple of weeks here and there. When I'm at the top of the really tall ladders, I have somebody to help me pick the grapes and put them in boxes to sell, round about August bank holiday.

My husband's a gardener, he's in charge of the front gardens over there. We've been married two weeks. I was on my honeymoon last week, but we didn't go away. I still worked my overtime, opening and shutting the vine, even though I wasn't at work during the day. There isn't anybody else who understands it. It's not that it's difficult, it's just that there's nobody who appreciates quite how it has to be done. So I was up at seven round here every morning, opening up the vents and the windows just the same as usual.

Window Dresser
Michael Roberts

When I first wanted to be a window dresser it was gasps of shock at home, well, actually it wasn't quite, they weren't that interested. I just knew that I wanted to be a window dresser. I used to live in Bournemouth and there was a big square by the sea front, and on one side of the square was a store called Bobbie's, which is now Debenham's. It was terribly old-fashioned, they used to do big theatrical windows and I remember going into that square from about the age of ten thinking, 'God, I would really like to be a window dresser.' When the careers officer came round and asked what we wanted to do and I said, 'A window dresser,' he said, 'Forget it, I have no openings for you.'

I hated school. I was in a really bad secondary modern. It was just awful, and as I knew all along what I wanted to do anyway, I told my parents, who I wasn't terribly close to, that I was leaving school, and I left at fourteen and a half or something crazy, walked into Bobbie's and asked if they had a vacancy in the window display department, and they said, 'Yes.'

I didn't do anything but clean for a year. But it was great, I was in the window and that was all I wanted – wonderful. I stayed there for four years and then came up to London.

I suppose for a gay person it's an avenue to express the like of fashion and colour and all the things that make up a creative job. The majority of display people I know are gay, male not female. That's not wishing to slot us all into some awful carrier bag, but I think if the majority of guys in the display business are gay, well, there must be something in it, surely. Oh, I love it, I couldn't think of anything else that I would rather be doing. I enjoy the feminine side of it.

People don't quite know what one does, especially here with shoes. They think you just sit a shoe in the window and that's it, go home. I'm not really concerned. I find people tend to put me in a slot. In other words, if you are in display you're gay, and you're a bit fey, you pin things up on walls and that's it. If that's what they think, let them. I don't have that confrontation a lot, because I stick to my own social circle, I don't go out into the working men's clubs and say, 'I'm a window dresser.'

I dress windows, but my title at Bally where I work is 'Display and Design Controller'. I'm not interested in shoes. Oh God, shoes are so boring I could just die. I like creating windows and props that go with the shoes. It could be any product. Say it was refrigerators. If you are going to flog a fridge and you want to do it well, you are going to have to present the fridge better than the man next door, otherwise, unless you are cheaper, which usually companies I work for aren't, you won't make the sale.

There is an awful lot to learn. There are colleges all over the UK, and they churn out an awful lot of people who are not very good, usually girls, because usually window display is a girl's job. Most fall by the wayside, the really good ones end up in Harvey Nichols, Harrods, Liberty's, Selfridge's and so on.

Well, you have to know how to display everything from silk to taffeta to chiffon to woollen fabrics, you have to understand modern furniture, antique furniture, silverware, china, glass, the whole range of merchandise, colours, groupings, graphics, and it goes on ... photography, screen printing, letrasetting. But display is something you can't learn, I think. You are either good at display or you're not. Say you're handling a lady's dress, you have got to understand how the skirt should fall, and how the jacket should sit and how the collar should be, and even with shoes you have to understand how to present them in the best way for them to look good to the public.

For example, you never show the inside of the foot, you always try and show the shoe from the best angle, which is the outside looking down on the shoe. Shoes are a lot easier to display than fashion or china and glass because they are solid objects. You can't turn and twist it as you can with a lady's dress or a man's suit.

At Bally I have got a lot of window space if you add it all up, because there are thirty-four shops, and each of those shops have a fairly big window, so altogether I've got about as much space as Selfridge's, but it's spread all over the country, from Chester to Salisbury.

We spend an awful lot of money and time to create an illusion, something to stop people from walking by our shoes, to actually say,

'Bloody hell, what's that, that's extraordinary,' then their eyes look down on to the stock. You're creating something to stop the passer-by and in doing that you're creating a fantasy, an illusion, a spectacle. Maybe you are hoodwinking to an extent, the illusion bit, but it's no more than combing your hair to look better.

You can do whatever you want in a job like mine. Where you have a big space to fill and a good company to work for and a decent budget, creativity is wonderful. I mean I've got enormous scope here that a lot of people don't have. In our Brompton Road shop, we have Italian marbled gardens with water fountains playing in the windows, and huge, enormous great leaves and trees, all hand-marbled and stippled, which is lovely isn't it? The windows before that we filled with four-foot bananas, and all the Arabs and all the tourists were saying, 'My, look at that,' and they all stopped, and then they looked at the stock.

If a window is wrong, I'll go and take the whole thing out again and change it. ... I'm a perfectionist, I couldn't live with it if it wasn't as I wanted it. No way.

Of course I'm not fulfilled. I don't think I ever will be because I'm not doing 100 per cent of what I want to do, because when you work for a company of this size 30 per cent of your life is spent running it and the actual creativity is never as much as you would like.

A dream window for me would be something like Bloomingdale's or Saks in New York. I'd love to do Galerie Lafayette in Paris, and just make it the most shining store in Paris, and everybody would come and say, 'Ahh ... this is what display is all about!' I would love a big run, a great amount of space to really play in.

Money is not that important to me. I'm not paid enough for what I do for them, but then again for the amount of fun I have, I think it's worth not earning another five grand. Anyway, I'm not going to stay in the job long because there is nothing worse than a forty-five-year-old display manager, is there? Or a forty-five-year-old hairdresser, for God's sake ... it's a young person's job, and has got to be a young person's job. All the famous names in display that you meet at parties or whatever, they are all retired, or should have done, and there are always young people coming up all the time who are more talented, who understand what is going on now.

I have just employed a guy here now who is twenty-two and he's very conscious of young designers coming through, young illustrators who I don't know about. I'm thirty-eight, and there are times when I feel out of touch, so it is good for me to have him here because he'll chivvy me up a bit.

I enjoy working very much indeed and I know I'm very lucky to have the job I've got. But I do resent the fact that I only have two days off a week and that's why I won't work after forty-five. I'm not working a nine-to-five job for a company after forty-five, I promise you, I'm getting out and I'm doing what I want to do, which might be running a small silkscreen firm, or, I don't know, who knows, I'm not concerned yet ... something will crop up.

My brother's an accountant, talk about boring, he hates it, he hates his job, and I think he secretly admires the fact that I have a job that I enjoy. And I also think, I don't know whether it's true or not, that all through his O-levels and A-levels and then accountancy exams, for all that sweat, he has now ended up in this rather plodding sort of job, and I just left school at fourteen and a half and was lucky. I suppose he draws a simile on that. All those years of sweating and he has ended up with a dumb job. I don't think he ever wanted to be an accountant, he actually wanted to join the Royal Navy.

I think he has a false idea of what I do; he's probably one of the people who thinks I just flit around and pin things on walls. He respects it an awful lot, but for the wrong reasons, because he is very impressed with material things, and we have more material things than he does. So he is probably thinking, 'My God, there is money in this job that my brother is doing *and* he's enjoying it.' I wonder if that makes him unhappy? I think it probably does.

Writer
Ian McEwan

Is it really work? It certainly makes you hungry, it does many of the things that I think work does, it makes you tired and you know when you've had enough. It's work *and* it's art which I suppose is one of its great satisfactions. Sometimes I cannot separate out sheer quantity from a sense of pleasure at the end of the day, that is to say, even though I know there's no relationship between doing two thousand words in a day and the quality of the work, I still feel the very crude pleasure of actually getting words down on a page, even though the next day they're junked.

I think living in a partially Protestant country, I just breathed in a work ethic like everybody else. My father was a soldier all his life, so he was a disciplined man, got up early every morning whatever he did the night before, and the idea of work was very strong in the household. My parents' generation and class felt the brunt of the Depression, so they had a very strong sense of the importance of work and the awfulness of being without work, and I suppose the school system and its disciplines gave me quite a strong sense of feeling uneasy when I'm not working.

I did holiday jobs, I was a dustman for a stretch. That's the longest job I've done, being a dustman, and it was when I had a year between school and university. Oddly enough it seemed quite romantic when I signed on for the job, I had nine months to waste and I didn't have any money, and I wanted to be outdoors. But actually it was awful and I felt very depressed because I wasn't at all good at it. On my first day I dropped a dustbin in the middle of the street. There was a huge mess and the traffic was held up, and at that age of eighteen I felt a great crisis about work, I thought, 'I can't even do this, this job which is the crappiest job you can imagine.'

I sort of drifted into writing, and the things I started with were rather strange. I wrote a film script, and yet I had no ambitions for it to be made. It was an adaptation of a Thomas Mann short story, and I never showed it to anyone. It was as if I was going in at a sort of shallow end, you know, it wasn't really a piece of my own work, I didn't have to rely on my own voice, it was almost a technical matter that started me writing. And then I messed around with long poems which were really completely imitative of Yeats.

I knew that all sorts of people had ambitions about writing, some even publish books but still carry on either being a teacher or a civil servant. I was slow to accept the idea that it was actually a profession, I saw the word 'career' and 'writing' put together and I was quite astonished. I thought, 'How can anyone regard this as a career?' For me at the time it was, I suppose, a sort of blundering, a kind of opening up which had no definite points, no moments of realization, and for a long time I had ideas that I might go and do a science degree. I still thought that I hadn't had a proper education somehow, reading English, and I wanted to go and learn something.

I was someone who wrote but oddly enough I didn't consider myself to be a writer until I published a book and saw myself described as '... something something the young writer', and I thought, 'My God, they mean me.' So it was at that point that I began to think that maybe that's what I was. But even then, in my mid-twenties, I still thought I might go off and do something else, I don't think it became fixed until I was in my early thirties when I had published three books and I actually realized I didn't want to do anything else.

It certainly has a great impact to hear yourself described as a writer, also finding what many writers call your own voice, this idea that you have got some distinctive way of saying something, a voice that you then begin to get keener and keener to want to use and find different forms for.

There are times when I belong with that camp of writers who would rather wash the dishes than go absolutely crazy in front of a blank sheet of paper. But I know that that's what has to happen. I am someone who has to sit around for a long, long time writing messages and so on to myself before I get something going. I rather envy those writers who just as they're finishing one novel are already shaping up the next one. I actually have to live through some more life, even though I don't regard myself as a particularly autobiographical writer, I have to go through changes before something else can begin.

I try to make sure that I'm sitting at my desk by nine or nine-thirty in the morning. I keep a very occasional notebook/diary and I find that's useful to sustain the illusion of writing when I'm not really doing it. I would say if nothing has happened satisfactorily after three or four hours then it's really time to do other things. You think you've stopped thinking about it but in fact when you come back to it you find the solution is offering itself. I think that it's a matter of diminishing returns after the first three or four hours, and my ideal rate of work is somewhere between four and eight hundred words a day, but say settling around five hundred words a day. Sometimes that takes all day to get done and sometimes those five hundred words are out in the first hour.

I'm disciplined once I'm excited about something, and getting pleasure from it. Then it's no longer a matter of discipline, I don't have to force myself to it, and if I've been out in the evening and come back at midnight I need to come and just look and see what I've been up to that day. I get insomnia when I'm working hard; I can't quite ever leave the thing alone, but I'm too tired to make any useful progress.

The fact that you're around in the house I think makes people feel that you're really just idling a bit. The trouble is that I'm someone who rather welcomes interruptions. Not always, but if I'm a bit stuck then I'm quite happy to drink a coffee with somebody. There is a danger that if you're around the house you're available.

It is a privilege to do what I do and it's very easy to forget that, but if ever I travel on the London Underground at rush-hour, then I remember what a fabulous privilege it is to tumble out of bed, go into the garden for a bit, walk up to your study and do the thing that most fascinates you.

I am very superstitious. Black ink always. Notebooks have to be from some obscure firm in Edinburgh, just simply because the first one was from there, and I want them all to look like that. I have to continue with the kind of paper I started on: if it starts on blank A4 then it must continue, and if it was lined A4 it must continue on lined A4. I never write the year on the notebook until that year is up, somehow I feel it's asking for trouble. Another emergent superstition is not giving anything a title until it's finished.

I suppose when I'm not writing I'm sort of on the lookout for things without even really knowing it. The one thing I have learnt is that however obvious an idea is, unless you write it down, you've had it, it's gone, so I carry round a pen and an envelope.

The other day, for instance, I was getting on the train and a porter, not that there are many porters left on Oxford Station, but a porter came along whistling 'Für Elise', with the most extraordinary heavy emphasis on the down beat. And I suddenly thought, 'That's just what I want for something I'm doing.' And when I looked at him, his manner was quite aggressive, and he turned this thing everyone plays on the piano when they learn to play into the most extraordinary sort of jack-booted march as he strode up the length of platform, and there just seemed a wonderful tension between what it was and where he got it from. Maybe he once learnt it on a piano, and he was doing it a sort of strange damage while he was doing his job and being efficient, and his heels were banging down on the platform, knocking out this incredible beat. Now I wouldn't have written that down had it not been for the fact that so many times things like that happen, and you think, 'That's just perfect,' and you don't write it down and they've gone, and you think, 'Now what was that perfect thing this morning?'

I went to a concert, I heard the Bach Partitas for violin, and it filled me with such elation that I wanted to run out and start a story. I didn't quite know what story, but at the same time I was thinking, 'The violinist is rather fat and she is very young. Is she unhappy? Does she overeat? Does she have a husband?' In fact, to our disgrace, my wife and I talked only of that in the interval, but I like those kind of things too.

I get bored like everybody else and I'm a compulsive daydreamer. Sometimes I can be staring out of the window and suddenly discover my pulse rate is incredibly high because I've imagined myself into some awful situation.

I don't sort of walk around feeling grand or anything being a writer, but I just have a habit of watchfulness, on the lookout for things, and plenty of times I'm on Oxford Station and all I care about is the fact that I'm late, I'm going to miss the train or I've left something behind, do I have time to go back and get it? It's like anyone else. When you do get the good things, well, you do feel virtuous because you wouldn't get it unless you were on the lookout, but also, I suppose, they have to come your way.

I'll tell you two areas where I look. One is how people are with their children, because that fascinates me a great deal, and the other thing is couples, married or otherwise. I saw, again on the station, a man who had come to meet his wife or girlfriend. She had a case, and he must have come on another train because he had a case, and he had a bike. And he really wanted to carry her suitcase, but he also wanted to push his bike and he also had to carry his suitcase, and he got into such a tangle. He finally settled it by putting both suitcases on the saddle and holding them down, and I was just intrigued by this chivalry because he was actually rather angry at the same time and it wasn't that he was doing this with some great display of extravagant behaviour, but he was in the grip of this behaviour, and the fact that she was offering either to push the bike or carry one of the suitcases made him immensely irritable. And then they set off and she was walking beside him looking rather meek and put-down and he was looking, well, put-upon. Those kind of things I like, people gripped by their behaviour rather than on top of it, but they are sort of distressing at the same time.

I think when you're writing, especially when you're writing prose fiction, you get terribly interested in gesture and the surface of things, and writing about it just feeds back into watching it and watching people.

I suppose in some way I'm writing out sort of maps for myself, but I do need these little touches to make them work, and the maps are really routes to material in my own head, conflicts, wish-fulfilments, dreads, my own past. It's often only very much later that I discover how, say, a short story is a very displaced and remote code for something that happened to me in the past, and I don't think of it in those terms at the time, but much later I can see why things are there and I can see that they actually are quite thinly veiled versions of real events.

I suppose I agree with the Czech writer Kundera, I mean I think that fiction writing is an incredible form of investigation, either of yourself or the outer world, which cannot really be rivalled by any other art form. I think it's one of the central forms of artistic expression. Theatre cannot come close to the way in which a fiction can create either an outer or inner world, can portray a state of mind, or measure the relationship, say, between an individual and his or her society, investigate the nature of a relationship between people, or can look at the way people change through time. Poetry can give you the state, but it can't give you that continuity of exploration; film can never take you inside in quite the same way. So if you asked me what it's for, then I would say it's a kind of investigation of understanding. There's also simply the pleasure of setting out to give something a shape; to give unarticulated feelings and thoughts a shape which can then live and exist independently of yourself.

I think the idea of a reader, the idea that something is going to be read, is very important to me, and I wonder if I would have been robust enough to go on hammering away, as I know a few people have done year after year, in fact right through their lives, writing novels that always get rejected. I think I might have just felt so frustrated that I would have found some other outlet, because my work needs to get beyond the drawer as far as I'm concerned.

The real pleasure I get from my work is the work that I've just done, the work I've completed that morning will give me pleasure although I tend to lose interest once it's over and it has left me. Putting the last dot on the last page is a pleasure which I constantly want to relive, even though it's fantastically brief, and it's two or three years apart.

Writers divide between those who simply write to find out exactly what it is that they think, and those who have to think of the sentence first, then put it down, and constantly agonize about the gap between the thought and the language that's going to embody the thought. I suppose I end up being more in the second camp. I spend an awful lot of time despairing of ever keeping shape to the thought, although that makes it all the more pleasant when it does happen.

You like to feel you're getting better at it. But this is not the case, and you only have to look at other writers' work to know that this isn't so. But I need this myth, otherwise it would be very hard to go on if you felt that your best work was behind you. I mean there's not much point in writing twelve books and only the first was any good. But there are things you can do when you are young which you can't do later on. I once wrote a story which I would find impossible to write now. It was called 'Butterfly', and it was narrated by a man who sexually assaulted a girl and pushed her into a canal. As a parent now, I find that my responses are so much more complex that it would take a lot more to take me into that situation, so I suppose you become warier about just what you are doing. Maybe you don't have quite the same freedoms that you have at the age of twenty-two. But in other ways I feel perhaps a little more daring, in terms of the different kinds of forms I'm prepared to work in and what I'd like to make them do. Also, another thing you lose is a certain unself-consciousness. If you've never been reviewed or had people feeding your stuff back to you in ways, you proceed with a kind of abandon. It's not that you carry around in your mind what the *Observer* critic said about your last book or anything. But cumulatively you begin to build up a picture through other people's eyes, of what other people think you're doing. It did make me want to stop writing in a way. It made me want to shift my ground, I didn't want to become just a 'writer of creepy stories' – if that's what they were going to be – where I didn't regard them as creepy stories at all.

That business of being in the public domain, it's not a conscious element when you're in the silence of your study, trying to write the next paragraph, but I don't think it can fail to have some effect, maybe even beneficial, like maybe encouraging you, but it's just that you stand in front of a kind of mirror, distorting or otherwise, flattering or otherwise, just the fact that you do cast a reflection has some kind of effect. I think I felt a slight diminishment of freedom in some way, although I'd be hard put to say quite what I didn't do that I otherwise would.

You discover that there is only a minority, a small chunk of people who have even heard of you. A few years ago I was staying in a hotel chalet, on a skiing holiday, and there was no organized seating arrangements so each night we sat on different tables, and I was asked what I did. People were announcing themselves as dentists and accountants and plastic surgeons, and I said I was a writer. And everybody said, 'Well, that's incredibly interesting, what's your name?' And there's nothing quite so awful as announcing your name to people whose eyes don't even register anything at all, and, this is the next question, although it's totally futile because if they haven't heard of you at this point ... 'Give me the name of some of your books,' they say, and you go through the most humiliating process of naming your books, and even as you do so the very titles sound absurd and you wish you hadn't written the titles. And each night I went through this, and after a few days, people would say, 'Oh, you're the writer chappie, aren't you, what was your name again?' And then I'd go through this sad litany of my work. And then on my last evening, when I'd gone through this again, this chap had heard me out through my titles, and he said, 'Desmond Bagley, now *there's* a writer,' and it was that emphasis, 'now *there's* a writer', as if to say, 'Where were you?' And those are chastening moments.

Zookeeper
Cliff Tack

This is something I have wanted to do from about the age of five, as long as I can remember really. I have always had pets at home and been interested in animals. I enjoyed walking around zoos, and I knew I would like to work in one. Glad to say I haven't been disappointed.

I suppose everybody says they work hard. In zookeeping, some days can be really hard and then another day can be quite nice. If the weather is against you and you have problems with the animals it can be a long day. For example, I might have to go back at night to check on a difficult calving, a possible breech birth or posterior presentation, where the legs get fouled up, and that means assisting her. You never know when you are going to have your dinner hour, nor, if something crops up, what time you'll get home at night. Several times I've said I will pick Mary up at a certain time and been late, but she understands, because she worked as a zookeeper and knows you just can't clock off at five and leave whatever is happening.

I look after mainly African animals at the moment, but a nice selection; bison, wolves, deer and several species of antelope. I try to think I haven't got any favourites and I like the whole spectrum, because in this job, to be fair to the animals, you've got to like them all, really. But I have to admit the rhinos are my favourite at the moment.

Every animal has got to be fed, watered, cleaned out, counted and checked over for any ailments. They are the constant things every day of the year, day in and day out. And looking after animals is a 365-days-of-the-year job. If it rains one day you take it in your stride, but if you have a week of wet weather or real cold snowy weather, by the end of the week you're just glad to get out of it for a while. But then on the other hand it's great to be out in the summer.

Zookeeping is a particularly low-paid profession. In Canada and Australia I think they get paid more what our profession is worth, but I'm afraid in this country we are still way behind. I think it is an injustice, but I suppose it is just one of those things that's gone on where the wages have not met the living standard. I suppose every profession in the country thinks they're underpaid, especially nowadays with the teachers thinking they're being hard done by, and nurses certainly are getting a raw deal.

I'm not particularly money-orientated, coming from an area where there is a lot of farm work and people are generally low-paid, but on the other hand when you are married and you've got children, some more money would be nice, to be able to afford some of the things that people take for the norm. But there again, I don't suppose that people are ever satisfied, and if you have more you want more. Even if I won the pools I'd still like to be involved with animals. Probably still the same job, mind you.

It doesn't worry me now, but I can see when Caroline goes to school and all her friends have got the colour televisions, video and things like that, she will probably feel left out of it. Personally, if I have got enough for the basic needs, I'm happy. I suppose I am selfish, like everybody is, to a certain degree. I'm not really interested in all this electronic wizardry. I mean a video is a case in point, generally if I want to see a programme I'll see it; if I'm not there, it's bad luck.

I've seen parents where the father will work all weekend or do overtime, and will never see the children, and he thinks because they've got a bike they're not hard done by. But surely that child would prefer to have its father there, and go out for the day and play with the father, than they would have a new bike? Well, to me the most important thing is being with my daughter as much as I can, and also trying to teach her that material things are not important.

For me as an individual, the enjoyment from my job is sufficient compensation for the lack of material possessions. What I'd be like with another job I just don't know. I think I'd certainly be a sadder, less buoyant person, because I'd be a nine-to-five person and anybody who is nine-to-five with their 'Monday morning feeling', I think it must take a lot out of them, well, it would certainly take a lot out of me.

I'd have said adamantly a few years ago that I would never change my job, and I still think I wouldn't, but if pressures became too much I'll have to, to be fair to my family. But if you can enjoy the job that you're doing you will have a much fuller life because you are enjoying each day as it comes, you're not thinking, 'Five o'clock... wait till that bell goes and then I can go home.'

I'm never thinking about what I'm going to do tonight after I clock off. I'm enjoying what's going to happen this afternoon. It could be a walk across one of the big paddocks, Valley Meadow or something, looking around for a young animal that has just been born, young fallow deer, or mouflon.

If I've had two days off or been on holiday I feel I've lost that contact, I want to go back and see what's happening, which animal's had a youngster, or how so and so is who wasn't too good when you went away. I'm always enjoying what I'm doing.

Well, zoo is a funny word nowadays. I think public opinion will go against small zoos where animals are kept in almost prison-like conditions. But at Whipsnade we've got large acreage to keep animals, particularly endangered species, in as near the right environment as possible. It is far better, in my opinion, to have an animal survive in a zoo, rather than face extinction because of the lack of habitat and loss of rainforest in its natural homeland.

I think of my job as a form of ecology work, really. It's all about maintaining the old environment. It's hard to put a measure on its worth, really, I mean you can say a nurse saves people, you can say a policeman does a good job, but a zookeeper, what actually does he do? Well, animals are still a part of life. People can be educated and entertained at the zoo. I know a lot of people think they can live in a world without animals and birds, but it would be, to me at least, a world not worth living.

Index of Interviewees